New Directions in Cultural Policy Research

Series Editor
Eleonora Belfiore
Department of Social Sciences
Loughborough University
Loughborough, UK

New Directions in Cultural Policy Research encourages theoretical and empirical contributions which enrich and develop the field of cultural policy studies. Since its emergence in the 1990s in Australia and the United Kingdom and its eventual diffusion in Europe, the academic field of cultural policy studies has expanded globally as the arts and popular culture have been re-positioned by city, regional, and national governments, and international bodies, from the margins to the centre of social and economic development in both rhetoric and practice. The series invites contributions in all of the following: arts policies, the politics of culture, cultural industries policies (the 'traditional' arts such as performing and visual arts, crafts), creative industries policies (digital, social media, broadcasting and film, and advertising), urban regeneration and urban cultural policies, regional cultural policies, the politics of cultural and creative labour, the production and consumption of popular culture, arts education policies, cultural heritage and tourism policies, and the history and politics of media and communications policies. The series will reflect current and emerging concerns of the field such as, for example, cultural value, community cultural development, cultural diversity, cultural sustainability, lifestyle culture and eco-culture, planning for the intercultural city, cultural planning, and cultural citizenship.

More information about this series at
http://www.palgrave.com/gp/series/14748

Jonathan Paquette

Cultural Policy and Federalism

Jonathan Paquette
School of Political Studies
University of Ottawa
Ottawa, ON, Canada

New Directions in Cultural Policy Research
ISBN 978-3-030-12679-7   ISBN 978-3-030-12680-3   (eBook)
https://doi.org/10.1007/978-3-030-12680-3

© The Editor(s) (if applicable) and The Author(s), under exclusive license to Springer
Nature Switzerland AG 2019
This work is subject to copyright. All rights are solely and exclusively licensed by the
Publisher, whether the whole or part of the material is concerned, specifically the rights
of translation, reprinting, reuse of illustrations, recitation, broadcasting, reproduction
on microfilms or in any other physical way, and transmission or information storage and
retrieval, electronic adaptation, computer software, or by similar or dissimilar methodology
now known or hereafter developed.
The use of general descriptive names, registered names, trademarks, service marks, etc. in this
publication does not imply, even in the absence of a specific statement, that such names are
exempt from the relevant protective laws and regulations and therefore free for general use.
The publisher, the authors and the editors are safe to assume that the advice and
information in this book are believed to be true and accurate at the date of publication.
Neither the publisher nor the authors or the editors give a warranty, express or implied,
with respect to the material contained herein or for any errors or omissions that may have
been made. The publisher remains neutral with regard to jurisdictional claims in published
maps and institutional affiliations.

Cover credit: © Ekely/Getty images/eStudioCalamar

This Palgrave Macmillan imprint is published by the registered company Springer Nature
Switzerland AG
The registered company address is: Gewerbestrasse 11, 6330 Cham, Switzerland

To my friends, Steven Trafford Taylor and Carl Dholandas, and their relentless and inspiring passion for political institutions and history.

ACKNOWLEDGEMENTS

I wish to thank my colleague and friend, Dr. Devin Beauregard for his comments on previous versions of this manuscript. I have been working with Dr. Beauregard for almost ten years now and have been a friend of his for almost as long, and I always feel very fortunate to be able to rely on his expert views to discuss my work. At the time I was writing this book, Dr. Beauregard was also teaching an important section on federalism at the University of Ottawa. This core course plays an important part in our curriculum. I was fortunate to be able to discuss my book (and vent) with him, as his mind was perfectly aligned with the topic of this project.

It should also be noted that this book was born from a number of informal discussions. Conferences are always a good place to circulate your work, but they have also been a good place to measure how much we understand one another. International conferences, in particular, have inspired this book. I am greatly indebted to my exchanges with scholars and friends from Australia, like Stephen Boyle (UNISA) and Carmen Reaiche (University of Adelaide), as well as American scholars like Kevin V. Mulcahy (LSU), Eleonora Redaelli (University of Oregon), and Rachel Shane (University of Kentucky)—exchanges for which the idea for this project began to take form. Our discussions on our institutional and cultural policy commonalities and (often huge) differences were an inspiration for this book. I would also like to acknowledge my colleague from the University of Ottawa, Monica Gattinger, whose work on provincial cultural policy paved the way for a better understanding of cultural policy at the subnational level. This was also an important inspiration in trying to engage with federalism at an international and comparative level. All of these encounters, along many others, were inspirational and convinced me of the importance of developing a resource for comparative research that could speak to a global audience of scholars working in the field of cultural policy.

INTRODUCTION

Institutions play an important role in defining the scope and possibilities of governmental actions; they enable certain decisions, while vetoing others. Institutions are also an important component of the political game. In order to influence governmental decision-making and pursue the good or policy they want, interest groups and activists must possess a certain knowledge of government institutions. For researchers, understanding institutions—their dynamics, their evolution, and the kinds of decisions they enable or constrain—can constitute an invaluable resource for explaining certain types of governmental policies. In Political Science, institutions have always been one of the key parameters mobilized by researchers seeking explanations for political phenomenon. In this discipline, after decades of predominance of behavioural approaches to politics, a noticeably greater emphasis has been placed on research programmes seeking explanations based on institutional frameworks and settings. In the late 1980s and 1990s, Political Science saw a resurgence of institutional analysis (Steinmo et al. 1992). The "return" to institutions (Evans et al. 1985) has had an influence on Political Science in general, but it also had a clear impact on the development and evolution of scholarship on public policy. In other disciplines, like Management Studies or Organizational Studies, the institutional turn has had an even more powerful impact, and today institutionalism and new-institutionalism have exerted a considerable influence on the evolution of the ways in which we understand organizations (Scott 2001).

x INTRODUCTION

When it comes to the study of cultural policy, the notion of institution has always had a crucial place. But, after three decades in which cultural advocacy has tried to bridge the gaps between the social support for cultural policy and the economic values or culture, cultural policy research has been more markedly influenced by the discursive dimension. Researchers have amply documented the normative transformations in cultural policy documents and strategies, looking at their alignment with economic and social rationalities that would naturally confer greater governmental support for the arts and heritage. Cultural policy research could only echo these important transformations at work in the actors' discourse. Over three decades, the world of advocacy and the world of politics have been defining culture and cultural policy in order to meet economic rationality and social demands. Around the globe, researchers have done an incredible work in capturing this important moment in the history of cultural policy. Whether any attempts to bridge the gaps between culture and economy in support of cultural policy—after three decades or relentless efforts—will ever produce the desired results expected by cultural advocate is left for discussion. Nonetheless, the creativity in cultural advocacy discourse has had an important effect in how actors talk about culture, and as a result, this important transformation has been captured by cultural policy researchers who have since insisted on research designs that emphasize interest-based explanations or models that privilege the influence of ideas on cultural policy development and change, to the detriment of institutional-based explanations.

That being said, this does not mean that cultural policy researchers are not interested in institutions. In fact, cultural policy researchers are very much interested by institutions; they document and study institutions, but rarely seek explanations for policy development and policy change in the broad institutional environment. When they study cultural policy, researchers engage with institutional transformation; they engage with the evolution of a ministry over time; they document the different milestones leading to the development of a national agency; they study the life of an art organization, whether it is a national broadcasting system, a national ballet or a museum. As such, they try to institutional change. Researchers also focus on the development of cultural organizations, and the ways in which they become more legitimate, gaining more resource and prestige vis-à-vis other policy sectors, like health care, environment or social services. In this case, researchers are interested in the dynamics of institutionalization. When they are interested in themes such as the democratization of culture, or when they pay attention to definition of culture that is implied by a national, regional, or local cultural policy, researchers are focusing on institutional outcomes. What if certain types of institutions or certain types of contexts had a profound effect on cultural policy development? Can institutions, and specific kind of institutions, influence the entire policy process, thus also influencing how cultural organizations can act, react, or how they are shaped?

It is with this context in mind that this book seeks to illustrate the value of the institutional factor in cultural policy research. In order to do so, this book focuses on one important institutional variable, the type or nature of the State, and presents the institutional and cultural reality of one particular kind of State: federations. By definition, federations (e.g. Canada, the USA, and Brazil) are different from unitary States (e.g. France, Italy, and China) insofar as they have subnational entities that possess their own powers and institutions—protected by the (State's) constitution—and suppose a division of (cultural) powers and responsibilities. Federations are complex assemblages of political and constitutional institutions. These (federal) institutions imply structures and—especially where culture is concerned—ways of handling social and political matters. In other words, federalism is a social and political philosophy that shapes the ways in which agents engage in and around cultural affairs. Simply put, the institutional configuration of federalism has become an essential component to understanding the explanatory power of institutions. But there are also other important and pressing reasons to pay attention to federalism. Federalism is a political and institutional reality for almost 40% of the world's population (Watts 1998: 1). More than 25 countries qualify as federations, not including all the countries that are theoretically on the fence or discussed as federations in development because of the evolution of their political system towards such an arrangement. Many important countries that we often use as reference in comparative work in cultural policy are federations. Canada, the USA, Australia, Brazil, Mexico are all federal countries whose cultural policies are widely discussed. With that in scope, this book tries to bring forward a number of element that may help a greater understanding of these countries, while providing material to help dissipate other misunderstandings.

Thus, the aim of this book is to explore how the institutional reality of federalism plays a unique part in creating dynamics for policy development and, eventually, the production of distinctive types of cultural policy. The book presents the influence of federalism on cultural policies through a variety of examples taken from different federations. Outside of a limited range of scholarship—a special issue of *Cultural Trends* in 2010 (volume 10, issues 1–2), a number of rich articles (Rius-Ulldemolins and Zamorano 2015; Lemasson 2015; Perrin 2012) and monographs (Saint-Pierre and Audet 2011; Beauregard 2018), and a selection of national case studies (Burns and Van der Will 2003; Gattinger and Saint-Pierre 2011; Bordat 2013; Hernández-Acosta 2013; Tabrett 2014) that have invariably engaged with the basic characteristics of the State and federalism—there has been very little scholarship linking cultural policy and federalism that emphasizes institutional explanations—and none that has taken an analytical distance to fully single out how federalism shapes cultural policy. Additionally, it should be noted that important professional resources, like the *Compendium of Cultural Policies*, provide descriptive resources on national governments, but do not take a distance, approaching these issues from a comparative outlook.

While this book insists on institutions and social philosophies pertaining to federalism, it does not aim to provide a complete cartography of cultural policy in every federal state. A project spanning the cartography of cultural policy would be more akin to a "handbook" of cultural policy and federalism—which is not the objective of this book. Rather, the purpose of this book is more analytical: it is a distillation of the essential principles of federalism that shape cultural policy. Building on examples from a variety of countries and contexts, this book focuses on the areas of cultural policy that are distinctive to a federal context. In federations, cultural policies are influenced by: a division/configuration of cultural powers and policy developments; an intergovernmental institutional landscape that influences cooperation, policy coordination, and policy implementation; intergovernmental competition (the politics of federalism); and cultural diplomacy. For these reasons, this book offers a number of takeaways for researchers in the field wishing to engage in comparative research on cultural policy—whether it is to shed light on federations or to compare a variety of institutional forms and settings. With that said, this book concedes an important limitation insofar as most of its cases and examples come from data investigating structures, policy, and institutions in Australia, Canada, Switzerland, Belgium, Latin American countries, the USA, Germany, Malaysia, India, Belgium, and, to a certain extent, Russia. Many federal countries—like Iraq, Nepal, or Sudan, for instance—are not extensively documented in this book.

Once again, this book is intended to provide a number of important references and ideas about institutional dynamics. The objective of this book is to help cultural policy researchers gain a better awareness about the institutional realities in which cultural actors evolve and in which cultural policies develop. While this book aims to convey general and basic principles about federalism and federations with regard to cultural affairs, it does not sacrifice anything to the ambition of explaining that there are, in fact, different types of federalism and different ideas about federations, and that these differences inform the development, and arguably, the very fabric of cultural policies. To give an example of what is meant, here, it can be suggested that federations are among the countries that offer the highest (Germany) and lowest cultural funding per capita (USA) (Canada Council for the Arts 2005: 1). If one tried to answer the question of whether federations invest more (or less) in culture than unitary states, they would probably find the answer to be inconclusive. Chances are that what really influences the level of cultural funding per capita—in general—is a better social disposition to social policy and the welfare state (see Esping-Anderson 1990). Esping-Anderson's typology might very well help in recognizing "three worlds of cultural funding" in relation to different societal and political structures that inform social policy. However, this book provides different kinds of answers than those of Esping-Anderson: it helps to understand why cultural funding is structured in a certain manner; it also helps to understand the strategies that advocacy groups employ in the cultural sectors. For instance, compared to Australians and Canadians, Swiss citizens can engage and constrain subnational and federal cultural policy by organizing a referendum. In 2018, the youth movement of the liberal-radical party organized a referendum against audiovisual taxes that could have, in fact, defunded their national broadcaster. All of these elements are rooted in the institutional levers of a political system.

Chapter 1 of this book aims to introduce federalism and alludes to a number of important questions that can stem from federalism as a system of institutions; it provides some important contrasts between federations and unitary States. Chapter 2 discusses one of the most important

xiv INTRODUCTION

elements for cultural power in a federation; it engages with the constitutional division of cultural powers. Chapter 3 moves away from constitutional issues and engages more closely with executive powers, looking at government capacity and administrations. This chapter focuses on intergovernmental relations. Chapter 4 brings forward the question of cities in federations; it discusses the intricacies of capitals and cultural institutions in federations, and also approaches the issue of the federal/municipal relationship in relation to cultural policy· development. Chapter 5 offers an original outlook on the nature of subnational cultural diplomacy; it provides some insights about different traditions and approaches when it comes to the presence of subnational States in cultural affairs. The last chapter provides a general conclusion and synthesis; it formulates four types of cultural federalism based on the parameters that are discussed throughout this book: division of power; intergovernmentalism; local/federal relations; and subnational cultural diplomacy and cultural relations. The value and limitations of this typology are also extensively discussed. With this in mind, this book was written with a certain comparativist ethos. By this, it is suggested that this book has sought to openly engage with multiple countries and that the results are informed by an analysis of institutional and public documents, press reviews, and many other material and tools commonly used in comparative research. Comparative research is never a perfect mediation, but researchers are always careful to make sense of their interpretations and are actively aware of the importance to distance themselves from their own natural readings of social and institutional realities. In other words, extreme care has been taken to make sure that this book does not overly reproduce the systems of reference and normativities that structure Canadian federalism. Attention and great care have been put in preserving the nuances that are necessary to understand the diversity of federal traditions across the globe, and essential distinctions between different federal States that may impact cultural policy development and implementation. Comparative research is, once again, never a perfect mediation between worlds and systems, but this book was produced with a special care not to be informed by frames of references that would be very natural to its author.

REFERENCES

Beauregard, D. (2018). *Cultural Policy and Industries of Identity: Québec, Scotland, & Catalonia.* London: Palgrave.

Bordat, E. M. (2013). Institutionalization and Change in Cultural Policy: CONACULTA and Cultural Policy in Mexico (1988–2006). *International Journal of Cultural Policy, 19*(2), 222–248.

Burns, R., & Van der Will, W. (2003). German Cultural Policy: An Overview. *International Journal of Cultural Policy, 9*(2), 133–152.

Canada Council for the Arts. (2005). *Comparisons of Arts Funding in Selected Countries: Preliminary Findings.* Ottawa: Canada Council for the Arts.

Esping-Anderson, G. (1990). *The Three Worlds of Welfare Capitalism.* Princeton, NJ: Princeton University Press.

Evans, P. B., Rueschemeyer, D., & Skocpol, T. (1985). *Bringing the State Back In.* Cambridge: Cambridge University Press.

Gattinger, M., & Saint-Pierre, D. (2011). *Les politiques culturelles provinciales et territoriales du Canada. Origines, évolutions, mise en œuvre.* Québec: Les presses de l'Université Laval.

Hernández-Acosta, J. J. (2013). Differences in Cultural Policy and Its Implications for Arts Management: Case of Puerto Rico. *The Journal of Arts Management, Law, and Society, 43*(3), 125–138. https://doi.org/10.1080/1 0632921.2013.817363.

Lemasson, G. (2015). Cultural Development: A New Policy Paradigm in the Cultural Policies of the 1970s in Québec. *International Journal of Cultural Policy, 21*(5), 593–610. https://doi.org/10.1080/10286632.2014.943753.

Perrin, T. (2012). New Regionalism and Cultural Policies: Distinctive and Distinguishing Strategies, from Local to Global. *Journal of Contemporary European Studies, 20*(4), 459–475. https://doi.org/10.1080/14782804.20 12.737663.

Rius-Ulldemolins, J., & Zamorano, M. M. (2015). Federalism, Cultural Policies, and Identity Pluralism: Cooperation and Conflict in the Spanish Quasi-Federal System. *Publius: The Journal of Federalism, 45*(2), 167–188. https://doi.org/10.1093/publius/pju037.

Saint-Pierre, D., & Audet, C. (2011). *Les Tendances et les Défis des Politiques Culturelles-Cas Nationaux en Perspective. France-Angleterre-États-Unis-Allemagne-Espagne-Belgique-Suisse-Suède-Pays de Galle et Écosse-Québec-Les Organisations Internationales.* Québec: Presses Université Laval.

Scott, R. W. (2001). *Institutions and Organizations.* Thousand Oaks, CA: Sage Publications.

Steinmo, S., Thelen, K. A., & Longstreth, F. (1992). *Structuring Politics: Historical Institutionalism in Comparative Analysis*. Cambridge: Cambridge University Press.

Tabrett, L. (2014). The Development of Cultural Indicators for Australia—Policy-Making in a Federal System of Government. *Cultural Trends, 23*(2), 82–92. https://doi.org/10.1080/09548963.2014.897449.

Watts, R. L. (1998). Federalism, Federal Political Systems, and Federations. *Annual Review of Political Science, 1*(1), 117–137.

CONTENTS

1	Federalism	1
2	Configuration of Cultural Powers	31
3	Cooperation and Competition: Cultural Governance and the Politics of Federalism	77
4	Cultural Policies, Federations, and Cities	123
5	Federations and Subnational International Cultural Relations	153
6	Conclusion: Governing Culture in Federations	183
Index		199

LIST OF TABLES

Table 2.1	Basic configuration and sources of cultural powers	69
Table 3.1	Influence of federalism on professional and advocacy groups	112
Table 3.2	Instruments of intergovernmental cooperation and competition in cultural affairs	114
Table 4.1	National capitals	126
Table 4.2	Concentration of cultural institutions in the capital	135
Table 6.1	Federal leadership type of cultural federalism	187
Table 6.2	Competitive cultural federalism	190
Table 6.3	Veto points cultural federalism	194
Table 6.4	Developmental cultural federalism	195

CHAPTER 1

Federalism

The purpose of this chapter is to introduce the basic definitions and principles of federalism. This chapter is meant to establish the parameters of what is meant by federalism and federal institutions; it is not meant to contribute further to the criteria that define a federation, but is simply meant to provide general conceptual boundaries of federalism. Federalism is a political and institutional reality for almost 40% of the world's population (Watts 2008: 1). More than 25 countries qualify as federations, not including all the countries that are theoretically on the fence or discussed as federations in development because of the evolution of their political system towards such an arrangement. As an institutional model, federalism is alive and strong, but world history is also full of experiences of failed federal projects: Yugoslavia, Czechoslovakia, Rhodesia, the West Indies Federation, and many others. While some countries like France or Italy are clearly not federations, their social and political history crossed paths with the idea—and although the idea never came to fruition in those states, it has been promoted by some of their politicians and philosophers (Biard et al. 2017). In sum, such an important element of institutional and political life as federalism ought to be better understood for its influence on cultural policy development and implementation.

The first two sections of this chapter present the two core characteristics of federalism: first, as an institutional form or structure for the State; second, as a social and political philosophy (Elazar 1979) that has

© The Author(s) 2019

J. Paquette, *Cultural Policy and Federalism*,
New Directions in Cultural Policy Research,
https://doi.org/10.1007/978-3-030-12680-3_1

numerous implications for politics, identity, and citizenship. The third section of this chapter provides empirical references to federalism; it provides a list of the main federal States, as well as some important institutional nuances and exceptions (e.g. European Union, quasi-federal States, devolution, etc.). The chapter concludes by raising and reasserting the importance of federalism—as an institutional variable and social philosophy—for cultural policy.

1.1   THE NATURE OF THE STATE: STRUCTURES AND INSTITUTIONS

Political scientists generally categorize States into two broad categories: unitary States and federal States. While there are a variety of political regimes and a number of nuances that could be made between these two broad categories, and while there are, in fact, many types of federal States, this basic dichotomy—differentiating between unitary and federal States—is essential to better understanding the subject. From an institutional perspective, unitary States suppose a structure of power that is generally assumed to be more centralized than that of federal States. By contrast, federalism implies a certain diffusion of power (Elazar 1987; Bagchi 2003). That diffusion or separation of power is operated at the level of subunits or subnational units. According to Karmis and Norman (2005), "In the most general sense, federalism is an arrangement in which two or more self-governing communities share the same political space" (p. 6). In other words, federalism supposes an institutional arrangement where two or more governmental units are federated—united—in sharing a national/federal level of government. In a related manner, federalism is not strictly an issue of institutional organization; it is also a political reality that has effects on citizens insofar as it may shape a sense of citizenship and belonging. Again, following Karmis and Norman's basic definition: "Citizens of federal states (or superstates, as in the case of the European Union) are members of both their subunit (sometimes called a province, canton, land, or, confusingly, a state) and the larger federation as a whole" (p. 6). In a federal State, citizens participate in the politics of their subnational and federal governments; they vote for and are governed by two political entities. A good way to understand federalism and to extend this definition is to approach and identify the logics of the alternative form of State: the unitary State.

In a unitary State, executive and legislative powers—in other words, governments and parliaments—do not need to share their decision-maker power with other subnational units. While unitary States do not have to share their power (with subunits), they have the prerogative to give (and take back) powers and responsibilities to other governmental bodies. For instance, unitary States will often rely on municipal powers or regional governments to oversee or deliver certain policies. France, Italy, and the People's Republic of China are good case examples of unitary States. In all three of these countries, the central government has given a certain number of decision-making powers to cities, and all of them rely on a very elaborate number of regional administrations to implement central policies. Looking more precisely at cultural policy research, it has been well-documented that France and Italy have also given a lot of cultural power to cities and regions and have decentralized some aspects of their cultural policies; cities and regions in these countries have taken not only a greater role in (cultural) policy implementation, but greater responsibilities in cultural decision-making (Friedberg and Urfalino 1985; Négrier 1997; Zan et al. 2007). In a unitary State, decentralization—handing over power or autonomy to another entity—is a voluntary process. In other words, subnational entities may well exist in political and administrative terms in unitary States—though their existence and relative power are often precarious.

In France, for instance, in 2016, the national government voted to reduce the number of regions in its metropolitan territory, from 22 to 13. This modification was driven by the national government and aimed at creating a more efficient structure for regional service delivery. Many well-known regions that had a long political reality in the post-World War II French administration and that people commonly associated or identified with have been amalgamated by what can easily be described as an ordinary act of government. As a result of this act, for example, two vast territories of western France—the former regions of Aquitaine and Poitou-Charentes—have been amalgamated into a single region called Nouvelle-Aquitaine (New Aquitaine). The same thing happened to a number of other regions in France. This example serves to illustrate how these regions—or subnational units—do not share the same level of power and guarantees that those found in a federal State do. This, however, does not mean that there is not a political price to the giving and removing of power to regional units. For instance, citizens of an amalgamated region may find their level of services to be diminished. Some citizens may even lament the fact that the amalgamation made it so that their city was no longer considered a capital of the newly minted region. Others may find that new regions, such as the new Occitanie region, may, in fact, convey a better sense of their local and regional identity than the previous regions did, while others may struggle to find themselves and recognize a sense of belonging and identity in a new mega-region like, for instance, Auvergne-Rhône-Alpes. The central government may well pay a political price in the short term for merging its regions—in the ballots, for instance; however, in principle, the reorganization of France's regions is perfectly within the range and nature of activities that the French (unitary) State is legitimately capable of undertaking. In a unitary State, "regions" and "regional governments" may be created, transformed, or eliminated, and the nature of their activities or power can be increased or decreased by a simple act of the national parliament. Regions in a unitary State do not benefit from the same power and protections as subnational governments found in federations. Unlike federated subnational governments, unitary State regions do not benefit from strong constitutional protections.

By contrast, in a federal States, executive, legislative, and judicial powers are constitutionally defined and distributed. From an institutional perspective, federalism is a form of division of power, where the constitution—the basic and fundamental law sustaining the political system—identifies and defines powers that are specific to the federal government vis-à-vis those that are specific to subnational entities. The vast majority of North American countries have federal States. Notably, Canada, the USA, and Mexico—the three largest North American States—all have federal political systems. Their federal governments and powers—housed in Ottawa, Washington, DC, and Mexico City, respectively—all have to compose with the existence of subnational governments (provinces in Canada, and states in the USA and Mexico) that have their own political space and powers. Subnational units benefit from constitutional protection, and the transformation of the federation—either by addition or removal of one (or more) subnational government(s)—is a very complicated process where subnational governments are actively involved. More importantly, the constitution also protects distinct areas of intervention; it defines, delineates, and protects powers that are specific to federal governments and those that are specific to subnational governments.

According to Lijphart, a "formal federal constitution" that guarantees powers specific to federal government and subnational units is the first and key condition for a federal State (2002: 177). To give an example, when it was crafted, the American Constitution defined powers specific to the federal government. In Article I, Section 8 of the constitution, 18 specific powers are bestowed upon Congress and the federal government, among which the most notable are associated with foreign affairs, national defence, citizenship, the national postal system, and finance—including the ability to establish a national currency. These powers are defined as the specific prerogative of the American federal government and subnational units—in this case, states—cannot intervene or act legitimately in these areas. These powers are constitutionally recognized as belonging to the federal government of the USA. Then, what defines state powers in the American Constitution?

Through the American Constitution, the Tenth Amendment of the Bill of Rights (1791) specifies the conditions of federalism in the USA: "The power not delegated to the United States [federal government] by the constitution, nor prohibited by it to the states [sub-national], are reserved to the states [sub-national] respectively, or to the people" (U.S. Constitution, amend X). This passage specifies that the state powers may be specified; but, by principle, all powers that are not defined as federal powers should be the authority of the states in the event that a governmental action or activity is deemed to be necessary. The constitution defines powers that are specific to each order of government and, often, defines who may be entitled to act in areas that are not explicitly covered in the document. The latter is often referred to as residual powers. As a result of this clause for residual powers, many of the USA's social policies are under the purview of state governments (Elazar 1990).

Similarly, the Mexican Constitution—which proceeds from a logic that shares many commonalities with the American Constitution—also clearly establishes the boundaries between federal and state powers (Rodriguez 1998) along similar terms. These provisions are mostly found in the second title, Chapter 2, Articles 42–48 and the fifth title, Articles 115–122 of the Mexican Constitution. The powers specific to the Mexican federal government cover similar areas to those covered by the United States' Constitution (i.e. defence, foreign affairs, currency, etc.). In the case of Mexico, however, Article 124 of the seventh title also suggests that "[t]he powers that are not expressly conceded by this Constitution to federal officials are understood to be reserved to the States" (Constitution of Mexico, art. 124, title VII).

The *Constitution Acts, 1867 to 1982* (2013) is Canada's main constitutional document. This document brings together the British North America Act of 1867 with the constitutional amendments that also introduced a Charter of Rights and Freedoms in 1982. As in the above-described cases, it is this document that delineates the capacities of both federal and provincial (subnational) governments; it also divides powers in terms of those that are exclusively federal, exclusively provincial, and "shared" between both branches of government (Verney 1995; Cameron and Simeon 2002). Some important powers are exclusively under the authority of provincial governments. For instance, the federal government has no say in education and educational policy as it is the exclusive jurisdiction of provincial governments. Municipal affairs and natural resources are also good examples of powers that are typically provincial in Canada. Each provincial government is responsible for its province's education policy and administers their education at will. Foreign affairs, national defence, employment insurance, census, fisheries, banking, aboriginal affairs, and many other areas are defined as exclusive federal powers. Old age pensions, agriculture, and immigration are defined as shared powers by the constitution, meaning that there must be a negotiation and agreements between governments. Powers undefined by the constitution as provincial or shared powers are residual powers. The disposition for residual power authorizes the federal government of Canada to act and intervene at will for the "good government of Canada" (Canada, Intergovernmental Affairs 2018).

These three cases present how federalism relies on constitutional grounds, and how the constitution is the main instrument that shapes this institutional reality. Federalism implies a relational structure between federal and subnational levels of government. In a related manner, the level of autonomy that is guaranteed by the constitution also informs us of another characteristic of a federal system, and that is that subnational parliaments' laws and policies may constitute a force that enables diversity or differentiation between different subnational spaces. In other words, federalism shapes power, but it also shapes the nature of the social, cultural, and economic relations established between the different subnational entities of a country. Federalism is also an institutional configuration of political forces that can confirm, maintain, and foster some social and cultural differentiations in a country.

For instance, in Canada, liquors, wine, and alcoholic beverages are subject to a federal tax if they are imported, but the commerce and production of alcoholic beverages are entirely a provincial prerogative. In the province of Ontario, the commerce of wine and spirits is entirely managed by a provincial government agency that holds monopoly over the sale of these products. In the province of Québec, the state has the monopoly over spirits sold in governmental agencies, but some wines and light alcoholic beverages can be sold by private businesses provided they meet certain criteria (Paquette and Lacassagne 2008). Some dispositions are also in place to allow flexibility in the sale of local wines and beers. In Alberta, the province has set the standards for the sale of alcoholic beverages and a governmental agency is responsible for verifying and enforcing the law; however, the distribution is managed by the private sector. These three important Canadian provinces have each created their own systems of alcohol management that reflects some of their respective social and political values. In federations, subnational political power may act as a force of differentiation; the lifestyle and economic and social conditions may also vary depending on where—that is to say, in which subnational entity—an individual resides.

Moreover, the institutional dynamics of a federation may not only contribute to shaping different living conditions for the federation's subnational entities, they may also act in a way that shapes politics and commerce between those entities. To build on the same example, we will say that in Canada, the commerce of alcohol between provinces is either forbidden by law or limited by provincial taxes and tariffs that treat them as imported goods. In other words, subnational relations are also a reality of federations; they are part of the political life of federations. To give an example, in 2018, as a measure of retaliation for the Government of British Columbia's lack of support for an important oil pipeline project that would have benefited the province of Alberta, the Albertan government imposed a temporary ban on the sale of British Columbian wine in its province. This is an example that speaks to the complexity of a federal system. For cultural policy, this means that the Canadian system is extremely fragmented and the federal government has no strong constitutional capacity to impose or oppose the cultural actions of its provincial counterparts.

In a federal system, the constitution is the most important source of power delineation and definition for federal and subnational governments. In principle, this division of power is respected; of course, in practice, there are notable exceptions, with a certain dose of creativity used by governments (at all levels) to circumvent some of the limitations imposed by their constitutions. As will be shown in Chapter 5, despite the fact that external relations are generally a prerogative of federal governments, some subnational governments have been increasingly active in promoting their (cultural) interests at the international level. Nonetheless, the constitution is intended to be the institutional instrument that informs every subnational member and their federal government of the rules of the game. The constitution states what can and cannot be done by member states. However, the constitution also has another function in federal systems: it clarifies the rules of membership and states the conditions for entering and, less commonly, the conditions for exiting the federation. The constitution is the key to the rules that have set the construction of a federation, and any modification to a constitutional law requires, in most cases, a special consultation of the federation's subnational governments. For instance, federations have clauses that can lead to the aggregation of new members. In recent years, the inclusion of the British self-governing colony of Newfoundland as a Canadian province in 1949 required constitutional amendments. In the case of the USA, under the American Constitution, the Congress can decide to include new states as part of the union (U.S. Constitution, art. 4, Section 3), but the Congress may not interfere with the affairs and, in particular, the boundaries of an existing state without its consultation and consent. Under this principle, and following this institutional trajectory, Alaska and Hawaii, which previously had the status of federal territories, became states on equal footing in 1959.

Federations not only grow, they can occasionally lose members and, at times, may even collapse. The politically complicated departure of Singapore from the Malaysian federation in 1965 is a good example of a territory that left to become a new nation of its own. Inclusion of new subnational governments or the secession of subnational governments (to become new independent States) happens, but are not extremely common occurrences. In post-communist Eastern Europe, federations have collapsed, thus rendering autonomy and sovereignty to their subnational members. The peaceful dissolution of Czechoslovakia in 1993 following the Velvet Revolution and the progressive evolution of a communist State to a liberal democracy is a good example. The same cannot be said of the dissolution of the Socialist Federal Republic of Yugoslavia in the early 1990s, which ended in a terrible bloodbath.

In this section, the intention was to establish some of the most basic institutional principles of federalism. It is argued, here, that federalism is more than an institutional reality; it is also a matter of social and political philosophy. Before moving further with this argument, it may be useful recall the basic principles of what is meant by federalism. In political science, there exist a host of rich definitions of federalism that present a number of criteria for recognizing a federation (e.g. Riker 1964; Birch 1966; Lijphart 1979; Watts 1998; Burgess 2006). Building on some of these ideas, while also avoiding an overly complex exegesis and comparison of these definitions and their theoretical divergences, this section, instead, offers a synthetic definition that should cover the essential elements for researchers who are specialized in the study of cultural policy and cultural affairs. First, federations are defined in contrast to unitary States. As such, federations are composed of two or more subnational governments. Second, these subnational governments (provinces, land, cantons, states, etc.) have an existence and political powers (legislative, executive, and, sometimes, judicial) that are protected by the constitution. In other words, in a federation, unlike a unitary State, the decentralization of power to subunits is guaranteed and protected by the constitution. Third, in federations, the constitution defines the basic rules of the political game. In particular, it defines which political entity is entitled to act in which matters; it defines the legitimacy of federal and subnational governments' actions over policy areas. Fourth, federations evolve over time; they are not static and the size of their membership may increase or, in some rare cases, decrease. The transformation of a constitution is also regulated by a process in which the subnational governments are often party, whether it is through a constitutional conference or an institution that aims to represent subnational governments at the federal level. In federal systems, the senate often acts as the legislative chamber that represents subnational governments. Changing the constitution, by addition of a member subnational state, for instance, implies changing the rules of the political game; these modifications always entail a form of consultation or consent from a representative of subnational governments. It should also be kept in mind that federations may also be dissolved or collapse. Fifth, federations imply power relationships and a political arena that operates on both the federal-subnational and subnational-subnational axes. That is to say, analysts and researchers of federative systems should be aware of the power relationships exerted between the federal and subnational governments, as well as the relationships between the subnational members. This is an important singularity of federations in comparison with unitary States. Finally, the degree of decentralization inherent to federalism may also contribute to social and economic differentiations between subnational governments. Federal systems are based on two opposing and sometimes contradictory tensions. On the one hand, federations protect forms of autonomy and distinctions between their subnational members. On the other hand, federal power often aims to equalize and normalize life standards across the country. This aim to equalize may or may not be successful; it may also be limited by other institutional constraints. Nevertheless, the aim to equalize should be seen as an institutional pressure common to all federal systems.

1.2　The Social and Political Philosophy of Federalism

Federalism has its roots in the history of political thought; it is a philosophy of the State. But, when thinking of federalism, institutional dynamics are what immediately come to mind. However, federalism is more than an institutional configuration or mechanic. A closer look at this institutional choice reveals, in fact, much more than a simple institutional assemblage: federal institutions are chosen over a unitary form of State for social, historical, and political reasons (Allen 1998; Rundell 2009; De Schutter 2011). The rise of federalism as an institutional form of government coincides with the emergence of a new, post-medieval political thought that engaged with antiquity and current history to question the ideal configuration of States.

In this section, a deeper understanding of federalism is offered, one that ties in with its philosophical origins. This section has two objectives. First, the section synthesizes and presents a number of dominant ideas and philosophies of federalism as they evolved throughout the history of political and philosophical thought. In its simplest expression, this first objective is to render explicit and acknowledge the links between institutions and fundamental political ideas of power and society. Second, this section will move past the acknowledgement that federalism is more than just an institution rooted in the world of political ideas. Philosophically, federalism emerged from political ideas and debates on sovereignty, democracy, and citizenship; its historical contribution was to further these debates. Therefore, the second objective of this section is to render explicit the basic principles of power and social organization that lie within federalism. While these ideas are rooted in a long history of political thought, their legacy is important, and their influence continues to inform many contemporary debates about State and society. Federalism, as a political philosophy, may also give a certain texture and flavour to notions of sovereignty, democracy, and citizenship which may also, in turn, inform some cultural policy orientations.

To these ends, this section will present the works of European philosophers Althusius and Montesquieu. This will be followed by an examination of the works of liberal thinkers, notably the works of Alexander Hamilton and James Madison and the work of John Stuart Mill as representative of different liberal perspectives on federalism. Similarly, the work of Immanuel Kant has been selected because it offers an essential perspective for contemporary debates in cultural policy, especially when it comes to engaging with the idea of cosmopolitanism. Finally, this section will present some basic ideas and works associated to Canadian philosopher Will Kymlicka. These works (and philosophers) do not cover the entirety of the question or scope of literary thought as it relates to federalism, but they were selected for their relevance to the question of cultural policy and because their contributions have a long-lasting legacy in political debates on the nature and purpose of political institutions.

One of the most prominent and oft-cited figures of federalism is the German lawyer and philosopher Johannes Althusius (1557–1638). Building on Greek philosophy, Althusius saw politics as the "science of those matters which pertain to the living together" (Althusius 1932 [1614]: lxvii), which is also indicative of his methodological stance on the best form and organization of the State: society is organic to human beings, where humans ought to live in symbiosis. Althusius' federalism (consociatio symbiotica) was informed by his understanding of society as consisting of complex layers of communities—a community of communities. Arguably, Althusius' views of politics were also implicitly relying on systemic metaphors of the social world. Unlike the thoughts of Hobbes or Rousseau, the latter of who also contributed to the debate on federalism, Althusius' political ideas did not rely on a form of sacrifice or surrendering of power, but on an idea of responsibility in sharing power. This is, in part, why Althusius' works are often cited as conveying the seeds of federalist thought in political philosophy. For Althusius, politics, as a practice, is the "art of associating" (Karmis and Norman 2005: 25). There is a normative conception, in Althusius' work, that associations are good because they are the purpose of politics. As such, federations perfectly achieve the purpose of politics as they are predicated on association. Interestingly, these basic principles are not without finding a certain echo in the political philosophy of contemporary times. In fact, the art of associating as the true nature and purpose of politics harkens to the more recent political works of Bruno Latour (2005; Weibel and Latour 2005). For Althusius, and certainly also for Latour, the purpose of politics is to assemble individuals and communities; it is about making links that recognize value in the association. Without going deeper into the works of Althusius, the principle that should be kept in mind is that there is a normative position on the nature of politics and of institutions in his work, and that federalism and federations explicitly achieve the ethical duties of politics. Federal institutions achieve the virtue and purpose of politics by being associations *par excellence.*

Another important contribution to the political philosophy of federalism comes from the work of French philosopher Charles-Louis de Secondat, Baron de La Brède et de Montesquieu (1689–1755). For Montesquieu, federations present a number of political advantages. Specifically, Montesquieu's views of federalism were more closely tied to the idea of "confederation", to the union of States who associate, but largely retain their sovereignty. Some of these essential ideas are conveyed in the first and second part of his work, *The Spirit of the Laws* (books VIII, IX, X). For Montesquieu (2013 [1758]), successful "federative republics" will share the same objectives and avoid wars between partners; they will commonly, in association, contract peace, and trade treaties. Looking at Holland, Germany, and at the Swiss Confederation, Montesquieu was persuaded that federations "combined the advantages of small and large States" (Karmis and Norman 2005: 54–55). For Montesquieu, small republics were more politically sound and less prone to corruption. In confederation, small republics could possess the power, influence, and forces of the greater monarchies. Confederation supposes sound governance at the level of the small republics and good capacity at the international level. If, for some reason, the confederation is dissolved, the States retain their sovereignty. The system described by Montesquieu—and some of the characteristics he identified—is echoed by the European Union. The recent British referendum for exiting the European Union (Brexit) in June 2016 shows some limitations to this model and is a reminder of the importance of the politics of federal associations. The majority of voters expressed a sovereigntist position, appealing to a desire to retain or reacquire more powers in Britain. As shall be discussed in the next section, the nature of the association between the member states of the European Union is not comparable to the federal arrangements between member states that compose Canada, the USA, or the current Russian Federation, for that matter. The case of the European Union provides an interesting debate as it, at times, challenges some of the conceptual ideas or common views about the nature of federalism.

Montesquieu was also adamant about the political value of the separation of powers (executive, legislative, judicials). For Montesquieu, power stopped power, or a power could limit another type of power to avoid tyranny (Riekmann 2007). Interestingly, it is in the American tradition of liberal philosophy that this idea of separation of powers meshed with the principles of federalism (Jewkes 2016). The American perspective on federalism also marks a theoretical and social turning point for federalism. According to Karmis and Norman, the American federation marks a transition from the earlier work associated with the idea of confederation and truly reveals some of the contemporary essences of federalism. More importantly: "For the first time in both practice and theory, the new Constitution [that of the United States] proposed a union not just of political entities, like states, but also of all citizens of all of these entities" (2005: 103). In other words, the American federation introduced the contemporary idea that the federal system was not simply a matter of association between States (that retained their sovereignty), but a matter of citizenship. Americans are both citizens (and residents) of the federation and of their individual subnational entities. The work of federalist thinkers (Alexander Hamilton and James Madison) is often associated with the *Federalist Papers*. The protagonists of these papers (which were published between 1787 and 1788) believed in the separation of powers and in the system of checks and balance that is now characteristic of the American political system. However, it is often argued that, from their normative perspective, the federalist thinkers were implicitly more in favour of a strong central government than a (weak) central federal government at the mercy of its subnational entities (Miller 1988: 107).

The Anglo-American tradition of federalism was seen, in this form of organization, as an additional means and tool to secure individual freedom through counter-powers against a central State. John Stuart Mill offers another fundamental perspective on federalism, and one that is, perhaps, best understood from the liberal-utilitarian position that is defended by Mill. Specifically, Mill's views of federalism, in his *Essays on Politics and Society* (1859), gain greater significance when they are recontextualized in the scope of a utilitarian position. For Mill, federations can be a viable solution for small States who wish for greater protection by uniting—whether it is to avoid war between them or to limit aggressions from other external powers. For a federation to be successful, it needs to meet a certain number of criteria. First, "there should be a sufficient amount of mutual sympathy among the populations" of the federating States (Mill 1859: 191). A shared language, religion, or culture offer better chances of success according to Mill. Second, Mill believes that federations are more successful in cases where an individual State (entity) relies on other partners of the union to protect itself from external aggressions rather than from its own power and strength. Third, "there be not a very marked inequality of strength among the several contracting states" (p. 191). Looking at these three conditions, it is evident that some of the utilitarian quest for the *summum bonum* (the highest good) is present. Federations are not normatively better than other forms of State, but they can, in some circumstances, be useful for organizing a good government. Mill's conditions also implicitly allude to potential limitations of federalism. Specifically, Mill's perspective points to the type of federation where one member would impose its strength over the others, or situations where a member is unable to benefit from the union because this form of association is unable to achieve outcomes that could otherwise be achieved by an individual or unitary State. This scenario also speaks to the potential value (and unequal power relations) of a (strong) State or political entity uniting with weaker States. The potential inequality of federations is an important theme, one which also informs about the internal dynamic, the inner political life, not to say the intergovernmental politics of federations.

Other thinkers and philosophers, such as Immanuel Kant (1724–1804), have seen in federalism a potential for global peace and stability between nations. In his *Perpetual Peace* (1795), Kant argues in favour of a global system where free nations avoid conflict through the establishment of a universal system based on the rule of law. For Kant, peace can only be achieved if nations form a federation that surpasses the sovereignty of individual States. According to Kant, perpetual peace cannot be achieved between States who would sign a treaty one day and decline to follow it the next. For this reason, Kant sought a more permanent structure to regulate relations between nations. To achieve this project, Kant outlines a number of principles to be followed. The first article of this treaty reaffirms the value of representative government and the importance of consulting the people (p. 121). The second article suggests that the "law of nations shall be founded on a federation of free States" (p. 129). The third article indicates that "the rights of men, as citizens of the world, shall be limited to the conditions of universal hospitality" (p. 137). According to Kant, these three principles ought to bring peace through a federation. There is, in Kant's idea of federalism, an ideal of universalism and benevolence that could be embodied in an international federal institution. Furthermore, the institutional development of a global federation should also give rise to a "cosmopolitan right or law" (p. 142). Institutions such as the United Nations immediately come to mind when engaging with these ideas. However, there are other important principles, here, to retain for cultural policy research. There has been recent reflection, in the field of cultural policy, on the conditions for a "cosmopolitan cultural policy" (Robbins 1992; Robins 2007), or on the cosmopolitan ideology of cultural policy (Jenkins 2004), or even the potential of cultural policy to federate and the capacity of culture to unite and achieve cosmopolitan politics through cultural practices (Skot-Hansen 2002; Alasuutari 2013).

In political philosophy, federalism has also crossed paths with a number of contemporary political ideas such as multiculturalism. The work of Canadian philosopher, Will Kymlicka (2011; Kymlicka et al. 1997), is a good example. While Kymlicka acknowledges that there are some important virtues in federalism, that it can be a space to provide sufficient room for some groups to express their cultural preferences, he also expresses concerns about the viability of federalism in multinational contexts. In particular, Kymlicka argues that the territorial logic of some forms of federalism may well lead to secessions. Kymlicka argues that his scepticism of federalism is based on the case of Québec in Canada, and by reference to what was also seen as a federation-in-the-making in Spain, where Catalonia, the Basques Country, and Galicia have acquired a form of autonomy. Against the most optimistic claims about federalism, multinational federations may become a "stepping stone for secession" (Kymlicka 2005: 110). Kymlicka (2011) further argues for a more creative form of federalism, where a multinational view of citizenship must be promoted, thus providing for a process of collective identity construction that acknowledge differences as a solidarizing force in federations.

Some of these ideas are not entirely novel. Looking back at the twentieth century, federalism—multinational federalism—was not only seen as an ideal for multiculturalism by liberal political philosophers, it was also promoted in the internationalist discourse and in socialist political theory. The former USSR and ex-Yugoslavia were both federations based on the diversity of nations and peoples. Thus, cultural diversity has been an important thrust in defining contemporary political thoughts on federalism.

As a political and social philosophy, federalism entails a number of values that exert a certain influence on how culture is understood and defined by institutions. With this in mind, it is useful to summarize and expand on some of the basic philosophical principles of federalism. First, federalism is often defined as a "counter-power", an additional protection against an omnipotent central government. This perspective is particularly salient in the American tradition of federalism. This philosophical perspective on political institutions can have a certain number of implications for culture as it acknowledges the importance or positive value of having different centres of decision-making; it is favourable to certain forms of decentralization. Second, while federalism offers "counter-powers", it can also offer a platform for reaching certain common values in the quest for greater social equity. On social issues, both Canadian and Australian federal governments are often seen as equalizers, trying to provide a certain form of equity for their citizens, notwithstanding the state or province in which they reside. For instance, the Canadian Broadcasting Corporation (CBC) was mandated by the federal government to provide information and culture to Canadians "from coast to coast" (Potter 2011). As part of its mandate, the CBC has rendered information and programming accessible to all Canadians, especially to remote areas of the country where private broadcasters saw no potential for earnings. Of course, in the decades following the introduction of the CBC, provinces like Québec and Ontario have introduced their own provincial public broadcasting corporations which have served to foster the provinces' own cultural aspirations. Third, whether the inclination is geared more towards decentralization or equalization, federalism is philosophically principled on the idea of diversity. Without implying it is inherently virtuous, federalism is, at the very least, a form of acknowledgement of a constitutive difference among the different parts or units of a country. This philosophical perspective has a number of implications for cultural institutions. Looking at the politics of heritage, this perspective implies that cultural narratives are presumably considering and making room for a form of diversity (i.e. cultural, linguistic, and regional). From a symbolic perspective, federal institutions often aim to mirror this diversity in their politics of representation, as cultural recognition is an important value. Fourth—and this point is made explicit by Mill—there is a potential for federations to become a space of political competition between members. Attention should not simply be paid to the legal foundations of federations, but should also be paid to the strength and weight of some of a federation's members. Federalism can imply both cooperation and competition between its constituent subnational entities.

1.3   Varieties of Federalism

More than 25 countries, comprising roughly 40% of the world's population, are governed under a federal system (Watts 2008: 1). Among these countries: Argentina, Australia, Austria, Belgium, Bosnia, Brazil, Canada, Ethiopia, Germany, Russia, India, Pakistan, Mexico, Nigeria, Sudan, Malaysia, the USA, Venezuela, Switzerland, and the United Arab Emirates. Smaller and less documented States have been organized for a good number of decades as federal systems—States such as St-Kitts and Nevis, and Comoros. Administrative reforms, constitutional reforms, and the emergence of new States and new "democracies" have also led to the development of new federations in recent years—often relying on federalism to account for profound cultural, religious (Burgess 2006), and political divisions in these countries: Iraq, Nepal, and South Sudan, for instance. Some federations have dissolved (e.g. the USSR, Yugoslavia, West Indies Federation, and Gran Colombia), or changed over time (e.g. Malaysia after the expulsion of Singapore in 1965). Looking at the above-mentioned countries and thinking about the proportion of the world's population that lives under this form of State, it becomes evident that federalism constitutes an important element of the political reality that must be addressed when thinking and talking about cultural policy. In this section, focus will be placed on the nuances of different accounts—whether it is on the account of history, of institutional mechanics, or of cultural diversity. Federal institutions and their functioning may be driven by different forces and differ from one country to another. In this section, we acknowledge the diversity of federalism and federations, or, to borrow from Béland and Myles (2012) or from Broschek (2012), we acknowledge the varieties of federalism.

Before going any further, it may also be appropriate to clarify the situation of three cases: The UK, Spain, and the European Union. Are these federations? The UK is a devolved State, having decentralized powers to

Scotland, Wales, and Northern Ireland. However, this decentralization is driven by the central government and has no strong and prior constitutional guarantees. While taking power back from Scotland, Wales, or Northern Ireland may prove to be politically costly, the UK remains largely and technically a unitary State (Peters 2001). Although there could be a case to be made for it evolving towards federalism (see Laffin and Thomas 1999), the UK is not considered a federation by most scholars. The absence of a constitutional guarantee is one of the elements that is often raised to disqualify the UK as a federation. Additionally, the policy areas in which Scotland and Northern Ireland, in particular, are competent are seen, technically, as powers that have been transferred to these devolved authorities by Westminster. Devolution is a form of decentralization.

Spain has been discussed in recent years as evolving as a de facto quasi-federation based on the power of autonomous regions (Sala 2014). According to Moreno, "The Spanish 1978 Constitution does not include the word 'federal' in any of its provisions, or in any subsequent legislation. However, since the 1980s the dynamics of the *Estado de las Autonomias* (State of Autonomies) are characterized by a latent federalization" (2007: 86). If federalism were to emerge in Spain, it would not be "the result of a well-defined constitutional separation of competencies and powers", it would develop "in an inductive manner, step by step" (p. 87). That being said, some authors do not share this point of view and suggest that many characteristics of a federal system are absent in Spain. The fact that federalism is not expressed in the constitution, the fact that the constitution does not clarify or clearly divide the powers between Madrid and the states, the fact that many regulatory powers remain centralized, and the fact that there are no federal instances to express the will of the states and autonomous regions—a function that the senate often accomplishes in federations—all point to a system that is, at best, quasi-federal (Maiz et al. 2010: 69–72). Additionally, the recent events of the Catalan referendum and the suspension of the Catalan government by Madrid in 2017 may require that political scientists revise their judgement of this case. The incident clearly shows that the Spanish government is leaning towards a unitarian conception of the State. In this case, the suspension of the Catalonian government is a denial of autonomy. Based on some of these reflections, Spain does not meet all the requirements of federalism.

As for the European Union, it is a federation of sovereign States; it is, in this view, a confederation, in the classical sense. Its processes and developments follow the patterns and objectives described by many of the aforementioned political philosophers, such as Montesquieu or Mill, of a confederation. While it is not a single State—rather, an association of many states—most researchers recognize (Burgess 1996; Mueller 1997; Kelemen 2003) that the European Union has characteristics of a federation; it shares commonalities with the political processes and institutional constraints that are typical to federations. Conversely, some countries official name may be misleading. The Canadian Confederation and the Helvetic Confederations, despite their names, have evolved into de facto federations; they are not, in practice, confederations.

These three cases (The UK, Spain, and the European Union) represent political entities or countries that have been extensively studied in cultural policy research. The UK is one of the more important case studies used in cultural research (see Gray 2000, 2004; Alexander 2007; Hadley and Gray 2017)—one from which a number of characteristics are usually derived—some of which make of it an archetype of cultural policy (Stevenson et al. 2010). In some cases, a certain type or approach to cultural policy has been defined as the British model (Gattinger and Saint-Pierre 2008; Gattinger et al. 2008). Similarly, Spain has attracted a lot of interest over the cultural rights of its national minorities (Basques, Catalan, and Galicians) (Bonet and Négrier 2008; Rius-Ulldemolins and Zamorano 2015). As for the European Union, it is also being extensively documented by researchers interested in issues of cultural governance and collective identity construction (Dewey 2008). These three cases are extremely important in cultural policy scholarship, but given the fact they sit in problematic standings vis-à-vis the more conventional understanding of federations and federalism, this book does not focus on them. Nevertheless, it is important to render explicit the reasons why these cases are not further documented in this book.

As for the rest of the countries that are often referred to as federations, and, in particular, those that were mentioned in the introduction of this chapter, it is important to introduce some of the important nuances. As is known, institutions enable and constrain cultural decision-making, but values (political and social philosophies) inform the normative frame in which agents approach these institutions. How culture is governed, in different countries, largely depends on institutional structures, social values, and the distinctive histories that shaped them. History and social values can significantly structure or alter how political institutions function. Suggesting what can sound like a relativistic aspect of institutions, however, is not to imply that the explanatory potential of institutions should be diminished; rather, it is to provide some nuances and cautions. Federal institutions are shaped by a variety of factors. It is not the intent, here, to proceed by systematic comparisons, but to offer some insights into the significance of these different factors in shaping the actual political life of federal institutions. To this end, three elements are insisted upon: historical developments, cultural diversity, and levels and extent of decentralization. These three themes, alone, are important and enough to support exercising caution when discussing federalism.

The historical development of federations is an element that shapes and informs how institutions work and the kind of constraints that agents must face. According to Burgess (2003), federations have often developed following two patterns: aggregation and disaggregation or devolution. For Burgess, the "classic example of federation by aggregation is the United States, which first broke away from the British Empire in 1776" (p. 379). Switzerland is another good example. The initial union of the cantons of Uri, Schwyz, and Unterwalden created the seeds of Switzerland. As reminded by Burgess, "[i]n contrast to aggregation, more federations have emerged via devolution. The British Empire has been the source of several successful modern federations, namely Canada, Australia, India, and Malaysia" (ibid.). These states were granted self-government—in part through an active desire from their federal and state governments to achieve imperial decentralization, but also through the British actively promoting the creation of federations between its different colonies. Canada and Australia are good examples of the unification of many self-governing colonies that shared interests and boundaries. Unlike the former British colonies, Germany, Austria, and even Switzerland, for that matter, have been shaped and reshaped as federations not through colonial processes, but through the evolution of the governance system of medieval Europe and the transformation of the Holy Roman Empire (p. 380). Federations are the result and inheritors of a long historical process. The question of the historical origins of federations takes its significance when researchers try to understand the patterns of evolution of a federation, as well as the basic logic and principles that federal institutions try to promote and protect. Additionally, the question of historical origins also gives a sense to the place and part that federal institutions play in the national history, in the collective myths that inform citizenship.

Cultural diversity is another important factor that shapes the dynamics of a federation. Some federations are often defined as being single-nation federations. According to Pinder (2007), "Australia, Austria, Germany and the USA may be called single-nation federations, within which none of the component states, with the exception of Bavaria, has a particularly enhanced sensitivity regarding its sovereignty, [...] on linguistic, cultural or ethnic grounds" (p. 6). Of course, the USA and Australia are much more diverse societies than is often assumed. In particular, both countries have a variety of Indigenous populations that have been living there since before the settlement of European settler societies. In the case of Germany, Bavaria is a good example of a member state with notable sensitivity regarding its sovereignty; however, there are other forms of historical minorities in Germany—including a Frisian language-speaking population and a Danish-speaking minority (Gorter 2008). In the USA, Louisiana has been a place where the French language has been widely spoken and used in the public space. In all of these cases, namely Australia, Austria, Germany, and the USA, cultural diversity was not considered in the design of their federations. Brazil and Argentina could be added to the list of States designed as single nation federations. By contrast, some federations have been designed and/or have evolved in consideration of cultural diversity. By cultural diversity, it is not so much a question of multicultural or pluralist societies shaped by contemporary migrations, but populations that have been recognized by a State as a different nation, culture, or population within the State. These populations are what would otherwise be referred to as national minorities (Beauregard 2018). Canada, Belgium, Malaysia, Switzerland, India, and Russia are good examples of multinational federations. These federations have been designed and/or have constitutions that have been greatly modelled to address issues of diversity, whether it is cultural, linguistic, or religious diversity. For instance, the Russian Federation has adopted a constitution where the multinational character of its subnations is recognized (Russian Federation, Chapter 1, art. 3) and where subnational governments have been designed on ethic bases rather than on territorial grounds. The Russian Federation is composed of 57 subnational governments based on territorial grounds and 32 based on ethnic considerations (republics and autonomous territories or *okrugs* and *oblast*). Since 2008, constitutional reforms have been made to change the inner dynamics of the federation. Vladimir Putin's political approach to the Russian Federation has been to diminish regional and subnational powers, and review any subnational legislation that may be in conflict with the Russian Constitution. Transformations to the Federation Council have also altered the possibilities for some regions and republics to have a voice in the evolution of federal affairs (Ross 2007: 123). Another good example of a multinational federation is Canada where the constitution recognizes the rights of a French-speaking minority of the population. For a long time, the Canadian federation has represented its creation as two nations coming together, namely the English and French-speaking population of Britain's North American colonies. The national mythology around the founding fathers of the Canadian federation heavily emphasize the relationship between John A. Macdonald and Georges-Étienne Cartier as symbolizing this union; it is not uncommon for public institutions (schools, airport, public spaces) to be named Macdonald-Cartier. Beyond symbolism, the Canadian federation has evolved in taking into consideration the religious and linguistic rights of the French-speaking minority. The disproportionate concentration of this population in three provinces (Québec, Ontario, and New Brunswick), and in one province in particular (Québec), has an impact on the provincial/federal governments dynamics. Constitutional dispositions on linguistic matters are also what shaped the evolution of Belgium, in the 1990s, into a federal system composed of regions and communities that reflect some of the divisions or different social and cultural aspirations of the country's Flemish, French, and German populations.

Third, federations may also differ on the level and types of power that are shared between the different entities of the federation (federal/subnational), and by the different degrees of decentralization of power that subnational governments benefit from vis-à-vis the federal government. For example, in Latin America, federalism has typically involved relatively low levels of decentralization and greater power vested in central institutions. In many cases, the constitution and political institutions give limited resources and capacities to subnational units to generate fiscal revenues. For instance, the Mexican Constitution and its party system have led to a more centralized form of federalism. A similar, more centralized form of federalism was also found in the Bolivarian federalism in Gran Colombia (1819–1831)—a federation, that lasted a little more than a decade, comprised of Colombia, Venezuela, Ecuador, Panama, and other territories (Brown 2006). These forms of federalism can be contrasted with the cases of Canada, the USA, and Switzerland (Vatter 2005), where subnational units benefit from greater fiscal autonomy and a greater number of powers.

Federalisms are not all the same; one could argue that, when taking into account values and history, there are, in fact, a variety of federalisms (Anckar 2003; Béland and Myles 2012; Broschek 2012). These elements have created conditions in which some federalisms imply greater fiscal autonomy to national subunits than others, while some simply have a greater number of powers and capacities to exercise them in their own jurisdictions. Political scientists have come up with the notion of asymmetrical federalism to account for federations where the constitution or political arrangements create a situation of exception for some subnational members (Beyme 2005). Countries like Canada, India, or Belgium are often considered as cases of asymmetrical federalism (Swenden and Jans 2006). In fact, most cases where there are particular dispositions for a recognized national minority would probably qualify as cases of asymmetric federations. Similarly, special measures to favour the German reunification may also have created conditions for an asymmetric federalism (Benz 1999). Fundamentally, the question of whether there are cases where federalism is both constitutionally and politically symmetrical can be raised. The USA is often described or thought of as a symmetrical federalism, but its system also has a number of interesting and important exceptions. The USA may be partly symmetrical between States with, for instance, two senators per state regardless of the population; but its political system also accommodates some associations that render the scenario more complex. Puerto Rico, for instance, is an associated state that, by virtue of this political and institutional arrangement, complexifies the view of the USA as a symmetrical federation.

Exceptions exist in the rules or practices of any federation. Now, that being said, the notion of asymmetric federalism should help with recognizing that there are some federal regimes where exceptions are made for subnational governments. If anything, this notion should serve as a reminder that federalism is not one single model, but a variety of institutional practices that may vary from one federation to the next.

1.4   Federalism and Cultural Policy

In this chapter, basic elements to consider when discussing federalism were presented. First, a basic definition of federalism was offered, based on a common contrast with unitary States. Additionally, the chapter pushed beyond an overly simplistic view of federalism as a single model applied universally across States. Next, this chapter introduced the long philosophical history of federalism in political philosophy. While this introduction may have been selective or cursory, it tried to present some of the main themes that have been brought forward by philosophers, most of which offer a normative (Karmis and Norman 2005) or favourable view of federalism. Political philosophers found different justifications for the adoption of federal institutions based on political context, cultural diversity, or, simply, based on the view that there should always be more protections or safeguards against an over-centralization of power. In reality, federations often evolve institutionally in search of a balance between moments where there are increasing pushes for centralization and moments where decentralization seems to be a solution for a political problem. Finally, this chapter cautioned the reader about a significant number of small nuances that render comparative work all the more complicated.

Different types of federalism and federal institutions have commonalities between them, but they respond to different historical processes; they are answers to different social configurations and the nature of their functioning and division of powers may vary significantly. Cultural policies are social policies, and a widespread belief in the relative importance of the State in social affairs may be the best indicator of support for social policies. This, in turn, may be the best predictor for more or less governmental spending in culture. Comparisons of cultural funding and structures between Australia and Canada are often made as they share a number of important commonalities. Finding similar outcomes between these two states is often unsurprising. Adding the USA into the mix makes comparisons more difficult. The governments of Australia and Canada typically spend five to ten times more per capita on culture than the USA does (National Endowment for the Arts 2000). As such, federalism, alone, may not be the best predictor for more or less spending. But what it can bring to the picture is the provenance of spending, or some spending patterns that may be hidden in comparative research when strictly looking at national levels of spending. Thus, there is, arguably, more to be understood in the relationship between federalism and cultural policy.

For cultural policy researchers, the most important and interesting element to consider when it comes to federalism is the nature of institutional designs and the specific forms of constraint that shape the politics of culture. Cultural policy in federations responds to different political expectations and follows different demands emerging from the political system. If culture is considered beyond the question of funding, and levels of funding per capita, then federalism can inform about a number of institutional constraints that emerge and shape cultural governance. In this book, the focus is on four particular areas on which federalism influences and structures the practice and politics of cultural policymaking and implementation. Namely, (1) the configuration of cultural powers; (2) cultural governance and the politics of federalism (looking at structures and at forms of cooperation and competition); (3) the place of local governments; and (4) the conduct of cultural diplomacy.

REFERENCES

Alasuutari, P. (2013). Spreading Global Models and Enhancing Banal Localism: The Case of Local Government Cultural Policy Development. *International Journal of Cultural Policy, 19*(1), 103–119.

Alexander, V. D. (2007). State Support of Artists: The Case of the United Kingdom in a New Labour Environment and Beyond. *The Journal of Arts Management, Law, and Society, 37*(3), 185–200. https://doi.org/10.3200/jaml.37.3.185-200.

Allen, B. (1998). Alexis de Tocqueville on the Covenantal Tradition of American Federal Democracy. *Publius, 28*(2), 1–23. https://doi.org/10.1093/oxfordjournals.pubjof.a029960.

Althusius, J. (1932 [1614]). *Politica Methodice Digesta*. Oxford: Oxford University Press.

Anckar, D. (2003). Lilliput Federalism: Profiles and Varieties. *Regional & Federal Studies, 13*(3), 107–124. https://doi.org/10.1080/13597560308559437.

Bagchi, A. (2003). Rethinking Federalism: Changing Power Relations Between the Center and the States. *Publius, 33*(4), 21–42. https://doi.org/10.1093/oxfordjournals.pubjof.a005011.

Beauregard, D. (2018). *Cultural Policy and Industries of Identity: Québec, Scotland, & Catalonia*. London: Palgrave.

Béland, D., & Myles, J. (2012). Varieties of Federalism, Institutional Legacies, and Social Policy: Comparing Old-Age and Unemployment Insurance Reform in Canada. *International Journal of Social Welfare, 21*, S75–S87. https://doi.org/10.1111/j.1468-2397.2011.00838.x.

Benz, A. (1999). From Unitary to Asymmetric Federalism in Germany: Taking Stock After 50 Years. *Publius: The Journal of Federalism, 29*(4), 55–78.

Beyme, K. V. (2005). Asymmetric Federalism Between Globalization and Regionalization. *Journal of European Public Policy, 12*(3), 432–447.

Biard, M., Ducange, J.-N., & Frétigné, J.-Y. (2017). *Centralisation et fédéralisme. Les modèles et leur circulation dans l'espace européen francophone,*

Germanophone et italophone. Rouen: Presses universitaires de Rouen et du Havre.

Birch, A. H. (1966). Approaches to the Study of Federalism. *Political Studies, 14*(1), 15–33.

Bonet, L., & Négrier, E. (2008). *La fin des cultures nationales? Les politiques culturelles à l'épreuve de la diversité*. Paris: La découverte.

Broschek, J. (2012). Historical Institutionalism and the Varieties of Federalism in Germany and Canada. *Publius: The Journal of Federalism, 42*(4), 662–687. https://doi.org/10.1093/publius/pjr040.

Brown, M. (2006). Not Forging Nations But Foraging for Them: Uncertain, Collective Identities in Gran Colombia. *Nations and Nationalism, 12*(2), 223–240. https://doi.org/10.1111/j.1469-8129.2006.00238.

Burgess, M. (1996). Introduction: Federalism and Building the European Union. *Publius: The Journal of Federalism, 26*(4), 1–16. https://doi.org/10.1093/oxfordjournals.pubjof.a029873.

Burgess, M. (2003). Canadian Federalism and Federation in Comparative Perspective. In F. Rocher & M. Smith (Eds.), *New Trends in Canadian Federalism* (pp. 375–397). Peterborough, ON: Broadview Press.

Burgess, M. (2006). *Comparative Federalism: Theory and Practice*. London: Routledge.

Cameron, D., & Simeon, R. (2002). Intergovernmental Relations in Canada: The Emergence of Collaborative Federalism. *Publius: The Journal of Federalism, 32*(2), 49–72. https://doi.org/10.1093/oxfordjournals.pubjof.a004947.

Canada, Constitutional Acts 1867 to 1982. (2013). Retrieved online from the Ministry of Justice's website http://laws-lois.justice.gc.ca/PDF/CONST_E.pdf.

Canada, Intergovernmental Affairs. (2018). *The Constitutional Distribution of Legislative Powers*. Retrieved online from Canada's Intergovernmental Affairs' website.

De Schutter, H. (2011). Federalism as Fairness. *Journal of Political Philosophy, 19*(2), 167–189. https://doi.org/10.1111/j.1467-9760.2010.00368.x.

Dewey, P. (2008). Transnational Cultural Policymaking in the European Union. *The Journal of Arts Management, Law, and Society, 38*(2), 99–120. https://doi.org/10.3200/jaml.38.2.99-120.

Elazar, D. J. (1979). From the Editor of Publius: Federalism as Grand Design. *Publius, 9*(4), 1–8. https://doi.org/10.2307/3329865.

Elazar, D. J. (1987). *Exploring Federalism*. Tuscaloosa: University of Alabama Press.

Elazar, D. J. (1990). Opening the Third Century of American Federalism: Issues and Prospects. *The Annals of the American Academy of Political and Social Science, 509*(1), 11–21. https://doi.org/10.1177/0002716290509001002.

Friedberg, E., & Urfalino, P. (1985). La décentralisation culturelle: l'émergence de nouveaux acteurs. *Politiques et Management Public, 3*(2), 215–226.

Gattinger, M., & Saint-Pierre, D. (2008). Can National Cultural Policy Approaches Be Used for Sub-National Comparisons? An Analysis of the Québec and Ontario Experiences in Canada. *International Journal of Cultural Policy*, *14*(3), 335–354. https://doi.org/10.1080/10286630802281921.

Gattinger, M., Saint-Pierre, D., & Gagnon, A. C. (2008). Toward Subnational Comparative Cultural Policy Analysis: The Case of Provincial Cultural Policy and Administration in Canada. *The Journal of Arts Management, Law, and Society*, *38*(3), 167–186.

Gorter, D. (2008). Developing a Policy for Teaching a Minority Language: The Case of Frisian. *Current Issues in Language Planning*, *9*(4), 501–520. https://doi.org/10.1080/14664200802364996.

Gray, C. (2000). *The Politics of the Art in Britain*. London: Palgrave.

Gray, C. (2004). Joining-Up or Tagging on? The Arts, Cultural Planning and the View from Below. *Public Policy and Administration*, *19*(2), 38–49.

Hadley, S., & Gray, C. (2017). Hyperinstrumentalism and Cultural Policy: Means to an End or an End to Meaning? *Cultural Trends*, *26*(2), 95–106. https://doi.org/10.1080/09548963.2017.1323836.

Jenkins, H. (2004). The Cultural Logic of Media Convergence. *International Journal of Cultural Studies*, *7*(1), 33–43.

Jewkes, M. (2016). Diversity, Federalism and the Nineteenth-Century Liberals. *Critical Review of International Social and Political Philosophy*, *19*(2), 184–205. https://doi.org/10.1080/13698230.2014.978639.

Kant, I. (1917 [1795]). *Perpetual Peace: A Philosophical Essay*. London: George Allen & Unwin.

Karmis, D., & Norman, W. (2005). *Theories of Federalism: A Reader*. London: Palgrave.

Kelemen, R. D. (2003). The Structure and Dynamics of EU Federalism. *Comparative Political Studies*, *36*(1–2), 184–208. https://doi.org/10.1177/0010414002239376.

Kymlicka, W. (2005). Is Federalism a Viable Option to Secession? In P. B. Lehning (Ed.), *Theories of Secession* (pp. 109–148). London: Routledge.

Kymlicka, W. (2011). Multicultural Citizenship Within Multination States. *Ethnicities*, *11*(3), 281–302. https://doi.org/10.1177/1468796811407813.

Kymlicka, W., Raviot, J., & Lee, S. (1997). Living Together: International Aspects of Federal Systems. *Canadian Foreign Policy Journal*, *5*(1), 1–50. https://doi.org/10.1080/11926422.1997.11014336.

Laffin, M., & Thomas, A. (1999). The United Kingdom: Federalism in Denial? *Publius*, *29*(3), 89–108. https://doi.org/10.1093/oxfordjournals.pubjof.a030039.

Latour, B. (2005). *Reassembling the Social: An Introduction to Actor-Network-Theory*. Oxford: Oxford University Press.

28   J. PAQUETTE

Lijphart, A. (1979). Consociation and Federation: Conceptual and Empirical Links. *Canadian Journal of Political Science/Revue canadienne de science politique, 12*(3), 499–516.

Lijphart, A. (2002). *Patterns of Democracy: Government Forms and Performance in Thirty-Six Countries*. New Haven, CT: Yale University Press.

Maiz, R., Caamaño, F., & Azpitarte, M. (2010). The Hidden Counterpoint of Spanish Federalism: Recentralization and Resymmetrization in Spain (1978–2008). *Regional & Federal Studies, 20*(1), 63–82. https://doi.org/10.1080/13597560903174923.

Mexico, Constitution of Mexico. Retrieved online from the Organization of American States' website https://www.oas.org/juridico/mla/en/mex/en_mex-int-text-const.pdf.

Mill. J. S. (1977 [1859]). *Essays on Politics and Society*. Toronto: Toronto University Press.

Miller, J. (1988). The Ghostly Body Politic: The Federalist Papers and Popular Sovereignty. *Political Theory, 16*(1), 99–119.

Montesquieu, C. L. (2013 [1758]). *De l'esprit des lois*. Paris: Flammarion.

Moreno, L. (2007). The Federalization in Multinational Spain. In M. Burgess & J. Pinder (Eds.), *Multinational Federations* (pp. 86–108). London: Routledge.

Mueller, D. C. (1997). Federalism and the European Union: A Constitutional Perspective. *Public Choice, 90*(1–4), 255–280.

National Endowment for the Arts. (2000). *Note 74*. Washington, DC: Research Division, NEA. Retrieved online from NEA's website https://www.arts.gov/sites/default/files/74.pdf.

Négrier, E. (1997). French Cultural Decentralization and International Expansion Towards a Geometrically Variable Interculturalism? *International Journal of Urban and Regional Research, 21*(1), 63–74. https://doi.org/10.1111/1468-2427.t01-1-00057.

Paquette, J., & Lacassagne, A. (2008). Terroir, politique et construction identitaire. Le marketing public du vin en Ontario. *Marketing et communication, 8*(2), 74–90. https://doi.org/10.3917/mama.052.0074.

Peters, B. G. (2001). The United Kingdom becomes the Untied Kingdom? Is Federalism Imminent, or Even Possible? *British Journal of Politics and International Relations, 3*(1), 71–83. https://doi.org/10.1111/1467-856x.00050.

Pinder, J. (2007). Multinational Federations: Introduction. In M. Burgess & J. Pinder (Eds.), *Multinational Federations* (pp. 1–17). London: Routledge.

Potter, S. J. (2011). Invasion by the Monster. *Media History, 17*(3), 253–271. https://doi.org/10.1080/13688804.2011.591757.

Riekmann, S. P. (2007). In Search of Lost Norms: Is Accountability the Solution to the Legitimacy Problems of the European Union? *Comparative European Politics, 5*(1), 121–137.

Riker, W. H. (1964). *Federalism: Origin, Operation, Significance*. Boston: Little Brown.

Rius-Ulldemolins, J., & Zamorano, M. M. (2015). Federalism, Cultural Policies, and Identity Pluralism: Cooperation and Conflict in the Spanish Quasi-Federal System. *Publius: The Journal of Federalism, 45*(2), 167–188. https://doi.org/10.1093/publius/pju037.

Robbins, B. (1992). Comparative Cosmopolitanism. *Social Text, 31/32*, 169–186.

Robins, K. (2007). Transnational Cultural Policy and European Cosmopolitanism. *Cultural Politics, 3*(2), 147–174.

Rodríguez, V. E. (1998). Recasting Federalism in Mexico. *Publius, 28*(1), 235–254. https://doi.org/10.1093/oxfordjournals.pubjof.a029950.

Ross, C. (2007). Russia's Multinational Federation: From Constitutional to Contract Federalism and the 'War of Laws and Sovereignties'. In M. Burgess & J. Pinder (Eds.), *Multinational Federations* (pp. 108–127). London: Routledge.

Rundell, J. (2009). Democratic Revolutions, Power and the City: Weber and Political Modernity. *Thesis Eleven, 97*(1), 81–98. https://doi.org/10.1177/0725513608101910.

Russian Federation. (2008). *Constitution of the Russian Federation*. Retrieved online from Oxford Constitutional Law website http://oxcon.ouplaw.com/view/10.1093/law:ocw/law-ocw-cd1023-H2008.regGroup.1/law-ocw-cd1023-h2008?prd=OXCON#law-ocw-cd1023-h2008-div2-1.

Sala, G. (2014). Federalism Without Adjectives in Spain. *Publius: The Journal of Federalism, 44*(1), 109–134. https://doi.org/10.1093/publius/pjt010.

Skot-Hansen, D. (2002). Danish Cultural Policy—From Monoculture Towards Cultural Diversity. *International Journal of Cultural Policy, 8*(2), 197–210.

Stevenson, D., McKay, K., & Rowe, D. (2010). Tracing British Cultural Policy Domains: Contexts, Collaborations and Constituencies. *International Journal of Cultural Policy, 16*(2), 159–172. https://doi.org/10.1080/10286630902862646.

Swenden, W., & Jans, M. T. (2006). 'Will It Stay or Will It Go?' Federalism and the Sustainability of Belgium. *West European Politics, 29*(5), 877–894.

U.S. Bill of Rights. (1791). Retrieved online from the United States National Archives' website https://www.archives.gov/founding-docs/bill-of-rights-transcript#toc-amendment-x.

U.S. Constitution. Article I. Retrieved from the Legal Information Institute, Cornell Law School's website https://www.law.cornell.edu/constitution/articlei#section1.

U.S. Constitution. Tenth Amendment. Retrieved from the Legal Information Institute, Cornell Law School's website https://www.law.cornell.edu/constitution/tenth_amendment.

Vatter, A. (2005). The Transformation of Access and Veto Points in Swiss Federalism. *Regional & Federal Studies, 15*(1), 1–17. https://doi.org/10.1080/13597560500083758.

Verney, D. V. (1995). Federalism, Federative Systems, and Federations: The United States, Canada, and India. *Publius, 25*(2), 81–98.

Watts, R. L. (1998). Federalism, Federal Political Systems, and Federations. *Annual Review of Political Science, 1*(1), 117–137.

Watts, R. L. (2008). *Comparing Federal Systems* (3rd ed.). Kingston, ON: McGill-Queens' University Press.

Weibel, P., & Latour, B. (2005). *Making Things Public*. Cambridge: MIT Press.

Zan, L., Baraldi, S. B., & Gordon, C. (2007). Cultural Heritage: Between Centralisation and Decentralisation. *International Journal of Cultural Policy, 13*(1), 49–70. https://doi.org/10.1080/10286630701201723.

CHAPTER 2

Configuration of Cultural Powers

One of the most singular and distinctive features of federalism is that it supposes a State that has two or more subnational entities with their own powers and their own legitimacy over certain areas of policy. In a federal State, the division of power is not only defined along the lines of executive, legislative, and judicial powers, but also defined in terms of federal or national versus subnational. In this chapter, an analysis on how the division of power between states is performed and what are the consequences for cultural policy across a number of federations is presented. Therefore, the focus of this chapter is on the basic "rules of the game" for cultural policy development. This chapter does not focus so much on the social forces, but, rather, insists on the formal institutional settings under which cultural policy and cultural administration develop.

More specifically, this chapter engages with the formal aspects of cultural policy by investigating two main dimensions. The first dimension looks at patterns of cultural administration; it looks at the evolution of cultural responsibilities alongside the process of State development. In particular, the first section focuses on the place of culture following the processes that led to the construction of federations. Did the creation or evolution of the federation transform cultural governance? This section provides insights into the consequences of federalism and federative processes on both existing and new cultural institutions. This first section of the chapter also brings forward the historical conditions behind certain federal States and problematizes the question of cultural affairs through

© The Author(s) 2019
J. Paquette, *Cultural Policy and Federalism*,
New Directions in Cultural Policy Research,
https://doi.org/10.1007/978-3-030-12680-3_2

31

the processes of State-formation; it attempts to reintegrate—as much as possible—an historical dimension to the evolution of cultural policy and cultural administration.

The second section introduces to a fundamental element: constitutional power. This section discusses cases and conditions in which cultural affairs are defined in constitutional matters as a federal, subnational, and/or shared (intergovernmental) power. The recognition of federalism, as a political structure, in the constitution is an essential and definitional element for identifying and recognizing federations; however, what about the place of culture and cultural policy in constitutions? What are the definitions of culture that are implicit in constitutional documents? Do these definitions insist on culture as an expression, as identity, or on the importance of cultural diversity and regional cultures? So, the questions raised are, on the one hand, who is responsible for culture and what is intended as culture? Third, after delineating through constitutions who governs and what exactly is being governed, additional constitutional documents and other public sector and governmental policies are analysed in order to situate any specific provisions that express the will to protect cultural, religious, and linguistic rights. These elements bring us further away from the realm of art and heritage in cultural policy, but they, nonetheless, represent an important element of cultural differentiation that, in turn, often informs cultural policies and their orientations. In some societies, language is not considered as a simple means of communication or tool to establish social relations; there are societies for which language is an essential cultural artefact or cultural mediator (Mulcahy 1995, 2017; Paschalidis 2009). Similarly, religion and religious rights are rarely studied in cultural policy research, but this element remains an essential identity marker in many societies. Religion informs identity construction, and it may also significantly inform certain cultural attitudes (Bennett 2009; Ahearne 2011; O'Neil 2011; Kuran-Burçoğlu 2011). On more practical terms, some dispositions for the protection of cultural rights may well, in fact, have a direct effect on a cultural policy subsector like heritage (Roszko 2012; Alexopoulos 2013; Astor et al. 2017). The constitutional protection of religion may come with special dispositions to protect religion and religious heritage.

In this chapter, focus is placed on the cases of the USA, Australia, Canada, Belgium, Austria, Malaysia, India, Germany, Switzerland, Brazil, Mexico, and Argentina. This chapter also engages, albeit on a more limited level, with other States, such as Russia.

2.1   Cultural Institutions and State-Formation

Federations proceed through the aggregation of different political entities. The process of constructing a federal State involves a series of political discussions or decisions that shape the powers and the nature of relationship between the federal legislature and government and the subnational ones. Federations are tied with a process of construction and reconstruction of States, and as such, the historical development of federations is not without influence or consequence for cultural policy and cultural institutions. The development of federal institutions is a political and historical process that provides many clues for understanding cultural policy. In the vast majority of cases, federalism is a political solution—a form of compromise—for what can be perceived of as a cultural problem in political terms. Here, in this section, it is important to acknowledge that a series of cultural institutions and even a number of manners in which to govern culture often pre-exist the birth of a new federation. The ownership or orientation of cultural institutions may be called to change under a new regime and a new constitutional order. In such cases, who owns and governs what was there?

In the USA, as shall be illustrated, there were limits, early on, to the presence of the federal government in cultural affairs. Culture was seen as an area to be governed by States or individuals. Nonetheless, the federal government has been active in securing participation in some areas of culture. The Library of Congress—the national library of the USA—was created in 1800 in support of congressional activities, but the mandate evolved to integrate cultural missions (Ostrowski 2004). A National Archives was created by an act of the federal legislature in 1934, and the federal government is also active in the museum sector. In 1836, the Congress accepted at the bequest of a scientist, a certain James Smithson, to create—according to his will—a museum and collection accessible to the public. One hundred years later, the National Gallery of Art creation in 1937 similarly followed the bequest of Andrew Mellon's collection of art to the federal government. In the 1960s, the government developed the National Endowment for the Arts (NEA) and the National Endowment for the Humanities (NEH). After the aggregation of the American states into a federation in the late eighteenth century, the federal government acquired or developed many cultural institutions of a national level. This development of the cultural sector follows a common pattern of State-building. Governmental activities—including cultural activities—developed at comparable paces at both the federal and state levels. The timeline of American history is such that governmental logics in both levels of government (federal and subnational) evolved at a similar pace.

The development of federations in the British Empire created a different scenario. State-formation in Canada and Australia involved the unification of self-governing colonies that had, at the time, a relatively well-developed cultural sector. In Canada, the development of museums, libraries, and the arts was driven by a variety of social forces in the early nineteenth century. At the time of their federation, Québec, Ontario, Nova Scotia, and New Brunswick already had a number of heritage institutions in place that flourished under the influence of learned society and political actors. In Québec and Ontario, the first public or governmental museums were both promoted and housed in their own legislatures (Paquette 2019). Following confederation, the federal government was, in fact, poorly equipped to address cultural concerns and develop cultural institutions relative to its provincial counterparts. As a result, the federal cultural institutions and sector evolved, after 1867, on new grounds and through a serendipitous process. For instance, the federal museums developed from a collection of geological specimens acquired from the Geological Commission of Canada (Paquette 2010). This eventually led to a National Museum that was, subsequently, subdivided into many distinct museums in the 1960s to constitute what is, today, Canada's federal museum sector. Compared to the provinces, the federal cultural institutions (museums, libraries, performing arts centres, etc.) were lagging until the 1960s. But the federal government's cultural efforts cannot be said to have been lagging in all areas. Much of the federal government's efforts prior to the 1960s had been devoted to the development of a national broadcasting corporation, which had begun in the late 1930s with the establishment of a national public radio and expanded in the early 1950s with the introduction of a national public television—both of which were offered in English and French. In radio-broadcasting, in particular, the federal government fully assumed a leadership position. Provinces like Ontario and Québec engaged in the broadcasting sector—and are still active in offering public television—but their efforts hardly rival those of the federal government.

In general, the late 1950s and early 1960s coincide with the growing efforts of the federal government to create a sense of (Canadian) identity. The Canadian cultural policy of the federal government is often said to originate from the recommendations of a federal commission (Massey Commission 1949–1951) that argued for a stronger federal presence in cultural affairs (Upchurch 2007). The report is also politically associated with a new form of Canadian nationalism constructed on the fear of the Americanization of its society. The report, which led to the creation of the Canada Council for the Arts in 1957—an arm's length arts funding institution—was heavily justified by the growing presence of American cultural charities on Canadian soil. The Centennial of the confederation in 1967—a celebration of the birth of the federation—could be seen as an ultimate turning point, where the federal government caught up and developed a number of important national institutions (Filewood 2018; Beaton 2017). In the wake of this anniversary, the federal government funded new institutions such as the National Arts Centre and the National Museum of Science and Technology, only to give a few notable examples. It is only, truly, in the 1960s that the federal government caught up with its provinces in terms of cultural development in areas outside of radio or television broadcasting.

In the Canadian federation, the province of Québec has always entertained a great interest in assuming a leadership position at the cultural level. The rise of a secessionist movement in Québec politics in the 1970s can explain, in part, an appeal to cultural themes, especially those of identity. But as Beauregard (2018) would argue, it is important to approach this case with all nuances necessary as themes of cultural policy have never strictly been the monopoly of parties or actors from the secessionist movement. In fact, institutions that were understood to be "national institutions" were created decades before the growth of a secessionist movement and can be traced back to the late nineteenth century. Cultural institutions—museums, libraries, archives, literature, heritage, and the performing arts—serve an idea of culture that works on the belief that there is a different sense of collective identity in Québec. In this context, it is perfectly accepted in Québec to have cultural institutions labelled as national ones, for example, Musée national des beaux-arts, École nationale de théâtre, etc. This is a political consensus, whether politicians or actors in Québec defend Canada or aspire to separate and create a new country. It is under a provincial Liberal Party government, largely associated with federalism, that Québec developed its first Ministère de la culture in 1961, the first ministry of its kind in Canada. For its part, the federal government only developed its Department of Communications—a department that ostensibly served the same purpose as the Ministère de la culture, but on a national level—in 1969. Cultural policy in Canada is traversed by different political views and different views of the federation. To classify positions towards governmental action in the cultural sector along a federalist versus secessionist dichotomy simply does not capture the complexity of this case.

The creation of the Commonwealth of Australia in 1901 followed a pattern that has a lot of commonalities with the Canadian experience. When the federation came to be, the Australian states, which were all self-governing colonies, had already established a number of significant cultural institutions. Again, looking at museums, libraries and archives, and institutions of the performing arts, Australia's state governments were better equipped than the federal one to offer and develop cultural services. New South Wales had a museum operating since 1827—the Australian Museum—that was eventually incorporated into the government of the colony by an act of parliament in 1853 along with its art gallery. The colony of Victoria has had a National Museum since 1854 and a National Gallery since 1861. South Australia—developed as a free colony and utopian project—was also active in the cultural sector and had a library and museum collection dating back to 1834. In Queensland, a natural history collection and museum had existed since 1871, while the National Gallery of Queensland was developed in 1895. The same goes for Tasmania and Western Australia, which each had State cultural institutions as early as 1843 and 1895, respectively. In Australia, efforts from the federal government towards developing cultural policies and institutions can be traced back to acts to memorialize Australia's participation in World War I. The Australian War Memorial, voted on by members of parliament in 1925 and opened to the public in 1941, constitutes one of the first attempts by the federal government to enter the museum sector. A national library was also created in Canberra in 1960. However, much of the Australian federal government's efforts in the museum sector come from two combined forces: the idea to create a rich cultural life in the country's capital city and the desire, in 1970, to commemorate the Bicentennial of Captain Cook's landing. The Australia Council for the Arts (act of parliament in 1975), the National Museum of Australia (created in 1980), and the National Gallery of Australia (created in 1968 and opened to the public in 1982) were all created under these dual forces. In terms of arts and heritage institutions, the Australian federal government has been catching up with its subnational entities for decades in all areas but one: radio and television broadcasting. Just like in the Canadian case, the Australian federal government has been active in developing a national broadcasting corporation (Australian Broadcasting Corporation) with radio broadcasts since 1932 and television broadcasts since 1953. Still, to this date, the public broadcasting corporations of Canada and Australia remain the single most important public sector expenditures of their respective countries (Statistics Canada 2010; Australian Bureau of Statistics 2014).

The dynamics of State-formation in Canada and Australia follow similar patterns; the evolution of their respective cultural policies also seems to follow similar logics. In both cases, the federal government's effort has been concentrated on mastering communication technologies through the development of an important public broadcasting project that also follows patterns similar to that of the British Broadcasting Corporation. Despite this fact, there was (and continues to be) an important and rich cultural life at the state level that is supported by the subnational governments of these States. Some of this reality of Canada and Australia's State-formation has left visible traces that can still be felt today. For instance, the National Gallery of Victoria (NGV) in Melbourne has retained its original pre-commonwealth name and institutional identity. The NGV is not a federal institution, but a subnational institution supported by the Victorian government. This may seem anecdotal, but it shows how the processes of State-formation are not without implications for cultural institutions. As shall be seen in coming chapters, an institutional structure that may seem antiquated and that is associated with the processes of federal development may well explain why Canadian provinces and Australian states are so active in subnational cultural diplomacy.

Federalism in India and Malaysia (Loh 2010), by contrast, is conditioned by postcolonial politics. The State-formation process in India and Malaysia responded to logic of independence from the colonial power. In these cases, the new national—federal—government established museums based on the existing colonial infrastructures; it built museums and libraries from the colonial societies and/or institutions that existed. Ethnographic and archaeological work conducted on their lands was taken back by the new national governments. In these cases, State-building and identity construction were essential; cultural institutions were developed from the former colonial collections. After its independence in 1947, India developed a series of cultural institutions; it developed a National Gallery of Modern Art in 1954, and a National

38   J. PAQUETTE

Museum in New Delhi was created from archaeological collections in 1957. The National Library act in 1948 created a new national institution based on the former Imperial Library, whose roots can be traced back to the mid-nineteenth century. In Malaysia, the Muzium Negara, the national museum, was also created from former colonial collections. In both cases, the most prominent collections and cultural institutions of the colonial era were transformed into national institutions and new national cultural organizations were created in the 1960s and 1970s as tools for identity construction and to assert and develop national competences and skills in these areas. The process of State-formation (and the federations that emerged) in India and Malaysia is rather different than the processes that were at play in Canada and Australia, for instance. National cultural responsibilities were defined in India and Malaysia for the federal government, while their constitutions created provisions to delineate the evolution of federal fields of authority vis-à-vis subnational ones. In Malaysia, it is especially true since Sarawak and North Borneo (Sabah) joined—with Singapore—the Malay Federation in 1963. Special protections for cultural rights were created in Malaysia to ensure that federal government's role in culture did not encroach on that of its new substates.

In Latin America, the State-formation process has been informed by strong leaders and political parties that shaped institutions in ways that have been more favourable to the central government. In other words, Latin American federations tend to be more politically centralized than federations in other parts of the world (Diaz-Cayeros 2006). Brazil, for instance, declared its independence from Portugal in 1822 and then followed a succession of transformations that ultimately led to the creation of a first republic (1889–1930) and federation. Beginning under the leadership and rule of Getúlio Vargas—and, in particular, the period referred to as the Estado Novo (1937–1945)—and even following his dictatorship, many military-led governments managed the Brazilian State. As a result, Brazilian federalism has been historically characterized by a strong central power (Selcher 1989). In Brazil, Mexico, and Argentina, the American Constitution was used as a template to create a new constitution for an independent State; however, the functioning principles and the politics of federalism were not in mind; as a result, these federations evolved to offer a different flavour of federalism. National cultural institutions were created as platform to celebrate national values, but they were also typically under federal power so they could be regulated or, more explicitly, controlled and, if needed, censored (Anderson 2002; Brune 2015). While there has been an important democratization of politics and societies since the 1980s and 1990s, Latin American federalisms have been carved by the turmoil of military governments and dictatorship.

In other cases, the development of federations corresponded with many historical layers of State-formation. For instance, many European federations—such as the German and Austrian federations, as well as the Swiss Confederation—developed on different layers of historical sovereignties and forms of government. These federations have been shaped by the old structures and ways of empires such as the Holy Roman Empire or the Austrian-Hungarian Empire. The articulation of these federations' central/subnational affairs and the boundaries of their territorial divisions are not only informed by a long history of medieval governments (duchy, counties, city-states), but are conditioned by linguistic and religious divisions. The old German Confederation (1815–1866) is quite informative of the visions and practices of federalism that develop in Europe. According to Broschek (2010):

> Under the institutional framework of the German Confederation (1815–1866) the German states became increasingly concerned with a modern form of state building. Almost everywhere the scope of policy activities increased considerably, especially after 1849. In particular, governments of the German states began to take a more active stance in areas such as education, economic and infrastructure policy. (p. 9)

This perspective suggests that forms of subnational autonomy were essential and part of the design of these federations. Commitment to principles of federalism in Germany dates back to governance principles of the Holy German Empire—though they remain highly entertained in modern political thoughts (p. 11). The democratic government that developed after World War II was also shaped along the lines of a federation. While the German State has been going through constitutional reforms since around 2006 that have led to greater centralization in many areas, cultural affairs remain an area where the *länder*—Germany's substate units—are the most competent powers. German reunification also represented a non-negligible element of State transformation, and one which had an impact on artistic careers and the institutional landscape of the cultural sector (Wesner 2018). The Austrian and Swiss States developed on similar historical grounds, layered in centuries of State-formation. In the Swiss context, cultural institutions have been attached to a long tradition of cantonal identity, and to a landscape characterized by an important linguistic diversity that is recognized by the constitution and in the conduct of public affairs, and which has had the effect of limiting the development of cultural institutions by the federal legislature. As for Austria, to quote a phrase often attributed to the famous and colourful French politician, Georges Clemenceau, "*L'Autriche, c'est ce qui reste*" (Austria is, what is left), in reference to the State that was created in 1918 in the ashes of World War I. From the Hapsburg Empire, through Austria-Hungary, the state that emerges from these important empires as a republic was more modest in terms of its power and territory. The federalism that developed in Austria followed the lines of a geography inspired by the medieval division of the lands that were known, but the constitution of the federation was a modern political instrument where the powers of both levels of governments were defined. As will be seen, the major cultural institutions in Austria were defined as federal properties, and a contemporary reading of the constitution suggests that culture is a power that was left to subnational governments—although, some elements can challenge this more or less established characterization of cultural powers.

Finally, the case of Belgium's federalism is also shaped by the European processes of State-formation; it was shaped by many political and historical forces. A Belgian revolution in 1830 gave rise to an independent Kingdom of Belgium. Historically, Belgium's political life has been dominated by a French-speaking liberal bourgeoisie; for decades, the country's political elite had been emerging from the French-speaking Wallonia region (Delwit 2012). Over the years, economic transformations—the industrial decline of Wallonia among them—and the transformation of political leadership among Flemish-speaking politicians and elite have transformed the political climate of Belgium and the patterns of governance that had been established since independence. In the 1970s, political crisis and difficulty in governing the country led to forms of political decentralization that eventually developed into a federation in 1993. As a result, cultural policy followed these recent transformations, and since many of the issues that led to Belgium's federation were of a cultural nature, cultural powers were transferred to the country's communities (Flemish, French-speaking, and German-speaking). In this context, the federal government retained national institutions it had built since Belgium's independence—some of which are royal institutions—and has worked to maintain and promote their multilingual nature. The rest of Belgium's cultural development has since been defined as subnational powers.

The historical processes at play in the development of federations have shaped the conditions under which cultural policies are made. These conditions have also influenced the development of both national and subnational institutions. Conversely, the State-formation processes—the processes that led to the development of a federal State—are also highly conditioned by pre-existing cultural conditions. In most cases, federalism is an institutional form made to accommodate cultural differences. In the following two sections, discussion will focus on two core elements of federalism that shape cultural decision-making: the place of culture in constitutions (culture as a governmental power) and the issue of languages and cultural rights—or protections and guarantees for citizens.

2.2   Constitutional Powers and Cultural Affairs

In democratic regimes, constitutions are the most important political documents. Constitutions explain the function of institutions, the structure of power, and the rights of citizens. While constitutions are not the only source of State power, they remain a significant one. As has been insisted, constitutions are crucial in defining the logics of a federal system. In this section, a number of questions are raised: Who governs culture? What place does culture occupy in a constitution? What is meant by culture? Constitutions reveal a number of things about the relationship between State and culture in federations. The constitution does not inform so much about the levels, the strengths, or anything that has to do with the amount of investment of a government; instead, it defines the government's rights, its capacity, and its legitimacy.

2.2.1   A Subnational Power

In some political systems, cultural powers are defined as subnational powers. In this category, the USA is certainly a good case to begin with—especially because it is often said that the USA relies on a largely private conception of arts, culture, and heritage. The predominance of private donors (or private money) is a key component of the American conception of the arts. This conception could definitely be further espoused, and there are plenty of sociological works that would support this widely accepted thesis. A more critical thesis would suggest that American philanthropy is not strictly humanitarian; rather, it is linked with the social dispositions—it is part of the habitus—of rich industrialists and American fortunes. In other words, the reasons why culture is so exceptionally supported by philanthropists and private interests may well have to do with a different relationship between cultural capital and economic capital, where cultural capital supports the value, recognition, and status of those who possess the economic capital; it validates and legitimizes their social position. Looking at the American Constitution may well reveal and confirm some of these theses once more. In this case, the constitution may both reflect and, in part, explain why the federal government is not typically active in cultural affairs. Culture is only scarcely part of the enumerated powers under the American constitution. The so-called enumerated powers are those that are strictly federal. In the first article of the constitution, it reads that the federal government has the power "to promote the progress of science and useful arts, by securing for limited times, for authors or inventors the exclusive right to their respective writings and discoveries" (US Constitution, art. 1, section 8). What this excerpt suggests is that copyright and patent regulation is a federal power. This is the only strict cultural power defined in the constitution as federal. The other federal cultural power is that which results from the Communications Act of 1934 (Paglin 1989). This act led to the development of a federal agency—the Federal Communications Commission—that oversees radio, television, Internet, and telecommunications broadcasting standards for all 50 of the country's states. From a constitutional perspective, the 1934 act was constitutional as it was under the federal government's authority to "regulate commerce with foreign nations, and among the several states" (US Constitution, art. 1, section 8). In sum, federal powers in culture are limited.

The *Tenth Amendment* of the US Constitution is also very informative and reveals an interesting element about the separation of powers between federal and state governments: "The powers not delegated to the United States by the Constitution, nor prohibited by it to the states, are reserved to the states respectively, or to the people" (US Constitution, *Tenth Amendment*). Juxtaposing section 8 of article 1 of the constitution with the principles expressed in the *Tenth Amendment* reveals that, in large part and principle, cultural affairs should be reserved to the states or the people. Cultural affairs are either private matters or an element that is under the purview of state governments. Of course, this disposition did not forbid the federal government from developing an elaborate network of federal museums in Washington DC, nor did it forbid them from using national parks as tools to construct national heritage or from developing national institutions such as the NEA and the NEH in 1965. The *Tenth Amendment* gives a sense of the theoretical limit of the federal government's powers in cultural affairs; it also reinstates the place of the people in the governance of its own affairs. In this sense, the constitution reflects cultural values, while also imposing limits to cultural powers. There is a constitutional principle behind the limited intervention of the federal government in cultural affairs.

The Swiss Constitution offers another interesting model where the subnational entities retain the majority of cultural powers. In contrast to the American Constitution, the Swiss Constitution is explicit: "cultural matters are a cantonal responsibility" (Swiss Constitution 2018: art. 69), and "the protection of natural and cultural heritage is the responsibility of the Cantons" (Swiss Constitution 2018: art. 78). By virtue of the constitution, cultural affairs are essential cantonal ones. However, the federal government allows itself to participate in these affairs should they be for the good of the federation. However, cultural leadership, in the name of the federation, is also structured as a power that should emanate from the cantons. Article 48 of the Swiss Constitution suggests that cantons may require the federal government to establish inter-cantonal agreements to develop "cultural institutions of supra-regional importance" (Swiss Constitution 2018: art. 48). Support for cinema and radio and television broadcasting standards is the only, albeit significant, cultural powers that are reserved to the federal government.

The case of Germany is absolutely interesting. Of all the world's federations, the German case has constitutionalized cultural powers as subnational ones. Culture is the responsibility of *Länder*. Germany has one of the most decentralized legislations on cultural affairs, where radio-broadcasting laws, typically, under the purview of federal legislations, are decentralized and administered by the subnational legislatures. This decentralization of cultural power is such that both matters of cultural diplomacy and regulatory issues may be delegated to a subnational entity, giving the power to act as a representative of the federation. According to the German Constitution (referred to as Fundamental Law):

> When legislative powers exclusive to the *Länder* concerning matters of school education, culture or broadcasting are primarily affected, the exercise of the rights belonging to the Federal Republic of Germany as a member state of the European Union shall be delegated by the federation to a representative of the Lander designated by the Bundesrat. The rights shall be exercised with the participation of, and in coordination with, the Federal Government; their exercise shall be consistent with the responsibility of the Federation for the nation as a whole. (Germany, Constitution 2017: art. 23, par. 6)

These dispositions of the constitution have arisen in relation to the development of the European Union; they speak to a high level of decentralization, but simultaneously to a high degree of intergovernmentalism. The only exclusive power of the German federation has to do with cultural property. Article 73, par. 5a of the German Constitution stipulates that the federal legislature has the exclusive power to safeguard "German cultural assets against removal from the country" (Germany, Constitution 2017). This power reasserts the place of the federal government in its role as a leader of cultural diplomacy in Germany, but it also gives to the federal legislature a power to administer the circulation of cultural goods through trade and export laws. In most countries, this disposition is associated with the federal legislatures' dominion over the rules for international trade and commerce, and cultural protections against export of culturally significant goods are often dealt with through a regular (and supplemental) piece of legislation.

The case of Belgium also falls into this category. Since the 1970s, Belgium went through a series of political and institutional transformation that culminated in the creation of a federation in 1993 through a new constitutional arrangement. This institutional structure aims to create a political compromise that overcomes the challenges of a diverse country where different cultures coexist, but have typically diverged in terms of social and political aspirations (Fitzmaurice 1996; Swenden and Jans 2006; Erk 2007). Belgium is the country of Dutch-speaking, French-speaking, and German-speaking populations. The German-speaking population of Belgium is considered a linguistic minority. In the Dutch-speaking region—Flanders—there has been a growing discontent with the federal government that resulted in the creation of a secessionist party and political discourses (Hooghe 1993; Béland and Lecours 2007). As a result, Belgium is constitutionally divided into regions and into three linguistic communities (Flemish, French, and German).

The federal constitution of Belgium has clearly transferred culture to the parliaments of the Flemish, French (Belgium, Constitution 2014: art. 127), and German-speaking community (Belgium, Constitution 2014: art. 130). Cultural and educational affairs are primarily defined as emanating from the subnational governments—in this case, the communities. In Belgium, just like in Germany, the radio-broadcasting regulation is a power that emanates from the communities, not from the federal government. Each community has its own regulatory body: Vlaamse Media Regulator (Flemish), Conseil supérieur de l'audiovisuel (French), and the Medienrat (German). These regulatory bodies have the power to grant licenses for public or private broadcasting and establish their own radio and television standards (Canadian Radio-Television and Telecommunications Commission 2009). The Belgian Constitution has also constitutionalized culture in order to clarify the place of communities in cultural affairs, and as a manner to offer a response to growing cultural aspirations from these different communities. Culture is also enshrined in the rights of all Belgian citizens (Belgium, Constitution 2014: art. 23), which creates an obligation for subnational legislatures to create acts in order to meet these cultural obligations. According to cultural policy researcher, Céline Romainville, there is a certain vagueness to this obligation of subnational governments with respect to the rights of their citizens, but it at least makes sure that the cultural institutions and support for culture are maintained to a decent standard. While the population may not be inclined to go to court to require more funding, this disposition acts as a way to clarify expectations for the legislator (Romainville 2009: 143). In this context, the formal power of the federal government of Belgium in cultural affairs remains limited to some of its pre-federation national institutions (museums, libraries, archives, heritage properties). Some of these institutions are conventionally associated with cultural policy; however, in the Belgian context, these cultural institutions are also, in part, regulated under the federal science policy, which should be understood as the federal cultural policy. Institutions that have been historically structured and bilingual have, in most cases, remained under the federal government's authority. In addition to the federal museums, libraries, and audiovisual centre, there are many laws concerning artistic labour that fall under federal competencies.

In some cases, the language of a constitution and its content may be misleading on first reading. The Austrian Constitution is a very good example of this. In matters of culture, prima facie, the Austrian

Constitution appears to be consistent with a model that privileges a subnational power over a federal one. Two elements would lead to this conclusion. First, there is an article in the Austrian Constitution that recommends that all powers that are not restricted to the federal authorities be devolved to the subnational entities. This article reads as follow: "In so far as a matter is not expressly assigned by the Federal Constitution to the Federation for legislation or also execution, it remains within the provinces autonomous sphere of competence" (Austria, Constitution 2015: art. 15, par. 1). Second, the article also delineates the federal dominion over a number of institutions that are under its supervision. Article 10, par. 13 of the Austrian Constitution recognizes the federal government's ownership over museums, libraries, archives, and many other collections, as well as theatres. Based on these two articles of the constitution, one could be led to believe that culture is primarily a subnational competence and that the federal government has limited reach in cultural affairs, reserving only a small capacity to intervene in culture. This interpretation is a common and defendable view of the Austrian Constitution as it relates to culture, one shared by a number of researchers in the field (see Compendium of Cultural Policy 2016, Austria). Additionally, throughout the 2000s, Austria's public expenditures in culture follow a pattern where the federal, provincial, and municipal government all share approximately one-third of the financial burden for culture (also see Compendium of Cultural Policy 2016, Austria).

However, there are other competing interpretations of Austria's federalism and cultural policy that may shed a different light on the country's structure of cultural governance. This could be seen as a cautionary case on the use of constitutions to define the space or instruments of cultural powers. That being said, there are other readings of the Austrian Constitutional that may offer a different take on the division of cultural powers. The Austrian tradition of federalism is much more centralized than it might appear at first glance. This tradition of centralization is an area where traditions and customs developing around the Constitutional Act are also very informative. Which leads to a first observation: Austrian federalism shares many commonalities with the types of federalism commonly found in Latin America. Just like in most Latin American federations, the Austrian Constitution defines areas where the federal level "legislates" and the subnational level "executes". More specifically, Austria is a federal system where many national policies are implemented at the subnational level. This may not be the case for cultural powers, but it nonetheless shapes the dynamics of intergovernmental relations in Austria; it creates a certain tradition and pattern of governance. These provisions of the constitution inform on the values behind the federation and the views of the national government and its constitutive subnational parts. The Austrian Constitution informs us of the culture of its federalism, where federal legislature has typically held a strong leadership capacity.

Second, education in Austria is a federal power. Historically, education has assumed important cultural functions. It has not been uncommon, in many countries, to see a Ministry of Culture emerging as a result of a separation or reorganization of a minister of education. France's Ministry of Culture is, to a certain degree, a creation from the Ministry of Education (Foulon 1990; Donnat 2003)—which is also the case in Austria. Also, typically, the Austrian national governments' attitude towards cultural affairs has been characterized as "centralist" and "paternalist" (Ellmeier 2003: 6).

Third, there has been an interesting argument about the Austrian case, where, according to Erk (2004), Austria is a federation without federalism. By this, Erk suggests that the evolution of the Austrian federation follows political and social patterns where the federation is given increasingly more authority by its subnational constituents. For Erk, there are no strong regional or cultural claims in Austria that would instil a political dynamic or strong claim for societal differentiation as would be found in many other federations. Even the political dynamics of American federalism, for that matter, answer some of the pressures of regional identities. According to Erk:

> Along with education, media is an important outlet for claims of societal distinctiveness. In federations with federal societies, media and education are the two most sensitive areas where substate units jealously protect their prerogatives and seek further competences. In Austria, however, there have been pressures in the opposite direction. (pp. 15–16)

In this case, the Federal Art Promotion Act of 1988 has been a force that helped to diffuse or emulate the principles of cultural policies at the subnational level. All of this suggests that Austria's federal legislature plays a role in cultural affairs that is, in fact, much more important than what is expected from the country's constitution. In principle, the Austrian Constitution reserves culture as a subnational power; however, in practice, this is not the case. It should also be noted that the contemporary—governmental—definition of culture as an area that is distinct from other forms of education or scientific pursuits could also help challenge this interpretation. Looking back at 1920, in the wake of the first Austrian Constitution, it would probably be expected that matters of culture would be understood as educational matters. In other words, Austria can, only reluctantly, be situated under the type of federation where cultural powers are primarily under subnational governance.

2.2.2   A Shared Responsibility

In some political systems, the constitution does not delineate too clearly the boundaries and scope of cultural powers. While some specific types of power are granted to the federation's legislature (often radio-broadcasting regulations), other powers are defined as being under the responsibility of the subnational legislatures. Former British colonies tend to adopt a model of cultural governance where the constitution gives room to both levels (federal and subnational).

When it comes to institutional and political affairs, Australia and Canada are often used to offer comparisons. In the case of Australia, under section 69 of its constitution, "postal, telegraphic, telephonic, and other like services" have been transferred from the states (former self-governing colonies) to the federal government and have been reserved as federal powers under section 51 (Australia, Constitution 2010). By extension, this article confirms the federal government's power over radio-broadcasting legislation. In most cases, the constitution remains relatively silent over the division of powers in areas of social policy. Education is defined as primarily under state authority—though not excluding federal interventions. The dynamic of Australian federalism is defined under sections 51–52 and 106–107. Beyond exclusive federal powers (section 51), Australia's states are generally competent in the (cultural) jurisdictions they had prior to joining the federation. The constitution suggests that culture is a shared power; it is an area in which both governments can legitimately intervene. As such, perhaps the case of cultural governance in Australia should be best understood along the same lines as the evolution of its tradition of federalism, and along the lines of a form of cooperation—in cultural affairs—where the states have an important leadership role, especially at the intergovernmental level.

While the Canadian Constitution may be more explicit than the Australian on the nature of the powers that belong to its federal government vis-à-vis its subnational governments, the structure of cultural power is similar. Culture is an area where both federal and provincial legislatures can intervene—with the exception of, once again, the radio-broadcasting laws that are reserved to the federal legislature. However, culture and heritage are referred to in two specific areas in Canada: education and multiculturalism. Education is a provincial power, though provinces are expected to respect the official languages of Canada (English and French) in educational matters. There is a great proximity between education and culture. In the case of the province of New Brunswick, the constitution recognizes that "the English linguistic community and the French linguistic community have equality of status and equality of rights and privileges, including the right to distinct educational institutions and such distinct cultural institutions as are necessary for the preservation and promotion of those communities" (Canada, Constitution 2013: art. 161.1). While culture has traditionally leaned towards provincial powers, the repatriation of the constitution in 1982, and its modification and inclusion of a Charter of Rights and Freedoms, has clearly reshaped the language around culture and heritage in Canada. Multiculturalism and "multicultural heritage" are now constitutional principles, while the Canadian Charter of Rights and Freedoms requires that the federal legislature and government act accordingly with multiculturalism.

The constitution of India defined culture and heritage as a responsibility of the State, defined as including "the Government and Parliament of India and the Government and Legislature of each of the States and all local or other authorities within the territory of India or under the control of the Government of India" (India, Constitution 2007: art. 12). The structure of federal/subnational responsibilities takes the form of a series of common and shared obligations; the language of the constitution insists on guiding principles that inform the legislators and governments of both levels (federal and subnational). Here, the responsibilities over culture are equivalent or symmetrical. These powers insist on the protection of heritage:

> It shall be the obligation of the State to protect every monument or place or object of artistic or historic interest, [declared by or under law made by Parliament] to be of national importance, from spoliation, disfigurement, destruction, removal, disposal or export, as the case may be. (art. 49)

This disposition proposes a cultural responsibility that is shared, but whose orientation is defined in terms of national responsibility rather than insisting on regional characteristics. In other words, the Indian subnational legislatures should work towards safeguarding national heritage. There is no precision or obligation defined as a duty towards heritage that would be of regional interest. Article 43 of the Indian Constitution also supplements the federal and subnational governments' cultural obligations—though not in terms of heritage, but in terms of leisure and quality of life. According to the constitution, the economic and work conditions of Indian workers should aim to provide good wages and decent standards of life, including the "full enjoyment of leisure and social and cultural opportunities" (India, Constitution 2007). This second component of cultural governance in the Indian Constitution indicates that the legislator recognizes the importance of culture as an element of social citizenship; it brings the importance of the cultural rights of citizens into perspective.

In Malaysia, most cultural powers are shared between the federal and state governments. The constitution also specifies that the cultural powers of the federal government apply in the federal districts of Kuala Lumpur and Labuan, and that special disposition for the management of cultural heritage and cultural industries can be taken in the states of Sabah and Sarawak. These special powers are not fundamentally different in their legal essence than those that the states possess, but their reiteration in the constitution supports the idea and principle that Malaysia is an asymmetric federation with respect to these two states. The separation of powers between the federal and state governments (Malaysia 2007: arts. 74–77) is given precisions in the ninth schedule of the constitution. The federal government has authority and rights over libraries; museums; ancient and historical monuments and records; and archaeological sites and remains (Malaysia 2007: ninth sched., art. 13b). State governments, including the states of Sabah and Sarawak, also have these powers; they mirror the federal powers in a sense. The same goes for the licensing of "theaters, cinema and places of amusement" (Malaysia 2007: ninth sched., art. 5f). The federal Ministry of Culture has its roots in the foundation of the Ministry of Tourism in 1959; it was developed for the first time as a Ministry of Culture and Tourism in 1987 (Malaysia, Ministry of Tourism and Culture 2015). In Malaysia, the constitution reserves telecommunications, film productions, censorship, prints, publisher printing presses, Internet, and other telecommunications as areas of federal authority (Malaysia 2007: ninth sched., arts. 15.6–15.8).

Finally, looking at the Russian Federation's Constitution would lead one to believe that culture is a shared power between the federal legislature and its components. This is the reading one could make of article 71—defining the powers of the federation—and article 72—defining concurrent powers of the federation and its components (Russia, Constitution 2008). The question can be raised, in this case, of what is the actual value of the post-soviet constitution? Who enforces the constitution? And does it really delineate and protect the power of its subnational governments? It is very difficult to evaluate the value of this separation of power in a context where the Russian Federation is often characterized as an authoritarian regime under the strong leadership and presence of a single leader for years. Assessing the value and worth of a democratic instrument in a non-democratic context is certainly not very fruitful (Lynch 2016). Freedom of speech—including artistic expression—and many other forms of dissent against the Russian State and Vladimir Putin, specifically, have been followed up with violent repression (Jonson and Erofeev 2017). In other words, a subnational government claiming autonomy that would contradict national orientations seems very unlikely. That being said, a linguistic and semiotic analysis of federal and subnational policies in the Russian Federation seems to indicate that—in less sensitive areas of cultural policy—in particular, in matters of offering access to cultural institutions (museums, libraries, archives, park, etc.)—there are expressions of cultural diversity and claims for representing regional differences and aspirations (Koptseva et al. 2017).

2.2.3   A Federal Leadership

Constitutions clarify the capacities and responsibilities of federal and subnational entities to legislate over culture. So far, we have seen that constitutions may define culture as a power that is primarily emerging from the subnational legislatures, and we have seen instances where power is defined as a shared responsibility. Apart from telecommunications and radio-broadcasting regulations, constitutions rarely exclude or forbid legislative or governmental participation—federal or subnational—in cultural affairs. Constitutions tend to specify the space where cultural leadership ought to be exerted. In some cases, the leadership belongs primarily to the federal legislature.

The constitution of Argentina offers a good example of a case where cultural leadership is defined in favour of the federal legislature. In the constitution, the Congress (lower chamber) is empowered to "enact laws protecting the cultural identity and plurality, the free creation and circulation of artistic works of authors, the artistic heritage and places devoted to cultural and audiovisual activities" (Argentina, Constitution 1994: section 75, par. 20). Following this right, and in the spirit of social citizenship and accountability, the Argentinian government must act accordingly to protect cultural values and diversity in its interventions. In order to offer good life conditions, the authorities shall make "[...] rational use of natural resources, [including the preservation of natural and cultural heritage" (section 75, par. 41). According to section 125 of the constitution, the provinces and the City of Buenos Aires "may promote culture". The spirit of the Argentinian Constitution defines culture primarily as a federal power; it does not exclude subnational governments, but it defines their intervention as supplemental and in the pursuit of federal objectives.

Similarly, cultural policy in Brazil benefits from the strong leadership position of its federal government. Again, the federal legislature has the constitutional powers to regulate broadcasting, grant licenses, and regulate and "classify" content along national standards of suitability for certain audiences (Brazil, Constitution 2013: art. 21). There are three important observations to be made on the constitutionalization of culture in the case of Brazil. First, the Brazilian Constitution is most certainly, by comparison with others, the constitutional document that has been the most concise about its relationship to culture, the cultural rights of citizens, and the nature of policy instruments and obligations of the government with regard to culture. Constitutional amendments between 2003 and 2005 were made to include further cultural obligations for the State (here both federal and subnational). Some of these changes have been made as an attempt to seriously engage with UNESCO values and appeals to protect and promote cultural diversity (Arruda 2003; Barbalho 2007; Simis 2007). The second observation to be made is that articles 23 and 24 of the constitution recognize that the federal legislature—the Union—the states (subnational legislatures), and municipalities can all, in fact, pass acts that will help the protection and access to culture. To quote the document:

The Union, the states, the Federal District and the municipalities, in common, have the power: (CA No. 53, 2006), [...]

III – to protect the documents, works and other assets of historical, artistic or cultural value, the monuments, the remarkable landscapes and the archaeological sites;

IV – to prevent works of art and other assets of historical, artistic and cultural value from being taken out of the country, destroyed or from being deprived of their original characteristics;

V – to provide the means of access to culture, education and science; (Brazil, Constitution 2013: art. 23)

and

The Union, the states and the Federal District have the power to legislate concurrently on: [...]

VII – protection of the historic, cultural and artistic heritage, as well as of assets of touristic interest and landscapes of outstanding beauty; (Brazil, Constitution 2013: art. 24)

This disposition of the constitution establishes that every level of legislature and government can legislate in common and concurrently on cultural matters. The interpretation of these capacities to legislate and act can be better understood when put in context with articles 215, 216, and 216a of the Brazilian Constitution. This leads to a third observation that these above-mentioned articles create a constitutional obligation to render culture accessible and to protect cultural rights. These articles have an executory clause where the production of a National Cultural Plan, "in the form of a multiyear plan" is required (Brazil, Constitution 2013: art. 215, par. 3). In other words, Brazil has constitutionalized cultural policy; it is a constitutional obligation. The Brazilian Constitution is extremely comprehensive and covers many areas of cultural affairs, including: artistic production, heritage protection and promotion, commemorations, access to culture, diversity, tangible and intangible culture, cultural rights, cultural employment, cultural management, cultural funding for the establishment of national heritage sites, training, cultural information systems, and, of course, the structure of cultural governance. The language of article 216a insists

54 J. PAQUETTE

on democracy, consultation, and collaboration: however, in reality, articles 215, 216, and 216a are all in support of the federal government's leadership in cultural affairs. The National Cultural Plan, as the federal cultural policy, creates the obligation to establish a National Cultural System where the states and municipalities of the major cities must contribute to the implementation of the federal policy in partnership with the federal government. The powers in articles 23 and 24 should largely be seen as providing subnational governments the flexibility to participate in the implementation of the policy. This interpretation of the constitutional act may seem theoretical in terms of its outlook on the obligations created for states; however, there is more robust evidence of the constitutional predominance of the federal legislature over the subnational ones in cultural affairs in some of the specific dispositions of the constitution. In article 215, it reads:

> Paragraph 6. The States and the Federal District may assign up to five tenths per cent of their net tax revenues to a state fund for the promotion of culture, for the purpose of funding cultural programs and projects, the utilization of such funds for the payment of the following items being forbidden:
> I – personnel expenses and social charges;
> II – debt servicing;
> III – any other current expense not directly related to the investments or actions supported by said programs.

This element represents—in a certain way—the creation of boundaries or an intrusion of the federal legislature in the rights described in article 23 and 24 of the Brazilian Constitution. This disposition constitutes both an implicit expectation and, most definitely, a constraint for the subnational legislatures' capacity to develop autonomous cultural finances or distinct cultural strategies. The limitation of the spending power of states (subnational governments) also prohibits some types of cultural spending. Beyond this constraint financial autonomy in cultural affairs, the Brazilian Constitution also specifies that the National Cultural System should be created by an appropriate federal legislation and that the states, the federal district, and municipalities must develop legislative instruments accordingly (Brazil, Constitution, art. 126a, par. 3 and par. 4). While the constitution is not the only space where cultural powers can be found, in the case of Brazil, it does provide some important indications about the structure of cultural governance. Despite the capacity of states and municipalities to legislate on culture, some articles specify the nature of these powers, wherein most of the cultural powers and leadership seems to have been vested in the federal legislature and government.

Finally, the case of Mexico offers another good example of a federation where cultural powers are essentially vested in the federal legislature and government. There are many reasons for coming to this conclusion. First, the centralization of governmental activity has always been a reality of the Mexican political system. In particular, the domination of a single party over Mexico's political life for many decades has contributed to a centralization of powers in the hands of the president (Ward and Rodriguez 1999; McCann et al. 2015). Additionally, the Mexican Constitution has an article that granted the federal Senate the power to bankrupt state governors, which gives a sense of the power balance (or imbalance) in favour of the federal level that has existed in Mexico. In a context of centralization around a single party and president, the subnational level of legislature and government is certainly less potent or capable to act autonomously in matters of social policy. Second, looking strictly at the definition of constitutional powers between the different levels of government, culture is also under the purview of the federal legislature. Article 73 of the Mexican Constitution defines the following powers as federal:

> To establish, organize, end maintain throughout the Republic rural, elementary, superior, secondary, and professional schools, and schools for scientific research, of fine arts, and of technical training; practical schools of agriculture and mining, of arts and crafts, museums, libraries, observatories, and other institutions concerning the general culture of the inhabitants of the Nation, and to legislate on all matters relating to such institutions; to legislate on matters concerning archeological, artistic, and historic monuments, the conservation of which is of national interest; and also to enact laws designed to distribute feasibly between the Federation, the States, and Municipalities the exercise of the educative function and the appropriations corresponding to this public service, seeking to unify and coordinate education throughout the Republic. The diplomas issued by the aforementioned establishments shall be valid throughout the Republic. (Mexico, Constitution, art. 73, par. XXV)

Looking closely at this paragraph defining the power of the Mexican Congress, the cultural powers of the federal legislature include arts and heritage. Some of these powers are also enmeshed with the educational mission and power of federal authorities. Moreover, article 73 suggests, in parts, that states and municipal governments should contribute or collaborate in the implementation of federal (cultural) missions. According to Elodie Bordat-Chauvin (2014, 2018), the democratization process in Mexico, along with an attempt to revive or rebuild a stronger collaborative federalism, has led the government to develop an authority of cultural coordination—the National Council for Culture and Arts (1988)—that favours cultural policy development and implementation at the subnational level (Bordat 2013). Since National Council's inception, there has been an institutionalization of cultural organizations operating at the subnational level in support of the broad objectives of federal policy and orientations. This largely explains why, states, like Jalisco, for instance, have a very developed institutional framework (legal and organizational) to supervise cultural interventions at the subnational level.

In the case of Mexico, article 124, which is a common provision in constitutional acts—and which suggests that powers that are not enumerated in the constitution should fall under the authority of the states—is of little use since culture is defined as a federal jurisdiction. This is the most decisive element that supports the thesis of a federal leadership in culture. That being said, there are other reasons to suggest that the Mexican system of cultural governance favours the federal level. One important reason—which brings us to our third element supporting the federal domination over culture—has to do with the constitutional concentration of taxation powers at the federal level; it is the federal level of government that collects income and sales taxes and then redistributes them to the states. This essential instrument certainly contributes to limiting the capacities of subnational governments in culture, but also in many other policy areas (Zamora and Cossío 2006: 430–431). Fourth, the constitution also structures the nature of the subnational/municipal relations; it dictates the framework to be used by municipal governments, the nature of their missions, the type of political institutions, as well as the power vested in them. This structuration of the subnational/municipal powers by the constitution further consolidates the top-down approach of this type of federalism—all the way down to the local level of government.

2.3 Languages, Religion, and Cultural Rights

This section reviews the conditions under which the constitution and political institutions create certain powers with regard to linguistic and cultural rights. Most constitutional provisions are meant to protect communities and their linguistic rights; in doing so, they define cultural, political, and institutional relationships between a diversity of communities. From the perspective of cultural policy research, these issues may seem to cover elements that are mostly associated with citizenship, basic human rights, and matters that are often associated with researchers interested in anthropological perspectives on culture more than on the arts or heritage aspects of culture. While there is virtue in setting limits on the construction of an object that is so complex that its boundaries could extend indefinitely (as culture's typically do), it is suggested that these issues are, in fact, directly relevant to experts of cultural policy for many reasons. First, constitutions and other types of acts by the State can create expectations in terms of protecting or promoting culture and a diversity of expressions. More than stating that cultural rights must be respected, these legal instruments can create conditions which render governmental action accountable for support of artistic expression. Second, these legal instruments can also entail State obligation towards the protection of minority rights in terms of cultural heritage. Said otherwise, minority rights (linguistic, religious, or cultural) may state the capacity of individuals to enjoy and live their culture freely, without fear or interference from the State; however, they might also involve cultural policy as an instrument for achieving active State engagement in recognizing minorities. In the context of a unitary state, this dimension is largely unproblematic since leadership is defined as the national government, but in a federal context, this raises a number of questions. What is the part played by the different levels of government? Do these rights require some cultural responsibilities from the subnational governments? These questions are, in fact, particularly salient in the context of asymmetric federations, since the institutional design of the federation may be informed by the political dynamics between majority and minority populations in a given society. In this subsection, the focus is on cases where these issues have more influence on the nature of cultural policy development and implementation, namely Malaysia, Brazil, Argentina, Belgium, Canada, and Switzerland. Discussion in this section will also focus on the issue of Indigenous culture and identity, particularly in the North American and Australian contexts.

58   J. PAQUETTE

To this end, cases will be divided and organized into three categories based on the special provisions they provide minorities. The first category is that which elaborates a complex and comprehensive system of obligations towards minority groups, which is labelled, here, as comprehensive cultural rights. The second category is that of ethnic and Indigenous rights, which excludes issues of religion or language. The third category reunites federations whose special provisions are restricted to linguistic diversity. Finally, this section ends with an overview and discussion of Indigeneity, cultural rights, and cultural policy.

2.3.1   *Comprehensive Cultural Rights*

When it comes to federations, there are two that have developed rather comprehensive systems to protect cultural rights in their constitutional acts. By comprehensive, we mean that many aspects of diversity are being addressed, including cultural rights, linguistic rights, and religious rights. In this category fit both Malaysia and Canada.

The Malaysian example is a good case in point. The Malaysian Constitution provides protection for many rights; while it affirms that other religions may be practised, it establishes that the Malaysian State is an Islamic state and Islam is its official religion. But the Malaysian Constitution also reserves certain religious and linguistic rights, particularly for the states of Sabah and Sarawak that sits in positions of exception vis-à-vis other states. Similarly, the constitution protects native customs and laws, with article 161 of the constitution recognizing the use of English and native languages as official languages of the States of Sabah and Sarawak. In this sense, a certain measure of autonomy is granted in cultural governance for these subnational governments. The nature of the constitution's dispositions and approach towards Sabah and Sarawak recognizes the difference and Indigeneity of these territories. As such, cultural rights exist in the constitution to protect and promote heritage, from a self-governance perspective, where these communities are called to use these cultural rights.

In addition to the unique cultures of Sabah and Sarawak, Malaysia is a multicultural society where important Chinese and Tamil communities exist. While article 152 of the Malaysian Constitution specifies that Malay is the official language of the State, and while a proper command of Malay is essential for any new migrants to gain citizenship, other provisions and dispositions are made in favour of the use of English as a second language in public institutions in order to facilitate communications with Chinese and Indian communities. The separation of Singapore from the federation, however, has had an effect on the constitutional protections of Chinese and Tamil languages. As Singapore became independent, these languages lost their place and protection as official languages in the Malaysian Constitution. The Department of National Unity and Integration is, in part, associated with these issues—more so, even, than the Ministry of Tourism and Culture, whose focus is more clearly geared towards its tourism folio. As reminded by Bakar: "[t]o ensure unity in diversity can be maintained, a combined economic, political and legal apparatus is indispensable. However, the use of this apparatus to unite multi-ethnic groups with complete cultural and religious differences would not last long if there was no self-awareness of the need to live together in peace and harmony" (2007: 81–82). Bakar expresses a certain skepticism for the future of the federation which he describes as an "unsettled federalism".

Looking at the Malaysian style of federalism, we can understand that an elaborate regime of rights protection exists to create peace and harmony, by delineating spheres that cannot be infringed upon by the federal government; it offers a minimum of guarantees for cultural rights. That being said, there is no engagement in terms of promoting cultural development, and the language of the constitutional text does not suggest that it is a requirement. The federal government is responsible for maintaining this unity, and the subnational government are enabled, by law, to act and legislate in the confines of their recognized cultural autonomies.

In Canada, religious freedom, linguistic rights, and cultural diversity are all part of the Constitutional Act, and a complex system of cultural governance ensures that these rights have a certain life that people can act on them or claim them if need be. This system developed over time, and through Canada's history. What Canada has today is the result of a system of cultural compromises that date back to the origin of the British conquest of the former *Nouvelle-France*, the French colony in North America. In this sense, Canada's protection of cultural rights should be understood, first, in the context of the British government of the former French territories of North America. After the British conquest of *Nouvelle-France*, and the recognition of its cession through the Treaty of Paris in 1763, the French population established itself and formed a society, with its convention, religion, and laws. Facing this organized society, the British had decided to concede that the population should not be disturbed and should be allowed to maintain their laws (French civil laws), religion, and language in the conduct of public affairs (Brunet 1953; Landry 1975; Simard 1986). History will confirm that this was more of a practical affair than an act of virtue as the then English-speaking population of the colony was primarily composed of militaries and colonial administrators. The situation began changing as soon as the American Revolution started and as a new population of loyalists to the crown came north. Without going into further details, it should simply be noted that the origins of this system date back to the early British colonial government of Canada. This element helps to understand some of the dynamics that are at play in cultural rights in Canada.

Early in the country's development, it was recognized that Canada could not be the land of a single culture. It should be noted that Canada has a long history of racism and repression of its population, and this includes—though is certainly not limited to—its French population (Couture 2001; Dagenais 2015). Treatment of Irish migrants in the 1800s and the internment of citizens of Italian and Japanese origins during World War II are other good examples of Canada's racist/repressive past (Iacovetta et al. 2000; Kunimoto 2004). More fundamentally, however, the treatment of the Indigenous population through the old, exclusionary system of reserves, not to mention systematic assimilation through the abduction of native children, is an example of Canada's historical experience when it comes to dealing with cultural diversity (Paquette et al. 2017). It would be difficult to talk about Canada's system of protection of cultural rights without first acknowledging some of these facts.

It should be noted that Canada never declared its independence from Britain. Rather, Canada successively acquired a number of rights that lead, de facto, to its independence. The last colonial tie Canada retained was its procedure of constitutional amendments, which remained in London until the early 1980s. Then-Canadian Prime Minister Pierre Elliott Trudeau decided to bring the procedure to Canada and, in the wake of this important change, make constitutional amendments—the most important of which was the inclusion of the Canadian Charter of Rights and Freedom (Morton 1995; Epp 1996). Most of Canada's cultural rights can be found in the Canadian Constitution and its amendments of 1982. Section 23 of the Charter recognizes bilingualism/English and French as the two official languages for federal public services and recognizes that the population should have access to education in both languages. The implementation of this element lies on a complex legal and administrative system. In the province of Québec, French language is in majority and English language education is systematically protected by the constitution. For the rest of Canada, this is more complex. Access to French public services and education relies on a system that has a lot of intricacies and may require the population to seek recourse through tribunals to establish their rights (Carey 1997; Cardinal 2000, 2008; Cardinal et al. 2008). In other words, this article of the constitution suggests recognition and equal treatment in principle, but the implementation does not mean that every French-speaking Canadian can access a service in his or her language wherever he or she lives. Freedom of religion is recognized in the charter, as are the ancestral rights and former treaties established between the Crown and Indigenous communities. Finally, section 27 of the Charter reads: "The Charter shall be interpreted in a manner consistent with the preservation and enhancement of the multicultural heritage of Canadians" (Canada, Constitution 2013). This section establishes multiculturalism and the multicultural character of Canadian society.

Multiculturalism in Canada is a symbolic theme associated with citizenship and heritage (Bissoondath 2003; Garcea 2009; Leung 2013). Implementation of this principle is also framed in the Canadian Multiculturalism Act (Canadian Parliament 1985). The principles of this policy establish the importance of recognizing the participation of a diverse population in federal institutions and society; it also suggests that the aim of this policy is to help economic, social, and cultural development of a multicultural society. The objectives of this law are broad, but are made clearer when it comes to defining the role and expectations of the minister (and ministry) in charge of implementing the act. According to the fifth title of this act:

5 (1) The Minister shall take such measures as the Minister considers appropriate to implement the multiculturalism policy of Canada and, without limiting the generality of the foregoing, may

(a) encourage and assist individuals, organizations and institutions to project the multicultural reality of Canada in their activities in Canada and abroad;
[...]
(e) encourage the preservation, enhancement, sharing and evolving expression of the multicultural heritage of Canada;

(f) facilitate the acquisition, retention and use of all languages that contribute to the multicultural heritage of Canada;

(g) assist ethno-cultural minority communities to conduct activities with a view to overcoming any discriminatory barrier and, in particular, discrimination based on race or national or ethnic origin;

(h) provide support to individuals, groups or organizations for the purpose of preserving, enhancing and promoting multiculturalism in Canada; and

(i) undertake such other projects or programs in respect of multiculturalism, not by law assigned to any other federal institution, as are designed to promote the multiculturalism policy of Canada. (Canadian Parliament 1985)

The question of multiculturalism is an issue of citizenship, but it also has significant implications for cultural policy in Canada. This perspective on identity shapes how public authorities envision their responsibility towards both creation and preservation of culture. The issue of cultural rights can be seen as a redefinition of the basic principles of Canada's cultural policy at both ideational and normative levels. The nature of the cultural projects Canada supports and funds all aligns with this important symbolic reference to identity. This approach to cultural rights is as significant to cultural policy, if not more so, than the legacy of the Massey Commission in Canada; it explains what cultural policy is about. Simply put, cultural policy in Canada is a politics of identity and recognition.

2.3.2   Ethnic and Indigenous

In South America, two countries have particular disposition towards the protection of cultural diversity enshrined in their constitutional acts: Brazil and Argentina. In Brazil, protections of minority rights have been constitutionalized. Article 215 of the Constitutional Act recognizes ethnic differences in Brazil and aims to promote and protect these differences at the cultural level:

Article 215. The state shall ensure to all the full exercise of the cultural rights and access to the sources of national culture and shall support and foster the appreciation and diffusion of cultural expressions.

Paragraph 1. The State shall protect the expressions of popular, Indian and Afro-Brazilian cultures, as well as those of other groups participating in the national civilization process.

Paragraph 2. The law shall provide for the establishment of commemorative dates of high significance for the various national ethnic segments. (Brazil, Constitution 2013)

The Brazilian State has obligations, especially in matters of heritage protection and promotion, towards Brazilians of African descent, Indigenous populations, and other minorities involved in the historical development of Brazil. The constitution is also aided by a number of legislative instruments that support, in principle, a fairer society and which fight against discrimination in State and social institutions. It should be noted that Brazil has many issues when it comes to cultural diversity: the society is significantly shaped by a very rigid, albeit implicit, race structure that perpetrates social and economic divides. Moreover, the constitutional ct does little to protect Indigenous languages (Shulist 2016; Murphy and Vencio 2009). That being said, the constitutionalization of cultural rights has implications for cultural policy in Brazil; it has defined some of its recent orientations, though it represents a challenge for subnational governments in their attempts to integrate the structure and implement cultural policy.

In Argentina, the Constitutional Act (1994) recognizes the rights of its Indigenous population. The constitution recognizes, symbolically, that the Indigenous population pre-existed European settlement. This is an historical fact, but it is also meant as a symbolic and political act of recognition—of the highest importance—in a constitutional document. This recognition (article 17) is followed by a statement that supports the distinct cultural education and provisions, including linguistic rights, for Argentina's Indigenous population. Article 17 also recognizes that the subnational governments of Argentina may—and should—help the federal government in its effort to offer services meeting these cultural rights. Once again, cultural rights have implications for education and cultural policy development at the subnational level.

2.3.3 Linguistic Rights

In some countries, diversity may be conceived of in cultural terms, but special protections and rights exist strictly on linguistic grounds. The two federations that developed a system of protection that focuses almost exclusively on linguistic rights are Switzerland and Belgium. In the Swiss Constitution, article 4 specifies that German, French, Italian, and Romansch are official languages in Switzerland (Switzerland, Constitution 2018). Additionally, in article 8 of the constitution, there is a provision stipulating that language should not be a basis for discrimination, while article 18 recognizes the right to use any official language. The most important article in the Swiss Constitution is article 70, which defines the role of the federation and the powers of cantons in linguistic matters. Cantons may decide and define their own official languages in their legislatures based on their traditions and customs. But, both federation and cantons must recognize the plurilingual character of the country and must work in good faith towards its preservation and fruition. Article 70 adds three additional obligations to the federal government in terms of linguistic rights. First, the federal administration must provide public services in all of the official languages recognized by the constitution. Second, the federal government must help and contribute to linguistic rights preservation and development in cantons that are bilingual or plurilingual. This provision does not apply in cantons where the population is defined as or has been historically unilingual. Third, a special effort from the federal government must be made towards helping the Italian language in the canton of Ticino, and the Romansch language in the canton of Graubünden (Switzerland, Constitution 2018).

In Belgium, linguistic rights have been instrumental in the construction of the federation. Therefore, and at the risk of restating what has already been established in this chapter, the Flemish, French, and German communities in Belgium rely on a system of constitutional protections. These linguistic communities possess cultural and linguistic rights that the federal government must also work to protect at the federal level (Uyttendaele 1999; Domenichelli 1999). When it comes to the regional level of government, the bilingual Bruxelles-Capitale is home to a series of complex social and linguistic issues. These issues have become particularly salient and politicized in the periphery of Brussels (or Bruxelles in French), where a suburban French-speaking population has been granted special rights despite the fact it evolves in an area associated with Flemish linguistic rights and priorities (Blero 2011). Nonetheless, the federation was constructed around two tiers of units: regions and linguistic communities. In practice, while some social and demographic transformations have tested the limits of this system in recent years, the institutions function relatively well under it.

2.3.4 Indigeneity

Beyond linguistic rights, federalism also adds to the complexity of Indigenous cultural governance. So far, this chapter has discussed Indigenous cultural affairs covered in the constitutional frameworks of Brazil and Argentina, but these issues are also important to many other federations—such as Canada, Australia, and the USA, who, like Argentina and Brazil, share a settler-colonial history. Indigenous populations evolve politically in a complex institutional situation where their federal governments take a predominant, albeit passive at times, role in the governance of cultural affairs. The historical settlements and current geography of Indigenous populations in these countries also raise important governance challenges when subnational and municipal governments are brought into the equation. In many of these countries, the deadlock between retrograde federal laws governing Indigenous populations, coupled with the absence of institutional alternatives for governance, has created very difficult political situations for these populations (Hawkes 2004; Wall 2010).

Canada has, in recent decades, started engaging a more reconstructive path in terms of protecting Indigenous heritage. The rights to Indigenous self-governance and the recognition of the value and distinct character of Indigenous cultures have come a long way in Canada, despite the fact that some of these transformations are effectively lagging in terms of their implementation and the resources may seem minimal in front of the imposing work that lies ahead (Coulthard 2007). Similarly, since Australia revised its constitution to recognize Indigenous inhabitants as citizens in 1967, there have been many important social and political transformations in support of better rights for the country's Indigenous population—including cultural rights.

Heritage institutions in Canada, Australia, and the USA have been proactive in developing strategies to help promote these rights and preserve Indigenous culture. Arts councils have adapted in order to facilitate the promotion and development of Indigenous arts and forms of cultural expression. Institutions have adapted and tried to develop spaces where cultural decision-making can include Indigenous actors and be informed by their voices. These endeavours are profound, and yet, to this date, incomplete and imperfect processes. Over the years, a number of cultural rights have been recognized by federal governments to Indigenous populations of Canada, Australia, and the USA, but these rights developed alongside or on the ruins of the repressive rights structures of reserves.

To keep in with the spirit and scope of this book, it is important to note that Indigeneity may represent a number of challenges to cultural governance in federal contexts, and it does so for many reasons. The first challenge concerns Indigenous population in these structures. Indigenous populations are spread out across the Canadian, American, and Australian territories. These populations often represent an important segment of a state or province. However, for understandable reasons, these populations have not been in a position to invest in the subnational institutions as a majority and have never been a politically majority in these institutions. In Canada, a territory like Nunavut may well be defined as a political entity that works under the leadership of Indigenous leaders, but, as such, Nunavut remains dependent on the federal government because it is not a province. In other words, there are no real subnational territories that Indigenous populations have successfully claimed as their political voice, to express their voice as that of a majority. In this sense, Indigenous powers and resistance have been developing largely in the margins of the politics of federalism. Historically, when opportunities for Indigenous people to claim a legitimate political space have come close to becoming reality, in the early days of these federations—especially in Canada and the USA—these movements were cast aside and/or severely repressed.

Second, Indigenous populations have been constitutionally "protected" under federal constitutions and federal legislations. This is the case in all three above-mentioned countries. Federal powers have, historically, regulated the living conditions and social services offered to their Indigenous populations. Participation of subnational governments in Indigenous affairs has been traditionally limited, for many reasons, but in part because of the State's legal and constitutional framework. When it comes to cultural affairs, many subnational governments have been proactive, in recent years, in helping Indigenous populations in matters of arts and heritage. Perhaps the fact that cultural affairs in Canada, Australia, and the USA have been more or less defined outside the strict realm of federal powers has helped in making culture a tool for better subnational/Indigenous relations. While the federal governments remain the main contact point for Indigenous social services, subnational governments have, at times, expressed good faith in nurturing better relations, with culture and cultural policy often serving as a space where

Indigenous voices can be heard. This is especially the case in contexts where federal powers are less prone to condemn, and will more often encourage subnational participation in a variety of cultural affair.

What needs to be reminded here, the main takeaway, is that Indigenous cultural affairs in Canada, Australia, and the USA have evolved simultaneously within and in the margins of the politics of federalism. According to Martin Papillon, "Indigenous people in Canada and the United States are a classic case of small, territorially defined, political entities that either chose not to participate in or were forcibly excluded from the original federal compact" (2011: 290). As such, what developed is a form of multilayer governance system. This system includes official representation of Indigenous populations, federal institutions, and other levels of governments, including subnational governments and local authorities. In Canada, for instance, the Assembly of First Nations represents Indigenous leaders from across the country, which liaises with the federal government on important policy issues. While this system of governance fosters participation in federalism and offers a practical solution for Indigenous governance, it also evolves in the margins of the conventional structures of federalism.

2.4 Conclusion and Synthesis

This chapter provides a framework for understanding the most essential sources of cultural power in a federation. In particular, this chapter focused on the most formal source of power, that of the constitution. The reasons for focusing on constitutions are twofold. On the one hand, constitutions offer a canvas of a State's basic rights and offer a relative sense of the importance and place cultural has been assigned in a political system. On the other hand, the division of powers is essential to understanding federations. The objective, here, was to understand the structures and patterns of the division of cultural power; to obtain this understanding requires a constitutional analysis.

By shedding light on the most basic source of formal power, this chapter has shown that the nature and structure of powers pertaining to cultural affairs are given a relatively important part in the institutional design of federations. In the case of Brazil, the constitution has reached an important level of precision in defining the attributions of the federal government over the subnational level. In some constitutions, this has to do, in great part, with the fact that the federation was founded as a way of structuring a network of complex cultural relations. This is particularly the case for Belgium and, to a certain degree, Malaysia, Switzerland, and Canada. Additionally, this chapter has shown that it is not uncommon for federations to stipulate that all powers not defined in the constitution as belonging to a level of government—often the federal order—belong to the subnational one. This is very much the case in the USA, for instance.

In addition to the analysis of constitutional documents, this chapter has contextualized federations in relation to their respective State-formation processes. The intention, here, was not to provide a detailed historical account of every State's history, but, rather, to present essential ideas that help contextualize these different countries. This approach was far from exhaustive, but it provided some essential keys to understanding the motivations and processes behind the creation of the federations covered in this chapter. These keys, in turn, help us better understand the will and intentions of constitutional acts. Constitutions are the result of historical processes and political compromises—including cultural compromises.

Finally, this chapter looked at whether constitutional acts pay special attention to some cultural rights—in particular rights towards minority groups. In federations, these rights are most often aimed at protecting a nationally recognized minority group. In the Americas, minority groups are often Indigenous populations, but they can also be descendants of European settlers. In Europe, minority groups are often defined on linguistic bases—such as in Switzerland and Belgium. Constitutional documents and legal frameworks often pay special attention to certain groups in federations—the Italian and Romansch in Switzerland or the German-speaking population of Belgium—and these often have consequences that typically reach beyond cultural rights and involve a certain level of care or attention at the level of cultural policy.

Table 2.1 summarizes some of the basic observations made throughout this chapter regarding federations, based on the following three levels of analysis: State-formation, division of cultural powers, and minority rights. Additionally, an important column has been added to reiterate the different cultures and nations that are recognized by each State's constitution and political system. In this context, minority rights do not refer to specific anti-discrimination acts geared towards better integration, acceptance, and protection of recent migrants; it refers to the rights that have been defined in a constitution for recognized national minorities or Indigenous populations in federal States.

2 CONFIGURATION OF CULTURAL POWERS   69

Table 2.1 Basic configuration and sources of cultural powers

Country	State-formation	Constitutional division	Cultures	Minority rights
Australia	Aggregation of self-governing colonies	Shared	European settlers—Indigenous, and Torres Strait Islanders	Indigenous rights
Austria	Dissolution of empire	Subnational[a]	Single nation	
Argentina	Dissolution of empire	Federal	European settlers, Indigenous populations	Indigenous rights
Belgium	Imperial dissolution. Recent federation 1993	Subnational	Flemish, French, and German	German minority
Brazil	Dissolution of empire	Federal	European settlers, Afro-Brazilians, Indigenous	Indigenous rights; Afro-Brazilian cultural rights
Canada	Aggregation of self-governing colonies	Shared	European settlers (English, French) and Indigenous populations	Indigenous rights; Multiculturalism Act; French language education/service
Germany	Dissolution of Empire, reunification	Subnational	Single nation	
India	Postcolonial	Shared	Pluricultural	Recognized freedoms
Malaysia	Postcolonial	Shared	Pluricultural and "natives"	Minority rights (Chinese, Indian); native rights (Sabah, Sarawak)
Mexico	Dissolution of empire	Federal	European settlers and Indigenous	
Russia	Imperial history; post-Soviet dissolution	Shared	Pluricultural	Autonomies

(continued)

70 J. PAQUETTE

Table 2.1 (continued)

Country	State-formation	Constitutional division	Cultures	Minority rights
Switzerland	Historical aggregation of cantons in confederation tradition	Subnational	German, French, Italian, and Romansch[b]	Bilingual cantons; Italian; Romansch
USA	Independence, aggregation of colonies	Subnational	European settlers, Indigenous populations	Indigenous rights

[a]From a constitutional perspective, culture is a subnational power in Austria on the basis of an absence in the enumerated cultural powers of the federation. This perspective, however, is debatable in practice and in view of this book's understanding of the scope of education powers as delineated in the 1920 Constitution

[b]Switzerland is a multilinguistic federation. Using the notion of "nation" to characterize them may not fit with the customs of cultural identification in Switzerland

REFERENCES

Ahearne, J. (2011). Questions of Religion and Cultural Policy in France. *International Journal of Cultural Policy, 17*(2), 153–169. https://doi.org/1 0.1080/10286632.2010.528837.

Alexopoulos, G. (2013). Management of Living Religious Heritage: Who Sets the Agenda? The Case of the Monastic Community of Mount Athos. *Conservation and Management of Archaeological Sites, 15*(1), 59–75. https://doi.org/10.1179/1350503313z.00000000047.

Anderson, L. F. (2002). Of Wild and Cultivated Politics: Conflict and Democracy in Argentina. *International Journal of Politics, Culture and Society, 16*(1), 99–132.

Argentina, Constitution. (1994). Retrieved online from the Ministry of Justice and Human Rights' website http://www.biblioteca.jus.gov.ar/argentina-constitution.pdf.

Arruda, M. A. D. N. (2003). A política cultural: regulação estatal e mecenato privado. *Tempo social, 15*(2), 177–193.

Astor, A., Burchardt, M., & Griera, M. (2017). The Politics of Religious Heritage: Framing Claims to Religion as Culture in Spain. *Journal for the Scientific Study of Religion, 56*(1), 126–142. https://doi.org/10.1111/jssr.12321.

Australia, Constitution. (2010). Retrieved online from the Parliament of Australia's website https://www.aph.gov.au/About_Parliament/Senate/Powers_practice_n_procedures/Constitution.aspx.

Australian Bureau of Statistics. (2014). *Cultural Funding by Government, 2012–2013.* Canberra: Government of Australia.

Austria, Constitution. (2015). Retrieved online from the Austrian Ministry of for Digital and Economic Affairs' website http://www.ris.bka.gv.at/Dokumente/Erv/ERV_1930_1/ERV_1930_1.pdf.

Bakar, I. (2007). Multinational Federation: The Case of Malaysia. In M. Burgess & J. Pinder (Eds.), *Multinational Federations*. London: Routledge.

Barbalho, A. (2007). *Políticas culturais no Brasil: identidade e diversidade sem diferença*. Conference papers. Encontro multidisciplinares em cultura, Faculcade the communicação/UFB, Savador de Bahia. Retrieved online from the the conference website http://files.ifestcircomira.webnode.com/200000080-ce313d025a/Leitores,%20espectadores%20e%20internautas.pdf.

Beaton, M. (2017). *The Centennial Cure: Commemoration, Identity, and Cultural Capital in Nova Scotia During Canada's 1967 Centennial Celebrations*. Toronto: Toronto University Press.

Beauregard, D. (2018). *Cultural Policy and Industries of Identity: Québec, Scotland, & Catalonia*. London: Palgrave.

Béland, D., & Lecours, A. (2007). Federalism, Nationalism and Social Policy Decentralization in Canada and Belgium. *Regional and Federal Studies, 17*(4), 405–419.

Belgium, Constitution. (2014). Retrieved online from the Federal Constitutional Court's website http://www.const-court.be/en/basic_text/belgian_constitution.pdf.

Bennett, O. (2009). On Religion and Cultural Policy: Notes on the Roman Catholic Church. *International Journal of Cultural Policy, 15*(2), 155–170.

Bissoondath, N. (2003). Selling Illusions: The Cult of Multiculturalism in Canada. *Peace Research Abstracts, 40*(5), 23–77.

Blero, B. (2011). Bruxelles-Hal-Vilvorde, couronne d'épines de l'État fédéral belge? *Pouvoirs, 136*, 97–123.

Bordat, E. M. (2013). Institutionalization and Change in Cultural Policy: CONACULTA and Cultural Policy in Mexico (1988–2006). *International Journal of Cultural Policy, 19*(2), 222–248.

Bordat-Chauvin, É. (2014). De la mobilisation à l'institutionnalisation: une analyse comparative historique des politiques culturelles au Mexique et en Argentine. *Pôle Sud, 41*(2), 49–64.

Bordat-Chauvin, E. (2018). *Les politiques culturelles en Argentine et au Mexique*. Paris: Editions L'Harmattan.

Brazil, Constitution. (2013). Retrieved online from the Supreme Court of Brazil's website http://www.stf.jus.br/repositorio/cms/portalStfInternacional/portalStfSobreCorte_en_us/anexo/Constitution_2013.pdf.

Broschek, J. (2010). Federalism and Political Change: Canada and Germany in Historical-Institutionalist Perspective. *Canadian Journal of Political Science, 43*(1), 1–24. https://doi.org/10.1017/s0008423909990023.

72   J. PAQUETTE

Brune, K. (2015). Subversive Instruments: Protest and Politics of MPB and the Nueva Canción. *Studies in Latin American Popular Culture, 33*(1), 128–145.

Brunet, M. (1953). Premières réactions des vaincus de 1760 devant leurs vainqueurs. *Revue d'histoire de l'Amérique française, 6*(4), 506–516.

Canada, Constitutional Acts 1867 to 1982. (2013). Retrieved online from the Ministry of Justice's website http://laws-lois.justice.gc.ca/PDF/CONST_E.pdf.

Canada, Parliament of Canada. (1985). *Canadian Multiculturalism Act.* Ottawa.

Canadian Radio-Television and Telecommunications Commission. (2009). *Approches internationales en matière de financement de la radio communautaire et de la radio de campus* (Rapport final). Ottawa. Retrieved online from the CRTC's website https://crtc.gc.ca/fra/publications/reports/radio/connectus0903.pdf.

Cardinal, L. (2000). Le pouvoir exécutif et la judiciarisation de la politique au Canada. Une étude du programme de contestation judiciaire. *Politique et sociétés, 19*(2–3), 43–64.

Cardinal, L. (2008). *Le fédéralisme asymétrique et les minorités linguistiques nationales.* Sudbury, ON: Prise de parole.

Cardinal, L., Lang, S., & Sauvé, A. (2008). Les minorités francophones hors Québec et la gouvernance des langues officielles: portrait et enjeux. *Francophonies d'Amérique* (26), 209–233.

Carey, S. (1997). Language Management, Official Bilingualism, and Multiculturalism in Canada. *Annual Review of Applied Linguistics, 17,* 204–223. https://doi.org/10.1017/s0267190500003354.

Compendium of Cultural Policies and Trends. (2016). *Austria: 5.1, General Legislation.* Retrieved online from the Compendium's website https://www.culturalpolicies.net/web/austria.php?aid=512.

Coulthard, G. S. (2007). Subjects of Empire: Indigenous Peoples and the 'Politics of Recognition' in Canada. *Contemporary Political Theory, 6*(4), 437–460.

Couture, C. (2001). La disparition inévitable des francophones à l'extérieur du Québec: un fait inéluctable ou le reflet d'un discours déterministe? *Francophonies d'Amérique, 11,* 7–18.

Dagenais, M. (2015). 'L'histoire dira que Lord Durham a préféré une petite faction, et l'exposera comme une des aberrations humaines de notre époque': Comment Lord Durham perdit l'appui des Canadiens français. *Bulletin d'histoire politique, 23*(2), 181–203.

Delwit, P. (2012). *La vie politique en Belgique de 1830 à nos jours.* Bruxelles: Les éditions de l'Université de Bruxelles.

Diaz-Cayeros, A. (2006). *Federalism, Fiscal Authority and Centralization in Latin America.* Cambridge: Cambridge University Press.

Domenichelli, L. (1999). Comparaison entre les stratégies linguistiques de Belgique et du Canada. *Globe: Revue internationale d'études québécoises, 2*(2), 125–145.

Donnat, O. (2003). La question de la démocratisation dans la politique culturelle française. *Modern & Contemporary France, 11*(1), 9–20.

Ellmeier, A. (2003). Cultural Entrepreneurialism: on the Changing Relationship Between the Arts, Culture and Employment. *The International Journal of Cultural Policy, 9*(1), 3–16.

Epp, C. R. (1996). Do Bills of Rights Matter? The Canadian Charter of Rights and Freedoms. *American Political Science Review, 90*(4), 765–779.

Erk, J. (2004). Austria: A Federation Without Federalism. *Publius: The Journal of Federalism, 34*(1), 1–20.

Erk, J. (2007). *Explaining Federalism: State, Society and Congruence in Austria, Belgium, Canada, Germany and Switzerland.* London: Routledge.

Filewood, A. (2018). A Confederation Minstrel Show: The Centennial Play of 1967. *Canadian Theatre Review, 174,* 48–51.

Fitzmaurice, J. (1996). *The Politics of Belgium: A Unique Federalism.* Boulder, CO: Westview Press.

Foulon, C. L. (1990). Des Beaux-Arts aux Affaires culturelles (1959–1969): Les entourages d'André Malraux et les structures du ministère. *Vingtième siècle. Revue d'histoire,* 29–40.

Garcea, J. (2009). Postulations on the Fragmentary Effects of Multiculturalism in Canada. *Canadian Ethnic Studies, 40*(1), 141–160. https://doi.org/10.1353/ces.0.0059.

Germany, Constitution. (2017). Retrieved online from the Parliament of the Federal Republic of Germany' website https://www.btg-bestellservice.de/pdf/80201000.pdf.

Hawkes, D. (2004). Indigenous Peoples: Self-Government and Intergovernmental Relations. *Peace Research Abstracts, 41*(2), 233900.

Hooghe, L. (1993). Belgium: From Regionalism to Federalism. *Regional & Federal Studies, 3*(1), 44–68.

Iacovetta, F., Perin, R., & Principe, A. (Eds.). (2000). *Enemies Within: Italian and Other Internees in Canada and Abroad.* Toronto: University of Toronto Press.

India, Constitution. (2007). Retrieved online from the National Portal of the Government of India's website https://www.india.gov.in/sites/upload_files/npi/files/coi_part_full.pdf.

Jonson, L., & Erofeev, A. (Eds.). (2017). *Russia-Art Resistance and the Conservative-Authoritarian Zeitgeist.* London: Routledge.

Koptseva, N. P., Luzan, V. S., Razumovskaya, V. A., & Kirko, V. I. (2017). The Content Analysis of the Russian Federal and Regional Basic Legislation on the Cultural Policy. *International Journal for the Semiotics of Law-Revue internationale de Sémiotique juridique, 30*(1), 23–50.

Kunimoto, N. (2004). Intimate Archives: Japanese-Canadian Family Photography, 1939–1949. *Art History, 27*(1), 129–155.

Kuran-Burçoğlu, N. (2011). The Impact of Islamic Sects on Education and the Media in Turkey. *International Journal of Cultural Policy, 17*(2), 187–197. https://doi.org/10.1080/10286632.2010.549562.

Landry, Y. (1975). Étude critique du recensement du Canada de 1765. *Revue d'histoire de l'Amérique française, 29*(3), 323–351.

Leung, H. H. (2013). Canadian Multiculturalism in the 21st Century: Emerging Challenges and Debates. *Canadian Ethnic Studies, 43*(3), 19–33.

Loh, F. K. W. (2010). Restructuring Federal-State Relations in Malaysia: From Centralised to Co-operative Federalism? *The Round Table, 99*(407), 131–140. https://doi.org/10.1080/00358531003656180.

Lynch, A. C. (2016). The Influence of Regime Type on Russian Foreign Policy Toward "the West," 1992–2015, *Communist and Post-Communist Studies, 49*(1), 101–111.

Malaysia, Constitution. (2007). Retrieved online from the Attorney General's Chamber of Malaysia's website http://www.agc.gov.my/agcportal/uploads/files/Publications/FC/Federal%20Consti%20(BI%20text).pdf.

Malaysia, Ministry of Tourism and Culture. (2015). *History.* Retrieved online from the Ministry of Tourism and Culture's website http://www.motac.gov.my/en/profile/history.

McCann, P. J. C., Shipan, C. R., & Volden, C. (2015). Top-Down Federalism: State Policy Responses to National Government Discussions. *Publius: The Journal of Federalism, 45*(4), 495–525.

Mexico, Constitution of Mexico. Retrieved online from the Organization of American States' website https://www.oas.org/juridico/mla/en/mex/en_mex-int-text-const.pdf.

Morton, F. L. (1995). The Effect of the Charter of Rights on Canadian Federalism. *Publius: The Journal of Federalism, 25*(3), 173–188.

Mulcahy, K. V. (1995). Public Culture and Political Culture: La Politique Culturelle du Quebec. *The Journal of Arts Management, Law, and Society, 25*(3), 225–249.

Mulcahy, K. V. (2017). *Public Culture, Cultural Identity, Cultural Policy: Comparative Perspectives.* New York: Palgrave.

Murphy, I. I., & Vencio, E. (2009). Maintaining Two Worlds: The Relevance of Mother Tongue in Brazil's Amerindian Societies. *International Journal of Bilingual Education and Bilingualism, 12*(4), 387–400. https://doi.org/10.1080/13670050802588506.

O'Neill, M. (2011). Religion and Cultural Policy: Two Museum Case Studies. *International Journal of Cultural Policy, 17*(2), 225–243.

Ostrowski, C. (2004). *Books, Maps, and Politics: A Cultural History of the Library of Congress, 1783–1861.* Amherst: University of Massachusetts Press.

Paglin, M. D. (Ed.). (1989). *A Legislative History of the Communications Act of 1934.* Oxford: Oxford University Press.

Papillon, M. (2011). Adapting Federalism: Indigenous Multilevel Governance in Canada and the United States. *Publius: The Journal of Federalism, 42*(2), 289–312.

Paquette, J. (2010). La réforme des musées nationaux du Canada: les défis professionnels et managériaux de la recherche. *Canadian Public Administration, 53*(3), 375–394.

Paquette, J. (2019, forthcoming). La politique muséale du Québec: Trajectoires historiques de l'évolution d'un service public. *Politiques et sociétés, 38*(1), 20 pp.

Paquette, J., Beauregard, D., & Gunter, C. (2017). Settler Colonialism and Cultural Policy: the Colonial Foundations and Refoundations of Canadian Cultural Policy. *International Journal of Cultural Policy, 23*(3), 269–284.

Paschalidis, G. (2009). Exporting National Culture: Histories of Cultural Institutes Abroad. *International Journal of Cultural Policy, 15*(3), 275–289.

Romainville, C. (2009). Les fondements d'une politique culturelle commune. *Études théâtrales, 46*(3), 142–146.

Roszko, E. (2012). From Spiritual Homes to National Shrines: Religious Traditions and Nation-Building in Vietnam. *East Asia, 29*(1), 25–41. https://doi.org/10.1007/s12140-011-9156-x.

Russian Federation. (2008). *Constitution of the Russian Federation.* Oxford Constitutional Law Online. http://oxcon.ouplaw.com/view/10.1093/law:ocw/law-ocw-cd1023-H2008.regGroup.1/law-ocw-cd1023-h2008?prd=OXCON#law-ocw-cd1023-h2008-div2-1.

Selcher, W. A. (1989). A New Start Toward a More Decentralized Federalism in Brazil? *Publius, 19*(3), 167–183.

Shulist, S. (2016). Indigenous Names, Revitalization Politics, and Regimes of Recognition in the Northwest Amazon. *The Journal of Latin American and Caribbean Anthropology, 21*(2), 336–354. https://doi.org/10.1111/jlca.12189.

Simard, J. J. (1986). L'envol du Québec anglais. *Recherches sociographiques, 27*(2), 275–286.

Simis, A. (2007). *A política cultural como política pública. Políticas culturais no Brasil.* Conference papers. Encontro multidisciplinares em cultura, Faculcade the communicação/UFB, Savador de Bahia. Retrieved online from the conference website http://www.cult.ufba.br/enecult2007/AnitaSimis.pdf.

Statistics Canada. (2010). *Government Expenditures on Culture: Data Tables.* Ottawa: Government of Canada.

Swenden, W., & Jans, M. T. (2006). Will It Stay or Will It Go? Federalism and the Sustainability of Belgium. *West European Politics, 29*(5), 877–894.

Switzerland, Constitution. (2018). Retrieved online from the Swiss Federal Council's website https://www.admin.ch/opc/en/classified-compilation/19995395/201801010000/101.pdf.

Upchurch, A. (2007). Linking Cultural Policy from Great Britain to Canada. *International Journal of Cultural Policy*, *13*(3), 239–254. https://doi.org/10.1080/10286630701556407.

Uyttendaele, M. (1999). *Constitution et régime linguistique en Belgique et au Canada*. Brussels: Bruylant.

Wall, S. (2010). The State of Indigenous America Series: Federalism, Indian Policy, and the Patterns of History. *Wicazo Sa Review*, *25*(1), 5–16.

Ward, P. M., & Rodríguez, V. E. (1999). New Federalism, Intra-governmental Relations and Co-governance in Mexico. *Journal of Latin American Studies*, *31*(3), 673–710.

Wesner, S. (2018). *Artists' Voices in Cultural Policy: Careers, Myths and the Creative Profession After German Reunification*. London: Palgrave.

US Constitution. Article I. Retrieved online from the Legal Information Institute, Cornell Law School's website https://www.law.cornell.edu/constitution/articlei#section1.

US Constitution. *Tenth Amendment*. Retrieved online from the Legal Information Institute, Cornell Law School's website https://www.law.cornell.edu/constitution/tenth_amendment.

Zamora, S., & Cossío, J. R. (2006). Mexican Constitutionalism After Presidencialismo. *International Journal of Constitutional Law*, *4*(2), 411–437.

CHAPTER 3

Cooperation and Competition: Cultural Governance and the Politics of Federalism

Cultural policy is defined as the result of government action in the cultural sector. To build on Clive Gray's general definition of cultural policies, they are defined as "the range of activities that governments undertake – or do not undertake – in the arena of culture" (Gray 2010: 222). To further precise what is meant, here, by culture, cultural policy is defined as the regulation of arts and heritage—including media and what people often refer to as the cultural industries. Cultural policies may imply direct provision of cultural goods or services; they may also imply indirect action through funding; or they may involve regulations and modes of control of cultural production. Finally, cultural policies are not simply the policies that regulate culture, they are also vehicles for cultural production. What this means is that cultural policy involves agencies, organizations, laws, and other policy instruments that participate and support the implementation of the policy. As a result, what we ask here is how and in what ways does federalism influence cultural policy development and implementation?

Federalism is a set of institutions that shape the rules of the game, and this section of the book presents the types of politics that typically emerge in a federal context. Following from the chapter discussing the division of cultural powers, this chapter addresses the development of institutions designed to formulate and implement cultural policies, as well as those designed to regulate and evaluate cultural sectors. More importantly, perhaps, this chapter discusses the form(s) (and place) of

© The Author(s) 2019

J. Paquette, *Cultural Policy and Federalism*,

New Directions in Cultural Policy Research,

https://doi.org/10.1007/978-3-030-12680-3_3

77

collective action, resistance, competition, and cooperation that federalism usually engenders. Competition and cooperation are essential and definitional dynamics in federations; they are expressions of the "real politics" that is at play in a given country. In other words, while the constitution sets, in part, the most basic rules of the game, actors play around these rules, often mobilizing or challenging them in the process. The institutional structure of federalism offers opportunities for cooperation, but it also offers opportunities for strategizing and for making political gains. Competition and cooperation might also be tied to traditions, values, practices, and bureaucratic routines that have developed through time, as actors learned to cooperate and coordinate their actions on certain matters. Federations, as institutions, can also be seen as places of customs, values, and norms. In sum, there are two general perspectives that engage with matters of competition and cooperation in federations: one inspired by economics theory and the other inspired by cultural approaches and theories of groups and societies.

One of the most popular economic approaches to the political dynamics of federalism is public choice theory. The public choice perspective focuses on the gains and losses of agents and, specifically, on the strategies they use to maximize their gains and minimize their losses. The calculation of losses and gains is often used to make sense of the power relations that develop in the intricacies of the institutional maze of federal countries (see Tullock 1969; Ostrom and Ostrom 1971; Rose-Ackerman 1981; Buchanan 1995; Migué 1997). Because of its link to classical economic theory, public choice theory almost systematically raises the question of cooperation in collective action. Why should an actor cooperate? Are there opportunities to cooperate? What gains are there to be found in cooperation? Is cooperation worth it? These questions are also conducive to an examination of the values of cooperation in the development of federations. Given the implicitly sceptical perspective on human nature conveyed by public choice theory, most of the perspectives that use the theory build on a rather dark or cynical view of the place of cooperation in federations. According to Breton, "[t]he 'proof' that co-operation in federations is beneficial has traditionally been based on sentimentalism and romanticism" (1987: 278). Again, according to Breton, cooperation implies a sort of romantic view of federations where every member effectively works towards a common goal—which is not the case in reality. Nonetheless, from a normative perspective, competition is actually a positive aspect according to many public choice theorists, like Breton; it can achieve, in principle, greater efficiency in public affairs (p. 274). Challenges and competition are important aspects of public life according to the tenets of this economic approach to federalism. For Breton, "the heart of co-operative federalism is secret deals, not the stuff on which a lively democracy thrives!" (p. 275). Moreover, for Breton, the idea that federalism should be cooperative is more or less an ideological perspective. This does not mean that cooperation does not exist for public choice theorists; it simply means that cooperation is also a matter of calculable interests and political preferences.

The work of Chad Rector on the motivations behind the construction of federations as a form of institutional cooperation similarly proceeds from a theoretical perspective that is largely inspired by public choice theory. Building on his work, it is believed that the motivations for joining or building a federation may also be instructive about the strategic landscape of federations. First, federations, as we know, are built on compromises, with the union being seen as a contract between different parties. This implies that some public goods or policy sectors are left out of the negotiation and, thus, help the parties—often subnational members—maintain their autonomy over certain jurisdictional areas of prime importance for their population/constituency. Second, "federations are never the first choice of all member states" (Rector 2009: 162). By this, Rector implies that federalism is the result of a constraint imposed on some member states who would have chosen or preferred to remain independent if they could have. Third, there is always an issue of "weight" and "strength" in federations. Some subnational states can achieve better results for their policies by cooperating through federal institutions, while others prefer keeping their autonomy in some jurisdictions, as this approach can prove more beneficial to them. Similarly, however, subnational governments may also decide to challenge—individually or collectively—federal government and legislatures. In sum, competition and cooperation reside in a calculation of interests between actors. The main questions that arise from an economics' perspective are: what are the gains of a collective action? Does it benefit states to cooperate through federal institutions or not?

Of course, there are competing explanations and ways to account for the dynamics of cooperation and competition in federations. The alternative to the economic model comes from what political scientists often refer to as institutionalism, and perhaps more accurately characterized as sociological institutionalism. Rather than focusing strictly on the question of interests, and seeing human beings and groups as interest maximizers, institutionalists focus on the values and norms that are tied to institutions (Lownpes 1996; Immergut 1998). In particular, institutionalists are interested in making sense of the cultural values that lie in social institutions and that ultimately inform decisions and behaviours (DiMaggio and Powell 1991; Searing 1991; Selznick 1996). Institutionalist perspectives insist on the power of culture, symbols, and beliefs in decision-making and actions (Paquette and Redaelli 2015). As such, cooperation and competition may be the result of traditions, of institutional rituals, and of bureaucratic routines. On the one hand, cooperation is implicitly the model and political purpose of federations. From an institutional perspective, the idea is not to suggest that—in any circumstances—cooperation is better and the outcome should be more favourable for every party who is cooperating. Competition, on the other hand, may have a logic in a political system, where some actors have an important tradition or a symbolic attachment to maintaining autonomy or in challenging federal institutions.

In Political Science and Public Administration, these dynamics of cooperation and competition also refer to a body of work and a notion known as intergovernmentalism (see Théret 2006; Cameron and Simeon 2002; Fabbrini 2017; Csehi 2017; Simmons 2017). If anything, to provide a partial answer to the questions raised earlier in this chapter, federalism influences how agents—politicians, public servants, and professionals—will formulate and implement their policies; it may influence how cultural policy will happen, and it may also inform the values and rationality at play in cultural decision-making. The nature of intergovernmentalism implied in federalism is one of the single most important and distinctive elements of federalism. Intergovernmentalism in a unitary State—like France or Italy—is often defined by a national/local or national/municipal relationship where the national government is institutionally, almost systematically, in a position of strength. The scenario may be very different in a federation, and the general aim of this chapter is to try to provide insights and observations on the different intergovernmental strategies developed in the cultural sector.

Therefore, in this chapter, discussion will focus on understanding how cultural policies, in federations, are shaped by the dynamics of competition and cooperation. In the process, this chapter will engage more broadly with the issue of intergovernmentalism. While the last chapter focused on the structure of powers and the legal dimensions that lie behind the structuration of cultural powers in federation, this chapter approaches this aspect from a governmental perspective—focusing on the executive power and the public administration. The first section of this chapter discusses an important issue in better understanding the cooperative and competitive dynamics of federalism: cultural nationalism. By cultural nationalism, we mean the ideational and normative aspect of a cultural policy that symbolically aims to characterize the State's cultural mission as a mission for the nation. In this section, we will discuss the normative frameworks at play and the reasons why—at times—federal governments decide to enter the cultural sector and develop a greater presence, whether this is part of their constitutionally defined powers or not. The second section discusses intergovernmental strategies. In other words, we identify the existence (or inexistence) of relationships established around cultural policy formulation and cultural policy implementation. This section also seeks to understand the nature and aims of these different strategies. The third section of the chapter revisits the sometimes important and definitive role federalism can have in shaping relationships between State and society in cultural affairs. Similarly, federalism has important implications for the structuration of professional groups in different sectors and fields. This structuration can affect the strategies and approaches to mobilization used by certain groups in their efforts to obtain certain types of goods or policy orientations from the government. Federalism may also influence the structuration of cultural associations; it may not only define their advocacy strategies, but instil a certain culture that can similarly shape the association or group. The fourth section of this chapter will end with a synthesis and discussion on some key observation regarding the nature of cultural cooperation and competition in federations. In this final section, we will systematize some of the strategies found at both State and societal levels.

3.1   Cultural Nationalism and Federations

In most federations, cultural powers are subnational or are shared by both levels of legislature and government. The question raised, here, is why are federal governments developing cultural policies or investing financial and institutional resources in cultural affairs? A common answer to this question would suggest that there is an economic dimension to culture, and that investing in culture is something that could be profitable (Gibson and Klocker 2005; Oakley 2006). That culture represents a non-negligible part of the economy and that it has a part to play in economic and regional developments can certainly be plausible reasons. And, in recent years, times have shown that economic and regional developments are certainly good reasons for government intervention into cultural affairs (Strom 2003). However, there is also another important reason for government intervention into cultural affairs: cultural nationalism is politically irresistible.

In every country, there is—somewhere in its social and political history—an appeal to the power of art and heritage as testaments of a nation's greatness and grandeur, or as instruments towards the construction of its own values—its unique contributions to the world. This is true for totalitarian and authoritarian regimes, and it is also true for liberal societies (Miller and Yúdice 2002; Belfiore 2006). This appeal is explained by the fact that cultural policies are made of symbolic material, and the fundamental values to which they appeal all inevitably find ramifications in discourse about identity. For example, the New Labour's cultural policy (Belfiore 2002; Newman and McLean 2004; Durrer and Miles 2009), using art as a tool for social inclusion, is largely about identity and social cohesion. Even appeals to the power of arts and culture that may not appear to be *prima facie* about identity are, ultimately, linked to a conception of identity and citizenship. Politicians, experts, and social activists debate arts and culture publicly, and these debates become part of the collectively accessible repertoire of norms about arts and heritage. Cultural policy is an integral part of the processes that shape what Anderson (2006) would call an "imagined community".

Cultural nationalism is defined, here, as an appeal to art and heritage—as both an expression of a nation's identity and a tool to achieve its ethos. Cultural nationalism is, as was stated, politically irresistible because no single country escapes the political mobilization of the intersection between culture (art and heritage) and politics. Even in countries that do not have a strong tradition of cultural policy or countries where the presence of the State in cultural affairs is generally seen as minor or problematic, cultural nationalism has played a part somewhere in defining or establishing the State's cultural policy. While it is not a phenomenon that is strictly associated with federalism—it is more often found in unitary States—cultural nationalism is an element at play in shaping the dynamics of competition and cooperation between subnational and federal legislatures and governments.

Building on the work of public policy researcher John W. Kingdon (1984) on policy alternatives and policy agendas, it can be said that cultural policy is, in most cases, put on the agenda because it is supported by two concurrent forces: problems and political will. On the one hand, culture is put on the political agenda because it has been identified as an area that should get more attention. This typically happens at times when governments rationalize the structure of their public services and/ or have a reach in a comprehensive number of social policy sectors. In other words, there is a governmental logic in the structuration of relationships between State and society. On the other hand, cultural policy is developed most often when there is strong political will. The best expression of this political will is cultural nationalism. As a narrative, cultural nationalism creates the political justifications for culture; it establishes the normativity of the arts in an instrumental relation to State and society.

In this regard, the cases of the USA and Switzerland are extremely interesting. Both countries value low intervention in culture by their federal level of governments. In both countries, in fact, there are strong institutional limits to further federal participation in the cultural sector. It has become commonplace to say that the American approach to culture values a very distant State participation in cultural affairs. As much as cultural policy researchers tend to agree with this view, there have been periods in American history when this was less the case, where political elites favoured a greater relationship between the State and the Arts. To support this assertion, below is an excerpt from a famous discourse by President John F. Kennedy at Amherst College on 26 October 1963:

> [...] Artists are not engineers of the soul. It may be different elsewhere. But democratic society–in it, the highest duty of the writer, the composer, the artist is to remain true to himself and to let the chips fall where they may. In serving his vision of the truth, the artist best serves his nation. [...]

> I look forward to a great future for America, a future in which our country will match its military strength with our moral restraint, its wealth with our wisdom, its power with our purpose. I look forward to an America which will not be afraid of grace and beauty, which will protect the beauty of our natural environment, which will preserve the great old American houses and squares and parks of our national past, and which will build handsome and balanced cities for our future.

I look forward to an America which will reward achievement in the arts as we reward achievement in business or statecraft. I look forward to an America which will steadily raise the standards of artistic accomplishment and which will steadily enlarge cultural opportunities for all of our citizens. And I look forward to an America which commands respect throughout the world not only for its strength but for its civilization as well. [...]. (Kennedy 1963)

This excerpt is a good example of cultural nationalism; it expresses the place and role of the arts in society: in support of the values of the nation. This discourse also suggests a greater role for the federal government in the arts and heritage. These expressions of political supports are what would later give thrust to the establishment of the National Endowment for the Arts (NEA) in the USA. That is to say, even in the USA where there were no strategic reasons and no supportive constitutional framework to do so, politicians still entertained—at one time—the idea that culture should be part of the federal government's purview.

A similar normative appeal to the arts can be found in Australian history. Gough Whitlam's government (1972–1975) is known to have made a number of important contributions to Australian arts and heritage. Perhaps most importantly, Whitham's government was responsible for the creation of the National Arts Council in Australia. Why should the federal government enter the cultural sector? Here, again, is a case of cultural nationalism exemplified through a speech—this time, delivered by Whitlam in 1972:

In any civilised community the arts and associated amenities must occupy a central place. Their enjoyment should not be seen as something remote from everyday life. Of all the objectives of my Government none had a higher priority than the encouragement of the arts, the preservation and enrichment of our cultural and intellectual heritage. Indeed I would argue that all the other objectives of a Labor Government - social reform, justice and equity in the provision of welfare services and educational opportunities - have as their goal the creation of a society in which the arts and the appreciation of spiritual and intellectual values can flourish. Our other objectives are all means to an end; the enjoyment of the arts is an end in itself.

[...]

Many of our finest artists were working overseas. Our national cultural institutions were embryonic or non-existent. Such institutions as existed in the States were largely relics of colonial or Edwardian times... the basis of a national arts and cultural policy did not exist. There were no major performing arts centres. [...] Touring of the performing arts to country districts was organised by State-based arts councils with limited access to funds. There were no regional theatre companies or galleries; there was no film industry; there were no State arts ministries. Aboriginal arts, and the crafts in general, were virtually ignored. (Whitlam in Gardiner-Garden 2009)

In Switzerland, the establishment of a federal cultural administration followed a political path linking the strengths of the arts to issues of national unity. Between 1967 and 1968, many groups expressed some limitations about the state of culture in Switzerland, and politicians like Hans-Peter Tschudi began to express the idea that the federation should be allowed to do much more in cultural affairs. As a result, in 1969, a federal commission was established—known as the Clottu Commission—to explore the development of a federal cultural policy. Looking at some excerpt from the report shows how cultural nationalism is important in establishing the federal policy:

[...] the field of application of a Swiss cultural policy is characterized by frontiers, by the reality and by the myth of a common history, and more importantly by the will of different ethnic and linguistic groups capable of recognizing themselves in a common destiny. Our cultures are organically linked to that of our neighbors, but it is in common considerably more powerful.

[...] it is the mission of a Swiss cultural policy to justify and reinforce the confederal links and strengthen the solidarity between regions that are culturally strong, and those that are less, and by doing so, we will give every citizen reason to defend this link. [...] It would be dangerous for a federal State that reunites different ethnic and linguistic groups, to be united only around a number of limited material interests, and to be submitted to the vicissitudes of history.[1] (Commission fédérale d'experts pour l'étude de questions concernant la politique culturelle Suisse 1975: 374)

Former Swiss politician Gaston Clottu was in charge of this commission, and despite the very technical content of this report—and the thorough analysis of the cultural sector—this excerpt conveys a certain sense of emotionalism towards the mission of the arts. The arts, here, are defined

[1] Translated from the French original text.

as providing an opportunity to help build a greater sense of belonging to the federation. Constitutional constraints were described in the report as one of the most important barriers to a federal cultural policy. As such, if Switzerland were to benefit from the arts, it would only be through a series of profound institutional changes that this could happen. The Swiss Constitution was eventually modified in 1999 to allow greater federal government participation in cultural affairs; however, the system largely privileges the former interpretation of the constitution, which provides more cultural powers to the cantons. The change in 1999 simply confirmed that the federal level of administration could effectively participate in the cultural sector, under limited conditions. The Clottu report, however, had called for a much greater participation of the federal administration in a new Swiss cultural policy. Nonetheless, what this case illustrates is how, even in a country where there have been many complications limiting federal participation in cultural affairs, there is still—at least—one instance where cultural nationalism was used in favour of culture. In this case, it is not so much the moral role of the artist that is described and called to play, but the moral duties of the confederation—if it so wishes—to sustain the federation through links and supports that are not only of a technical nature. The arts, here, were seen as being there to support or provide "soul" to Switzerland.

In Canada, the most important thrust for the federal government's participation in the arts has been cultural nationalism. In the period following World War II, the Canadian government was interested in the role of the arts in supporting the social fibre and excellence of a nation. The Government of Canada called together a special commission—led by Vincent Massey—whose work, between 1949 and 1951, was to investigate the place and role of culture and humanities in Canadian society and to assess some of its strengths and weaknesses. In the terms of reference that guided the work of Massey and his commission, one can read:

> "It is desirable that the Canadian people should know as much as possible about their country, its history and traditions; and about their national life and common achievements; that it is in the national interest to give encouragement to institutions which express national feeling, promote common understanding and add to the variety and richness of Canadian life, rural as well as urban." (Royal Commission on the Development in the Arts, Letters and Science 1951: 4)

This serves to clarify the intentions of the commission. The arts and culture are questions of identity. But the cultural nationalism that lies behind the commission is probably not the kind of cultural nationalism one would expect today. In fact, little of it is about the challenges brought about by a diverse population, by the French-speaking population or Indigenous populations. These populations are identified as part of the fabric of Canadian society. However, this has nothing to do with the place of culture in preserving the unity of Canada from collapsing from within. The cultural nationalism that motivated stronger federal interventions in culture came from challenges from outside the country. In this respect, the report could not be clearer:

> But apart from these problems of dispersal we face, for the most part without any physical barriers, a vast and wealthy country to which we are linked not only by language but by many common traditions. Language and tradition link us also with two mother countries. But from these we are geographically isolated. On this continent, as we have observed, our population stretches in a narrow and not even continuous ribbon along our frontier–fourteen millions along a five thousand mile front. In meeting influences from across the border as pervasive as they are friendly, we have not even the advantages of what soldiers call defence in depth.

> From these influences, pervasive and friendly as they are, much that is valuable has come to us, as we shall have occasion to observe repeatedly in this chapter and indeed throughout this entire survey: gifts of money spent in Canada, grants offered to Canadians for study abroad, the free enjoyment of all the facilities of many institutions which we cannot afford, and the importation of many valuable things which we could not easily produce for ourselves. We have gained much. In this preliminary stock-taking of Canadian cultural life it may be fair to inquire whether we have gained a little too much. (Royal Commission on the Development in the Arts, Letters and Science 1951: 13)

This passage is just the beginning of a very long series of pages lamenting the presence of American media, foundations, books, newspapers, etc., in Canadian public spaces. The cultural nationalism behind Canada's federal government's presence in the cultural sector was motivated by a fear of Americanization. Americanization was seen as a problem for Canadian sovereignty. Effectively, cultural sovereignty was an issue of social and political sovereignty. The scenario of an ever-growing presence

of American interests in Canadian cultural affairs was something reinforced by English-Canadians' cultural anxieties. It is often said that
English Canada was born of a desire not to be American—in reference
to the arrival of Loyalists to the British crowns after the American War of
Independence. If we agree with this principle, then cultural sovereignty
becomes an important political project.

In Malaysia, the National Department for Culture and Arts—
eventually the Ministry of Tourism and Culture—is responsible for
a policy on cultural identity. This policy was elaborated in 1971 as the
National Culture Policy. The policy discusses the place of art and heritage, but clearly insists more on delineating the contours of what is culture and national identity in Malaysia. The policy establishes guiding
principles to clarify norms and values about culture that ought to guide
the government in cultural affairs, as well as in many other competing
sectors. Nonetheless, according to Mandal, "[i]n contrast to many other
former colonies, the nation was actively sought in Malaysia after the
independence rather than before. The NCP [National Culture Policy]
was therefore a belated effort at seeking national identity through the
arts" (Mandal 2008: 274). The policy was developed in response to a
series of ethnic uprisings in the late 1960s; culture and cultural policy
were intended as tools for national unity. Below are the three pillars of
the National Culture Policy:

1) The national culture must be based on the indigenous culture of this
region:

[...] The Malay culture today is a way of life and symbol of identity of
more than 200 million people who speak the same language. As such, the
culture of the indigenous people from this region, which, in a wider or
narrower sense, refers to the Malay culture, forms the basis of the National
Culture Policy.

2) Suitable elements from the other culture may be accepted as part of the
national culture:

Culture is a dynamic phenomenon, always changing through the on-
going process of adaptation and assimilation. This principle takes into
consideration the multi-cultural aspects in a multi-racial society. Hence,
cultural elements of the Chinese, Indians, Arabs, Westerners and others
which are considered suitable and acceptable are included in the national
culture. Such acceptance must be in accordance with the provisions in
the Constitution and the principles of Rukun Negara, as well as national

interest, moral values and the position of Islam as the official religion of the country.

3) Islam is an important component in the formulation of the national culture:

Religion or the belief in God is important in the development process of a country and also in the personal development of her people. Islam provides guidance to mankind and fulfills the physical and emotional needs. Hence Islam should be an important element in formulating the National Culture Policy based on its position as the official religion of the country. (Malaysia, National Department for Culture and Arts 2018)

Why are federal governments supporting culture? In this section, it is illustrated how culture and nation cannot be dissociated. In States that do not have a strong tradition in cultural affairs, in pluricultural States, where culture and nation can be seen in tension, the intersection between culture and unity or between culture and nation cannot be avoided. In this section, the cases of the USA, Switzerland, Australia, Canada, and Malaysia were singled out as good examples for their capacity to express cultural nationalism with a variety of nuances. Based on these cases, it becomes clear that cultural policy in federations—like those in unitary States—cannot escape the intersection between culture and nation.

The purpose of this section was also to state that, despite the fact that culture is organized along a series of constitutional divisions of power, the politics of culture is an important factor to acknowledge. In federations, where powers are divided and culture is in the realm of either or both a government and legislature, culture is caught in forces that sometimes evade formal institutional constraints. The above-mentioned cases serve to illustrate how cultural policies in federations are already politically problematic. While federations are about the coexistence of many, cultural policy tends to be about the nation—about something superior, even if it acknowledges differences. As such, cultural policy already sits in the dynamics of cooperation and competition, between ideas about culture entertained at the federal or subnational levels. In the next section, we depart from this ideational or ideological perspective of culture to turn our focus, once again, on institutional matters. This next section should help us understand, beyond the ideological appeal of culture, the influence of institutions and how subnational governments cooperate or contest their federal government on institutional grounds.

3.2 INTERGOVERNMENTALISM AND CULTURAL GOVERNANCE

The literature on federalism in Political Science and Public Administration has developed considerably over the years, and the creativity of the authors is remarkable. The nature of intergovernmental relationships is described using a vocabulary that is remarkably creative and constantly evolving. Fenna (2012a) has identified more than ten expressions used to describe federal/subnational relationships. "Cooperative federalism" is a very common expression; it characterizes cooperation between different levels of government and, in some uses, implicitly conveys the idea of federal powers' reliance on subnational authorities for policy coordination—as is the case with Germany (Benz 2007). In the American context, the expression "dual federalism" has a historical overtone: it refers to a time where federal and state powers were seen as jealously protected by their respective levels of authority; it implies that both levels will try to protect their own constitutional powers (Kincaid 1990, 1996). There is an almost normative undertone to this characterization that leaves the impression of stubbornness on the part of both governments that this is implicitly negative. The notion of "pragmatic federalism" implies that public powers are collaborating or in conflict—based on pragmatic issues more than issues related to values or political ideology (Hollander and Patapan 2007). Australian federalism is described by some (Smullen 2014; Fenna 2012b) as a pragmatic federalism. "Regulatory federalism" conveys the idea of a relationship where the federal government develops a legislative or regulatory office that exerts pressures on subnational governments to obtain conformity with federal legislations (Majone 1992). Radio-broadcasting laws can be defined as institutions that participate in regulatory federalism. "Coercive federalism" follows a more or less similar logic. Other notions include "adaptive federalism", "conditional federalism", "executive federalism", and "opportunistic federalism". The problem with these notions is that most of them convey the idea of a "management style" or style of relationship that is extremely fluid. A very cursory overview of the literature on federalism reveals that these labels have all been used to describe American federalism, and many of them have even been used to describe Australian federalism. This should be a reminder that these labels may or may not be that useful. They may be useful in terms of providing a sense of the style of federalism, but they may not always be mutually exclusive and should be used with caution. To simplify the matter, in this book, we will distinguish between two broad categories of intergovernmental behaviours and relationships: cooperative strategies and competitive strategies.

Cooperative strategies in cultural policy suppose that the governments who engage in policy development or implementation have a common understanding of culture; it supposes that the governments collaborating also have common interests in working together. While cooperation does not mean that all members participating in intergovernmental relationship will be unanimous in their decisions—some will surely benefit more than others—the implication remains that there is a certain general level of agreement among agents who enter such relationships. Competition, on the other hand, involves a relative level of conflict or disagreement between members of a federation over cultural affairs. The basis for these conflicts may be a difference in ideas about culture and the nature of cultural policy; it may be a divergence over the policy instrument used or the values that are implied in cultural policy; it may also be driven by conflicting economic, legal, or cultural interests. Some competitive strategies involve the quest for gains, while others simply reflect a protective attitude and a reluctance to cooperate in cultural affairs. Albeit mildly competitive, the strategies implied in dual federalism—where agents are preserving their powers—remain, nonetheless, positionally defined as a competitive strategy. In a single federation, depending on issues, values, and era, these cooperative and competitive logics can coexist; they are, more or less, part of a federation's dynamic, and it should be expected that a sector as broad and diverse as culture may be simultaneously built on and shaped by both tensions.

When it comes to cooperation, transfers are one of the most common instruments used (Puetter 2012; Bulmer and Padgett 2005). Transfers are usually defined as financial goods; they are, in most cases, viewed as a relationship where the federal government redistributes fiscal revenues to subnational governments as a mean of equalization—to provide a better balance between members of a federation to ensure that no subnational government is dealing with societies whose living conditions are dramatically different from the rest of the country. Transfers can also be done as an agreement between a federal government and its subnational component in exchange for assuming responsibility for the implementation of a social policy, for instance. This is often referred to as fiscal federalism (Oates 2005; Weingast 2009; Gervasoni 2010). In the cultural sector, financial transfers tend to be associated with normalization and harmonization projects that aim to ensure that arts, culture, and heritage sectors are serviced on relatively similar standards across the country, that no single citizen or professional suffers because they are living in one region over another. In other words, the aim of these policies is to provide a minimum standard across the country. In the cultural sector, this invitation to collaborate is motivated by a certain political idea or sense of the value of culture among federal decision-makers. Monetary transfers also tend to be associated with distinct, punctual funding and, in most cases, can be seen as seed funding. This view of collaboration through a financial instrument is not without reminding some of the strategies common to the European Union in terms of cultural funding. Nurturing the development of cultural capacities among members of a federation is a common practice.

The American cultural system provides a good case to see dynamic of transfers at work. In the USA, there is no ministry of culture; the federal education department does not operate in areas that are commonly associated with arts and heritage. The only federal institutions that govern cultural affairs are the national museums, the National Park Service (created in 1916 and operating, since, under the Department of Interior), and the NEA. The creation of the NEA takes its roots in a federal employment programme—the Works Progress Administration—that tried to support job creation in the cultural sector, among many others. According to Pleshette (1998), this programme "laid the groundwork for the NEA"—with which "John F. Kennedy's New Frontier administration transformed the nation's art agenda from the guise of employment relief into a vision of cultural policy" (p. 12). Again, according to Pleshette, President Kennedy entertained a vision of citizenship and of the American identity that gave full recognition and importance to the arts. In 1965, President Johnson's administration fulfilled this vision— with the aid of Congress members who also shared this vision—and obtained the funding and resources necessary to create the American arm's length arts funding agency. However, the federal government was not the first to develop an arm's length arts funding agency in the country. As reminded by Kevin Mulcahy, arm's length arts funding agencies already existed in many American states: "The Utah State Legislature established the first state arts agency in 1899" (2002: 68). New York State developed its arts council in 1960, and "[b]y 1965, five additional states – California, Georgia, Minnesota, Missouri and North Caroline – had established state arts agencies, bringing the total to seven" (p. 68).

Rather than furthering its vision of arts and culture and developing a stronger institutional framework at the national level, the executive mobilized the NEA and used it as a catalyst to achieve this through the subnational level. Again, according to Mulcahy: "'little NEA's' were established at the state level", [...] The 1967 annual report of the NEA noted that in its first year of operation the Endowment had provided the stimulus for the fifty states and the six special jurisdictions to survey their cultural resources and to provide cultural programs, [...] (p. 68).

In its first years of existence, the NEA directly funded the states to help them structure their arts and cultural sector. This funding had two consequences. The first consequence was that it helped implement a federal vision and policy at the subnational level; it was an appeal to voluntary collaboration. The second consequence was that it institutionalized cultural governance at the state level; it created an institutional structure which, as is often the case, was politically difficult for states to retreat from. When Mulcahy conducted his study—based on 1990s data and pictures—every state, associated jurisdiction (Puerto Rico) and territory (Guam, American Samoa, Mariana Islands, and Virgin Islands) had an arm's length agency loosely based on the model proposed by the NEA. Still to this date, in a climate aversive to the arts, the situation remains unchanged: States continue to pursue their obligations and role in the artistic sector, and these institutions still exist. The subnational level of cultural policy is extremely important; to understand the cultural sector in the USA, one has to pay close attention to the states (Mulcahy 2002; Rosenstein 2018).

In some countries, transfers are an important element of the federal/subnational relationship. Special funds may help subnational governments engage in new areas or further national mandates at the subnational level. In Austria, for instance, the federal government has taken a leadership role in sustaining cultural institutions at the subnational level; transfers from the federal government to the provinces are not uncommon. Financial transfers may be highly politicized in federations, and available cultural funding may also initiate competitive strategies among subnational states in order to prioritize their projects over others. Transfers offer a form of cooperation between the federal and subnational governments, but they can equally offer potential for competition between subnational members. In Austria, in an attempt to limit the growing cultural ambitions of the federal government, some provinces developed a new approach to cultural funding in which money would be redistributed in a cooperative manner, in support of existing provincial initiates (Wimmer 1992: 6). While this may be true for the arts, there was a paradoxical demand—from the provinces—to federalize funding and administration of heritage (p. 160).

It should also be noted that transfers—from a federal government—for cultural purposes may also be more common on symbolic occasions. In the USA, the build-up for the Bicentennial in 1976 gave place to a funding opportunity—City Spirit—that was open to subnational and local governments in support of cultural initiatives at the municipal level (National Endowment for the Arts 2012: 10). Similarly, the Centennial of the Canadian Confederation in 1967 and the Australian Bicentennial Anniversary in 1988 of the European settlement were both occasions where the federal government offered grants and funding for a variety of cultural projects developed by local and subnational governments. Symbolic milestones are important in the life of culture, and while this is often true for heritage—since these are meant as forms of commemoration—the art sector has also benefited from the funding that has come from milestone grants.

Transfers from the federal to subnational level are one of the many ways in which intergovernmentalism is practised in a federation. Interministerial or interdepartmental conferences are also a very common mechanism for cooperation. In Germany, the *Kultusministerkonferenz*—or Standing Conference of the Ministers of Education and Cultural Affairs, which have existed since 1948—acts as a coordination institution for establishing common goals and strategies in education and culture among German subnational states. This coordination conference has become increasingly important in the Europeanization process as it helps formulate a subnational position on which the federal government can act at the international or European levels. While this conference has traditionally worked towards resolving pressing educational matters, its cultural folio has also been increasing. Developing a common position and subscribing to international instruments in the cultural sector, such as those pertaining to intangible heritage, for instance, require significant effort on the part of the members of this conference. This conference is vital, especially when considered in the context of Germany's constitutional division of powers over culture.

In the USA, the National Assembly of State Arts Agencies (NASAA) is another good example of horizontal collaboration between subnational entities in the cultural sector. NASAA is an institutional form of cooperation between states through a not-for-profit organization that acts as a coordination body, reuniting every state arts agency or council. The NASAA offers its members opportunities to develop common strategies vis-à-vis the federal government; it also offers a space for disseminating knowledge between members. Both cases suggest a horizontal form of intergovernmentalism primarily involving similar subnational institutions and representatives. In the German case, the *Kultusministerkonferenz* represents a certain form of executive federalism in the cultural sector because it brings together members of the executive branch of governments to work together on common positions and challenges. As for the American example, the cooperation is based on administrative practices; it reunites agencies and public service organizations.

In Australia and Canada, such coordination institutions also exist; however, the federal representative, in these cases, is seen as an active participant and often assumes a leadership position in the forum. In Australia, the intergovernmental arena in the cultural sector originally came in the form of the Cultural Ministers Council (CMC), created in 1985 as a branch of the Council of Australian Governments—an umbrella organization whose mandate is to provide a forum for intergovernmental affairs. CMC evolved over its first five years into a regional interest organization; the form of intergovernmentalism it saw fit for culture also involved the participation of New Zealand as a full member, and Norfolk Island and Papua New Guinea as observers. The organization also grew to include territorial entities and representatives of local governments (Kyne and Morton 2017: 5–6).

In 2011, the CMC held its final meeting, and a new platform was created in its place—Meeting of Cultural Ministers (MCM). The MCM stepped back from the CMC's regional aims, to refocus on Australian cultural matters. The MCM continues to reunite the executive branch, but has evolved into a coordination platform that relies more heavily on cultural experts and senior public servants. Moreover, the MCM is now working under the federal Department of Communication and the Art of Australia, and over the years, has been a platform for discussing a number of issues pertaining to aboriginal culture and cultural governance among Indigenous and Torres Strait Islanders communities across the country; it has been a platform for discussing the issue of inclusion in the arts and, in particular, the question of the accessibility of cultural institutions in the context of disability; and it has also been a platform for discussing sectorial challenges pertaining to the music and film industries. The increased participation of public servants from the cultural services, and the inclusion of sectorial members as occasional participants, has contributed to transforming the style of the MCM meetings over the years. In a certain sense, the sustained presence of high-level experts from the public service and the institutionalization of cultural statistics over the years have also made the MCM a space in cultural issues are socialized. In other words, the MCM is a space that contributes to the creation and dissemination of collective "referentials" (Muller 2000; Sabatier et al. 2000; Lascoumes and Le Galès 2018). In doing so, the MCM shapes what is a cultural issue, what kind of values are implied in the current cultural debates, and what kind of policy instruments are used and considered. This institution has clearly created a culture of cultural affairs; it has helped generate common views and ways of referring to cultural affairs.

In Canada, the Canadian Intergovernmental Conference Secretariat was developed in 1973 as a platform to facilitate discussion across different levels of government. The first conference of federal and provincial ministers of culture was held in 1980. The transformation in federal ministries in 1993 that led to the creation of the Department of Canadian Heritage—replacing the former Department of Communications—was a turning point for this conference. The mandate of this new department was more recognizably cultural, which gave federal leadership in cultural affairs a new wave of energy and excitement. Since then, the meetings of the Canadian federal-provincial-territorial ministers responsible for culture and heritage have been dealing with issues similar to those outlined in the Australian context. The ministers' conferences have been used to develop common strategies to reinforce heritage protection, discuss pressing issues in the cultural industries, and discuss the place of Indigenous cultures in the process of reconciliation between the State and Indigenous populations. While there are some commonalities between the Canadian and Australian cases, in Canada, the work that is done through these meetings remains very focused on the development of common positions and the recognition of problems. As such, these conferences remain a platform that is focused on the political actors. Unlike in Australia, this platform cannot be seen as a learning or socialization platform; it does not have the same status or institutional continuity that is found in Australia.

In Switzerland, the federal government has a very modest level of cultural action. Under the Department of Interior, the Federal Office for

Culture is responsible for federal cultural affairs. Beyond the portfolios of national institutions it has under its direct supervision, the federal office is also in charge of intergovernmental cultural affairs. In the Swiss system of cultural relations, the constitutional and institutional frameworks of cultural governance posit the Federal Office of Culture as a partner of the cantons; the initiatives of a federal intervention must come from one or many cantons. As such, cantons play an important part in shaping the federal approach to culture. This form of cultural federalism requires a form of bottom-up initiative and participation in cultural affairs.

In other circumstances, there is a structural asymmetry between federal and subnational governments in cultural affairs. Limited spending powers at the subnational level in Mexico, for instance, make it difficult for subnational cultural departments to work outside the collaboration and recognition of the Federal Secretariat for Culture—the Conaculta (Bordat 2013: 231–232). Conaculta acts as a coordinating office; it is directly responsible for many of the federal government's cultural organizations, but it is also a liaison agency for a variety of institutions, which creates a more centralized type of cultural governance in Mexico. Similarly, the system developed in Brazil is based on cooperation between the federal and subnational entities, but this cooperation is—in principle—obligatory. Therefore, in Brazil, there is a division of cultural labour where the federal administration is in charge of the national cultural policy and the subnational governments are responsible for implementing it. Decentralization in the Brazilian cultural system does not mean decentralization of decision-making power; rather, it implies a greater proximity and accessibility of services at local levels through subnationally administered programmes. Similarly, the policy formulation process in Brazil is defined as participative, but this participation does not capture any federalist principles. Since 2007, the development of the *Conselho Nacional de Política Cultural* represents an attempt to develop and maintain a national cultural policy that is informed by the diversity of the cultural sector of the country (Barbalho 2016). Representations are based on two principles: ethnocultural representability and sectorial representatives from artistic disciplines or heritage professions. The idea of regional and subnational representation is not enshrined in the functioning principles of this policy formulation forum. By contrast, Argentina, who also typically has a more centralized form of cultural governance, has integrated some principles of executive federalism into the structures of its secretariat for culture. The *Dirección de Coordinación*

Federal is in charge of coordinating cultural actions with subnational partners, but it is also responsible for developing common frameworks and establishing common principles. It should be noted that this institution is not strictly for the cultural sector; the Argentinian Secretariat of Culture has replicated an administrative structure that exists in many other secretariats—including agriculture and economic development, among others. Therefore, the culture of cooperation in this case is built into the institutional tradition of federalism at the federal level. In most cases, in Latin American federalism, cultural policy is potentially subjected, by constitution, institutional developments, and resource asymmetry to a form of policy transfer (Radaelli 2000) that operates from the federal level to the subnational level.

National programmes may also be developed as a mean of disseminating common standards or harmonizing practices in the field. This is, of course, a very common occurrence in federations, but it is not exclusive to federations. In Malaysia, the development of a Human Capital Development Unit under the Ministry of Culture in 2001 served as a means of disseminating expertise through the professionalization of the sector. Similarly, the development of the Canadian Conservation Institute in the wake of the development of Canada's museum policy in 1972 is also another case in point. The institute's function was to develop capacity in conservation for the federal government and to experiment and test new methods and strategies for preserving heritage. However, the institute was also meant to serve as a place that could professionalize the sector while serving subnational institutions as well.

In other cases, the intergovernmental cultural relations may be developed at an interorganizational level. For instance, in India, the National Mission for Manuscripts introduced in 2003 to unearth and save India's traditional books as cultural heritage was developed as a federal agency. While this agency is strictly governed by federal entities and experts recognized by the federal administration, some of its projects have involved the participation of subnational governments. To this end, the National Mission for Manuscripts has collaborated with many subnational institutions—including the Department of Archeology of Tamil Nadu. These collaborations are practically oriented, but, nonetheless, show project-based interorganizational forms of cooperation. Interorganizational collaborations and meetings are also one of the most important bases of cultural federalism in Malaysia. Specifically, in Malaysia, the federal department of culture has always been strongly associated with a tourism mandate. Since the late 1980s and early 1990s, the prevalence of tourism in Malaysia has been fluctuating. In recent years, the country's arts and heritage components have been of a declining interest for federal politicians. As a result, there has been more continuity at the level of big national institutions, such as the Muzium Negara. It should be considered that both countries share a vision of cultural policy that has a strong focus on heritage and, specifically, intangible heritage. As such, the cooperative dimensions of federalism should be found more closely around the professional networks and interorganizational spaces where professionals, working for different entities, congregate. These collaborations are rarely politically motivated.

Direct subnational relations based on bilateral cultural interests are far from common. Regional subnational relations between members of the same country are much more common. In the USA, for instance, NASAA organization members are organized under a number of regional conferences, and they develop strategies and cooperate on regional grounds. While bilateral cultural relations are not common in a single country, there are some exceptions. For instance, the Canadian province of Québec has developed a number of representations in other provinces that act as a contact point between its government and those of other provinces. The Government of Québec's delegations in the provinces of Ontario and New Brunswick have a cultural component to their mission: they administer the Québec government's programme in support of Canadian *Francophonie*; these delegates actively support French-speaking cultural and educational institutions in these provinces as part of its bilateral relations in the federation. Québec's delegation in Toronto, for instance, funds festivals and cultural events that cater to the French-speaking minority of Ontario. Federalist politicians in Québec have always believed that sustaining French outside the province was part of Québec's cultural mission in the federation. Similarly, in Belgium, where the federation was constructed on cultural differences—not to say antagonisms—the governments of the Flemish and French communities have developed a common agreement for cultural cooperation. In this case, this bilateral agreement has practical aspects for artists and professionals working in the fine arts sector, as well as an important practical dimension for libraries. More importantly, however, the agreement signed in 2012 also has an important symbolic and political value (Lowies and Schrobiltgen 2016).

Financial transfers and inter-ministerial forums are some of the most important mechanisms for cooperation. There are many traditions and approaches to inter-ministerial forums: some are designed in a horizontal fashion; some ought to be seen as platforms for advocacy; while others are spaces where important decisions must be made and consensus must be created vis-à-vis the federal level of government. In some circumstances, asymmetries in the power structures of these forums can also establish the conditions for policy transfers. This is particularly the case in Latin American federations. Of course, the nature of the relationship between the federal and subnational actors in these cases is uneven. The process is not deliberative or based on negotiations so much as it involves a series of expectations in terms of implementing policies at the subnational level. Cooperation can be created on an interorganizational level and may be channelled by the public services' professional cultures and agents. Often, these agents will approach cooperation on an operational level. The European process, in some countries, requires an important degree of intergovernmentalism in cultural affairs. In Austria, Germany, and Belgium, where culture has strong foundations in subnational jurisdictions, both levels of government must establish paths to cooperate and liaise in order to adequately participate and comply with European legislations and policies. The confederation model that is theoretically implied in the European Union requires that subnational and federal governments coordinate since the process relies on international affairs, where federal authorities are typically competent. Finally, cooperation may also be articulated around the creation of common norms and standards. This approach tries to instil what new institutionalists would characterize as a normative isomorphism (Howlett and Ramesh 1993; Gupta et al. 1994; Gooderham et al. 1999; Bachmann 2001) or as a natural alignment with common standards. This voluntarist approach to cooperation can be witnessed in the alignment with national norms in subnational institutions. Education and training offered by federal governments' cultural institutions can act, in this sense, as a catalyst towards greater adhesion to national standards and practices.

There are few regulatory agencies in the cultural sector. In most cases, the regulatory agencies federations tend to possess are those associated with radio-broadcasting laws. In the vast majority of countries, these laws are under federal rule. These agencies represent a structure whose aim is to regulate content by providing national standards for radio, television, and the Internet. In general, these institutions tend to normalize cultural production while aiming to set standards for a nation, and, therefore, they are, by definition, more coercive than cooperative. In Belgium and Germany, these powers are vested in the hands of subnational governments who are sovereign in their own jurisdictions. In the USA, where the jurisdiction is primarily federal, there is a disposition in the processes that can create joint federal-state boards to regulate matters that are of local concerns. According to some researchers, telecommunications in the USA are also an area that evolved from a dual federalism to a cooperative federalism (Lawton and Burns 1996).

Regulatory agencies in the cultural sector may cover areas and policy issues where both cooperation and competition can occur. In Canada, for instance, the provinces have occasionally tried to engage with the federal government over a shared power in the administration of telecommunications, but very little has been accomplished. The Canadian Radio-television and Telecommunications Board remains the basic regulatory agency, determining the nature of the content and fixing quotas for Canadian content to be met by television and radio stations. These quotas must be respected or broadcasters risk losing their licence to broadcast. Provinces have tried to increase their participation or part in the administration of these regulations. Even if the USA is characterized, by many, as a cooperative federation in terms of cultural affairs—including telecommunications—there have been some instances and legal cases (e.g. Louisiana Public Service v. FCC in 1983) where the power of the federal government was challenged by the states in court (McKenna 1987).

Before going further in this transition from cooperation to competition, there is a question that must be raised: why would either the federal or subnational governments compete over cultural affairs? Culture is often described as a minor policy area (Gray and Wingfield 2011) and it is commonly considered as such by politicians. Cultural policy may be an area of controversy, but it is generally rarely considered an area where politicians would engage in a territorial war. To this question, there are, of course, a number of valid answers; however, in federations, there are two general reasons to explain why this is. First, governments and legislators in federations tend to want to preserve or acquire more rights, not less. History has shown that economic, social, and technological changes can create conditions in which a policy area or power would or could seem trivial one day, but become quite strategic the next. For instance, the regulation of commerce across the country or between states in the USA—a federal power—was also the foundation of the federal government's constitutional power in the area of communications and, ultimately, became the government's foundation for regulating radio-broadcasting and telecommunications standards across the country. Exerting one's own jurisdictional power is essential to protecting or claiming that power when it becomes strategic. Additionally, not exerting power, or letting another level of government act in one's jurisdiction, can come with a political cost: in matters of culture, such power may be used politically in issues of national/regional identity to feeds on important political symbolism. Second, many federations are built on pluricultural grounds. In a number of cases, recognized national minorities are a majority in subnational social and political institutions (Beauregard 2018); culture, in these circumstances, may already be an important political issue.

Competitive strategies in federations can take many forms. However, generally speaking, courts are an important and often powerful instrument in challenging power. Courts can confirm and reinstate constitutional rights over a federal or national jurisdiction. In some systems, courts can be used to reinstate or validate a minority right. In Canada, courts are often used to challenge provincial governments' decision in cultural and educational affairs, especially with regard to the protection of minority rights (Cardinal 2008). Tribunals are also spaces where the cultural rights of French-speaking populations in Flanders have been tested. The highest courts of justice are often called to intervene and provide interpretations in terms of protections for national or linguistic minority rights. These tribunals can, more or less, confirm some rights or interpret the nature of the legislator to understand if a jurisdiction is acting on its right or is incompliant and not fulfilling its duties.

Another good example of the use of tribunals in federal/subnational affairs can be found in the history of public television in Germany. After World War II, the federal government tried to establish a national broadcasting corporation. By the 1950s, the system was, relatively, a collaboration between the federal and *Länder* governments—as both had established collaborations around a public broadcaster (Deutsche Welle). However, by 1960, the federal government had ambitions; it tried to diminish the number of land-based broadcasters and proposed a federal act to regulate the sector; it also tried to develop a new national broadcaster through the acquisition of parts in a private broadcaster. The *Länders* united and challenged, with success, the federal government in court. The federal powers claimed that—based on article 73—they could act in this capacity, but the court confirmed that the broadcasting laws—the regulation of the sector—were a matter of subnational jurisdiction. According to Erk, the court offered a strong response with respect to a friendly form of federalism and to the jurisdictions (2007):

> It is interesting to note that the ruling of the High Administrative Court also included a section which criticized the federal government for not cooperating with the Länder. The issue here seems to be the independent action of the federal government, not the level of governance. The court ruled that the federal government offended the principle of federal friendly behavior. As a consequence, Deustchsland Fernsehen GmbH was abolished. But Deutschlandfunk and Deutsche Welle remained due to their international mandates. (p. 63)

Competitive strategies may also entail the development of new institutions. In some instances, occupying a power, using it to claim a jurisdictional capacity to act in the long term, can be seen in the repertoire of strategies mobilized by governments. In Canada, the provinces of Ontario and Québec have developed their own public broadcasting systems, more or less, as a political response to the presence of federal public broadcasting through the English Canadian Broadcasting Corporation and the French Radio-Canada. In the 1970s, the Government of Ontario created TV Ontario (TVO) in English, with a French section in operation until the full development of a provincial channel in French (TFO). Similarly, and also in the early 1970s, Québec's legislature and government decided to establish a public corporation, Radio-Québec (now Télé-Québec). Both cases evidence a certain attempt by provincial governments to offer a response to what was provided by the federal public corporation. These projects were, and remain, attempts to provide a distinctive provincial voice in public affairs and education (Laurence 1982; Bernier 1989; Nielsen 1995). Similarly, after World War II, Bavaria was very active in the cultural sector, developing standards for radio-broadcasting which privileged local music, as well as content associated with "high-culture", as a mean of reaching an ideal of identity. This ideal was in clash with American popular culture. This response from Bavaria was singular as it was a rapid response and use of cultural powers compared to other subnational jurisdictions, and it offered views that were also strikingly different from those entertained at the federal level (Monod 2000).

Federal and subnational legislatures and governments can enter into a variety of competitive strategies in order to protect or further their power over cultural affairs. Requesting more powers can be seen as a competitive strategy in cultural affairs. In Austria, where the subnational governments are generally sympathetic to the intervention of the federal government in cultural affairs, there have been cases where discontent was expressed and subnational governments (re)claimed some of their cultural powers. The province of Vorarlberg, in 1979, launched an initiative to reclaim powers in education, broadcasting, and other cultural affairs—including monuments protection—that had slowly been taken by the federal government (Erk 2004: 10–11). This is exceptional in the Austrian federal system, but it highlights how important it is for a jurisdiction to use its power. In Canada, provinces are commonly requiring more powers from the federal legislature. In recent years, provinces like Québec and New Brunswick acquired some rights to conduct international cultural affairs as members of international institutions, such as UNESCO or the Francophonie organization. On other matters, provinces like Ontario, Québec, and British Columbia have required more powers from the federal government in areas such as digital media as a way of both ensuring their producers have access to new digital platforms and increasing their taxation capacities to fund their creative industries. The taxation of big international corporations—such as Netflix—has become a point of contention in the federal/provincial relationships in Canada.

Requesting more power is a more conflictual approach to cultural governance; however, at times, it may prove to be a productive and creative strategy. In most cases, federal and subnational governments tend to protect their powers; they do so by developing solutions to problems if they were lagging in doing so, or they simply maintain their own system in place. In India, where federal and subnational cultural policies rely on intangible cultural and, more importantly, archeological heritage, subnational governments have made efforts to maintain their presence in the archeological sector. After the Indian federation was declared and organized, archeological services were not centralized and the subnational legislatures and governments kept their own services active. To this date, half a dozen subnational governments have a strong institutional framework to conduct archeological work, from preservation to research and communication. While the organizational cultures of the different archeological institutions in India are quite different, and while there are no conflictual elements or strong controversies in India's archeological institutions, subnational governments actively occupy their power in this sector. This is part of the reality of federalism, where when a power is not defined constitutionally as belonging to one level, it is often more strategic to be active in the area and establish or validate precedence.

Finally, another level of competitive strategy—which can be taken as a normative differentiation—can be found in policy documents. Different ideas about culture, identity, and citizenship can be expressed through policy documents—documents which convey a different political sense of what art and heritage can mean for a government or society. In this area, every policy is subjected to the ideational and cultural dynamics of institutions; every cultural policy builds on materials and references that make it a statement recognizable as cultural policy. On the other hand, every cultural policy is a statement of unicity and authenticity; it is a claim for expressing something distinctive about a nation or subnational territory's culture and social aspirations (Faure 1995; Hassenteufel and Surel 2000; Jobert 2004; Palier and Surel 2005; Durnova and Zittoun 2013). Cultural policies operate on a variety of referentials and these simultaneously open to a common body of cognitive references; they bring us back to a common world of policy ideas, while also expressing differences.

3.3 Federalism and Professions and the Public

So far, this chapter has addressed the realities of federations as both legal and political institutions. This chapter has also explored how these institutions were rooted in political philosophy, resulting from a variety of historical and social processes. Moreover, this chapter has discussed how this institutional structure and configuration operate on a division of power that can shape the political game at both legislative and executive levels. Similarly, this chapter has also discussed how judicial powers can play a part in federations. What has not yet been fully addressed is society. Federations shape cultural policy and cultural affairs—not only through their institutions and political elites, but through their populations. Going back to Karmis and Norman's (2005) basic definition of the phenomena, one can say that a federation is a political entity where individuals are citizens of both their country and subnational entity. In other words, citizens of a federation belong to (at least) two political communities. There are three important implications to this duality. The first implication is linked to identity and belonging, and the second is linked to the social and institutional realities of public service demands and delivery. The third implication has to do with the political expectations and practices of federal institutions. There is a symbolism to federalism that is incarnated in its ways of dealing with citizens, its views on access to services, and its perspective on participation. In federations, public services are often organized in a manner that mirrors the subnational societies of the country. From public service employment, to the symbolism of public information campaigns, federalism is often trying to reflect the diversity of the country in its structures and actions. While diversity is often approached in cultural and linguistic terms, there are instances where subnational representation is an objective; it is part of the politics of symbols that is typical of federalism.

In terms of identity, in some countries, subnational governments are associated with strong cultural and political projects vis-à-vis the federal government or the opinion of the rest of the members of the federation. In countries where federalism was not built on profound cultural differences, subnational governments may choose to build on a different sense of regional identity. In Australia, Queensland and West Australia can be seen as areas where there is a strong attachment to the national identity and the Commonwealth, but where there is also a strong expression of a distinctive sense of selfhood. Likewise, South Australians like to remind others of their distinct history as a free settler's utopian colony—unlike the rest of the country whose European settlers came as convicts. Regional identities are also important in the American system. North and South has been a historical divide in the USA, but so too has East and West. In the USA, the society is traversed by a diverse sense of regional differences. Some of these strong identities are also part of the social and political realities of states. Texas has been typically seen as a state where there is a strong reference to a distinctive character and sense of identity (Ely and Barr 2011). Beyond the case of Texas—which can almost be seen as a stereotype of regional identities—there are, in fact, many expressions of regional difference and culture in American society (Ryden 1999; Huddy 2001; Conforti 2001). In Germany, Bavaria also plays an equivalent role as a state that has traditionally held a different sense of identity that is often seen as being in sharp opposition to the kind of identity and social culture witnessed in the rest of the country (Ford 2007; Hepburn 2008). In Switzerland, people may identify as Swiss, and the federation may be built on linguistic divisions more than on cultural lines, but there are occasions where the population of certain cantons feel they are different from the rest of the population.

In other federations, the civil society may have a sense of identity that is strikingly different from a portion of the population; it may also be, quite simply, a culture that is officially recognized as a different one. In India, there is a diversity of culture and religion. Federalism, in India, is built on different states that cover populations who have different senses of selfhood. In some cases, there is also a growing sense of alienation among certain populations (Baruah 2009). While diversity may be widespread, some regions may embody their populations' strong sense of resentment against the central government (e.g. Assam, Manipur, and Nagaland). Similarly, in Malaysia, in addition to a multicultural society where a Malay majority coexists with Chinese and Indian minorities in Peninsular Malaysia, there are also strong senses of identity in Sabah and Sarawak. In Canada, there are also different senses of regional identity. There are different social aspirations in Western Canada; Alberta, for instance, has commonly been identified as a province sceptical of any federal intervention. Québec has a different culture, and its sense of nationhood has been recognized by the federal legislature. Québec's society is also divided on its sense of belonging—and, specifically, whether it should even belong in Canada. A similar scenario can be found in Belgium where a sense of identity is profoundly marked by linguistic differences. In Flanders, there is a secessionist movement that would ultimately like to see Flanders as an independent country. This does not forbid other citizens from feeling a strong attachment to Belgium or to the federation through Bruxelles-Capitale. In Australia, Canada, the USA, Mexico, and South America, Indigenous populations very often express that they do not feel they belong to any of the levels of government of their country. Many of them have different cultures, languages, and traditions, and the political system offers them very few alternatives or opportunities to thrive politically. In some cases, these systems structurally constraint the Indigenous population's full political participation. Even if some federations are more culturally homogenous, it is inescapable that there will be a different sense of identity and belonging in some regions, cultures, or subnational states (Simon et al. 1995). Difference is part of every society and political system; however, in federations, this difference takes on a different texture.

Identity is the most essential part of the reality of federations: individuals are citizens of two political entities and communities. The other important element of this reality is the structure of public services. Depending on the legislation, individuals will have to transact with one level of administration or the other to obtain their public services. In some cases, both administrations have paid for services or public goods, and, typically, both will try to get social and political credit for their governmental participation (Liesbet and Gary 2003). Peoples' social learning towards public institutions is shaped by this reality.

This is true for citizens at the individual level, but it is also true for groups. In federations, political advocacy is caught in the intricacies of federal and subnational politics. Advocacy groups need to develop an understanding of the best strategies to use in order to mobilize their base and in order to obtain the changes they want from either level of governments. In some cases, this involves developing a strategy to bridge the policy gaps between both levels of government or to try to obtain more collaboration from federal and subnational levels. In other contexts, activism may target federal or subnational levels of government and require that either of the governments normalize their policy or take over the policy area from the other levels (Lens 2001; Solberg and Lindquist 2006; Riverstone-Newell 2012). Symbolically, subnationally based activist groups can form a broad national coalition with other like-minded groups to obtain change—thus giving more heft to the collective action and ensuring that the action appears to be representative (Lewin and Derzon 1982; Chua and Poullaos 1993; Gray 2004). Professional groups also often engage in activism and with political powers. Therefore, these groups are not immune to the politics of federalism: it can be a trust or constraint for a professional group. Similarly, professional groups also exist in federal contexts, and their structures are often developed in ways that mimic the political structures. In some cases, national institutions have subnational committees and one national executive. In other circumstances, national organizations exist alongside a constellation of subnational professional institutions.

What does it mean for the cultural sector? For cultural collective actions, federations imply a number of challenges. For artists and heritage professionals, a federation implies that resources are distributed and available through different levels of government. Commonly, in federations, artists have to liaise and engage with both federal and subnational governments in order to secure resources. Resources for cultural activities and institutions are often spread across the different layers of government. However, just as there are challenges in a federated system for artists, so too are there benefits: artists and heritage professionals can find sympathetic cultural patrons in their subnational governments if the federal government is not supportive or less inclined to support a project (or vice versa).

In many respects, the politics of federalism shape cultural organizations much in the same way as they often do with professional organizations (Constantelos 2010; Karper and Boyd 1988; Prince 2006). National professional organizations federate a number of agents who come from different regional and cultural realities, and have different needs based on their conditions or resources that their subnational governments make available. This diversity of interests can, however, hinder—at times—the capacity of professional organizations to unite and be successful when it comes to influencing cultural policy. Sometimes, federal professional organizations also exist in the social and political space with subnational organizations whose objectives may be different, if not competing. As such, there is a diversity of issues traversing the professional world, and there are a variety of ways in which to collaborate and compete.

In terms of establishing collaborations at the professional level, associations have invited and experimented with different institutional models and strategies. In Canada, the Museum Association, the main national association representing Canadian museums at the national level, has focused its advocacy on the federal government and has collaborated with every provincial museum association in the country. This principle of collaboration is enshrined in the by-laws of the association, but is also a working principle in practice. In other areas, like the visual arts, there are different ways to reflect Canadian federalism in the functioning of the organization. The Canadian Artists Representation/*Le Front des artistes canadiens* (CARFAC) represents the interests of artists in the visual arts since 1967. CARFAC has different provincial representations throughout Canada, but for Québec it has preferred to develop a working relationship with the *Regroupement des artistes en arts visuels du Québec* (RAAV) in order to build on the existing institutions and acknowledge the difference in needs that may arise for this specific community. In this case, the association has espoused an interpretation of federalism that acknowledges some asymmetries; it is a recognition in practice of asymmetric federalism in professional organizations and representations.

A good example of federalism in professional and institutional culture can be found in the functioning of the Indian Library Association. This national institution, representing the professional and institutional interests of libraries in India, is one of the most important bodies representing cultural professions in the country. In the Library Association's statutes, one can read the following articles:

110 J. PAQUETTE

For election to Six posts of Vice-Presidents, there shall be reservation of one post for each of the following zones:

Southern Zone: Tamil Nadu, Kerala, Karnataka and Andhra Pradesh.

Western Zone: Maharashtra, Gujarat and Rajasthan

Central Zone: Chhattisgarh, Madhya Pradesh, Uttar Pradesh, Uttarakhand, Bihar,

Jharkhand, Orissa

Northern Zone: Punjab, Haryana, Himachal Pradesh, Jammu & Kashmir

Eastern Zone: West Bengal, Assam, Meghalaya, Nagaland, Arunachal Pradesh, Sikkim

Union territory Zone: Delhi, Chandigarh, Pondicherry, Goa, Andaman & Nicobar, Mizoram, Manipur, Tripura and others

If there are any changes in geographical boundary or status of the territory, the Council of ILA is empowered to change the placement of the states/ union territories to the proper zone. (India Library Association 1987)

Institutionally, the Indian Library Association has integrated, into its functioning and governance, some of the characteristics typical to federations, at least in terms of securing regional representation of the profession. The six vice-presidents of the Indian Library Association must come from one of the states in the designated zones. The vice-president function embodies the idea of federalism insofar as it acts more or less as some senates do in federations; it is there to ensure that the profession's interest is covered, more or less, throughout the country. This example is a case of a strong institutional adhesion to federalism because it creates an obligation for the executive and members of the association. The note following the regional division also allows the Council of the Indian Library Association to modify these divisions based on any formal transformation in the political geography of India; in this respect, it tries to mirror the political subnational divisions of the country.

Museums and Galleries Australia, the national professional institution in the Australian Museum sector, has similar requirements in its constitution to those of the Indian Library Association (Museum Galleries Australia 2013: 6). The board has an executive composed of four persons (president, vice-president, secretary, treasurer); it is also supplemented by six members from museum institutions—at large—and eight positions represented by the subnational states. The last category also acts, in a sense, like the senate in political institutions: it ensures that the association is representative of the country's political geography by building on its states.

Similarly, the Asociación de Revistas Culturales Independientes de Argentina (AReCIA) is another good example of professional and activist federalism in the cultural industries. With representatives in Córdoba, Tucumán, Misiones, La Plata, Mendoza, Mar del Plata, and Patagonia, AReCIA aims to develop resources at the local level and mobilize its members at both local and national levels. In this case, federalism is expressed in the spirit of decentralization, as a way to ensure that subnational issues and differences can be heard.

This is just a sample of thousands of activist movement and professional associations that can be found in the cultural sectors of federations. Studying the influence of federalism on these associations, alone, would be the work of a single career. Nonetheless, the above-mentioned examples are meant to introduce the implications of federalism on arts and culture, from the vantage of civil society.

Table 3.1 provides a summary of the effects of federalism on professional associations and arts advocacy groups. Depending on their degree of institutionalization—whether they have formal rules or rules that are more established customs—and depending on their degree of adherence with the social philosophy of federalism, professional associations, and arts advocacy groups in federations will be influenced by federalism along one or many of these five dimensions: strategy; structures, symbolism, organizational culture, and modes of representations.

Again, this is not to pretend that regional divisions and representations are only to be found in professional associations and advocacy groups in federations. There are certainly important forms of decentralization in the function of professional organizations in the UK, France, Italy, or any other unitary State, for that matter. What is meant, here, is that in federations, the federal/subnational divide is more than a functional element; it is almost a second nature of these societies. A federal society means that citizens engage with arts and heritage institutions that are governed by federal or subnational administrations, which may imply a very different experience of arts and culture depending on where one lives. Questions regarding the publics of culture and participation in arts and heritage are also similarly shaped by this institutional reality. Additionally, the institutional context of federalism may also be conducive to preferences for some forms of collective actions and cultural activism over others. Likewise, professional groups not only evolve in a strategic space shaped by a dual—federal/subnational—system, they may also try to replicate these institutions in their own modes of functioning.

112   J. PAQUETTE

Table 3.1   Influence of federalism on professional and advocacy groups

Dimensions	Aspects
Strategy	• Strategies are shaped according to the division of powers (federal/subnational) • Organizations may cooperate, divide their labour (between national and subnational), and try to avoid overt conflicts in some situations
Structures	• May replicate the structure of the federation • Forms of decentralization may be allowed in the functioning of the association • National associations may try to develop formal partnerships with existing subnational organizations • Divisional structure, with the antenna and branch of association in different subnational regions, for member services
Symbolism	• Aims at being representative of different parts of the federation • Aims to have annual conferences in a way that creates proximity with its membership across the federation • Symbolic of the "whole and the parts" in organizational documentations, organizational spaces, etc.
Organizational culture	• Makes sure that the traditions of different parts of the country are being respected or integrated into the association • Recognizes the differences in regional/subnational culture
Modes of representation	• Requires representation of subnational membership in constitution • Requires that the executive or board retains a certain measure of subnational representation • Reserves seats for subnational members on the executive

3.4   BALANCING COMPETITION AND COOPERATION

In a federation, the institutional configuration is developed, in part, to consider a measure of diversity. In most cases, federations are developed to take into consideration cultural, regional, or linguistic differences. The political geography of federalism is shaped by these forms of difference, which also take part in further strategies of differentiation (Karmis and Maclure 2001; Weinstock 2004). For governments, professionals, and cultural activists, federalism supposes a number of constraints. The fragmented nature of governmental and professional institutions in federal contexts requires that agents adjust their strategies to an institutional landscape that can often discourage change or collective action. For these different stakeholders, federalism requires a certain dose of leadership; possessing the capacity to navigate in this context creates the necessary conditions for leaders to balance cultural interests. Federations reside in a dynamic of cooperation and competition; they are, by definition, structures of cooperation. But, in reality, as we have seen with many authors, including Rector (2009), federations are never—in every circumstance—a structure of unanimous agreement. Federations are complex social and political assemblages, where many partners may at times have conflicting interests. This is reinforced in federations that are built around cultural and linguistic differences. Arguably, even in federations that are assumed to be more homogenous on cultural grounds, there are still noticeable differences and forms of regionalism that exert a pressure on federations. Therefore, cultural affairs may well be an area of contention between subnational members and/or between the federal level of administration and its subnational members. In this chapter, it has been insisted that, despite the division of powers in the constitution, there is always a moment in a federal nation's history when the federal government will succumb to the temptation of exploiting the intersection between culture and identity. Cultural nationalism is an attraction of every society—including those who privilege a greater distance between State and culture. Alone, this aspect is responsible for the dynamics of cultural policy as being always in balance between states of competition and cooperation between governments.

Finally, in this chapter, we looked at the forms in which the executive levels of government and administration engaged in cooperative and competitive strategies, and identified many instruments and practices of cooperation in cultural affairs (see Table 3.2). The most used cooperative mechanisms in federations are transfers. In general terms, transfers were examined as a form of financial redistribution of fiscal revenues from the federal to the subnational levels of cultural administration. Some funding is negotiated in support of operations, while others are made on a project basis. Unique funding—through a single lump sum—is often associated with pivotal (celebration, employment stimulus package, etc.) moments where funding can come in support of a subnational cultural project, as seed funding, or as a unique infrastructure investment. However, as was discussed in the cases of Mexico, Brazil, and Argentina, these transfers can also involve the transfer of practices; they may also involve a transfer of expertise or obligations which subnational governments must often conform with. The intergovernmental relationships in Mexico, Brazil, and Argentina have evolved since the 2000s in the form of policy transfers from the federal governments.

114   J. PAQUETTE

Table 3.2   Instruments of intergovernmental cooperation and competition in cultural affairs

Strategy	Instruments	Objectives
Cooperation	Federal transfers (financial)	Developing capacities at the subnational level Developing new programmes and institutions Harmonizing the cultural sector across the country
	National training programmes or national standards	Harmonizing and creating common standards across the country through professionals and professional practices
	Conferences (interdepartmental)	Formulating common strategies, learning, and making collaborative decisions in cultural affairs
	Policy transfer	Creating obligations to be administered at the subnational level
	Interdepartmental organizational collaborations	Creating capacities, formulating common strategies, and learning through professionals and cultural organizations
	Subnational cooperation (bilateral or regional)	Horizontal cooperation to develop cultural capacity or to organize collective action vis-à-vis the federal level of government
	Regulatory agencies	Coercive collaboration to standardize the cultural sector
Competition	Courts	Gain or confirm cultural power
	Cultural development	Developing a cultural capacity and exerting cultural power
	Public opinion	Collective action based on public opinion to gain more power or resources from a level of government
	Normative differentiation	Establishing cultural policy on different norms and referentials

National training programmes, national standards, and interdepartmental collaborations at the organizational level are also important tools for cooperation in federations. These are common tools of cooperation in India and Malaysia, where capacity development is key for professionals in the cultural sector. Executive conferences reuniting different cultural policy ministers in a federation are also an important instrument of cooperation. As we have seen in this chapter, there are many approaches to this instrument. In Australia, this perspective is driven by the federal level as a tool to construct common grounds. In Canada, the approach is more politically driven; it attempts to find common strategies, but also to establish the shares of federal and provincial governments' participation in some areas over others. In Germany, this approach is clearly meant to develop a common subnational answer and position to be communicated to the federal administration; it is crucial given the country's respect for the separation of powers. Also, as we have seen, direct subnational cooperation may be less common, but it also shapes some of the realities of the cultural sector. Direct bilateral cultural relations in a federation are arguably rarer than subnational international relations—as we shall see—but it also exists in the repertoire of cultural cooperation in federations.

When it comes to competition, there are four basic instruments. First, courts play an important role in confirming powers; it can also be used by a government to seek additional powers. Second, cultural development is also an important strategy. While a state developing its cultural sector in its own right may not seem, on first glance, to be a form of competition, it can, in fact, be a way of occupying a sector, developing precedents, or making sure that its power will not eventually be challenged when it becomes strategic. The case of provincial broadcasting corporations in Canada is a good example. While the regulation of radio-broadcasting is a federal power, the provincial governments were left with the capacity to develop their own public broadcasting systems; it was not forbidden by the legislation. Provinces like Ontario and Québec were quick to legislate on the matter, but slower at developing their public broadcasting systems. As a result, the interventions of these provinces remained minimal in the face of the vast public broadcasting corporation developed by the Government of Canada. Nonetheless, the existence of TVO/TFO and Télé-Québec constitutes a precedent that serves provincial governments' cultural ambitions, while making sure that their capacity to engage with the sector can be resumed too simply by the federal legislature and its regulatory agency. Dual federalism is a simple form of competition that does not have to be conflictual, per se.

Finally, public opinion and normative differentiations are also important strategies in the repertoire of cultural instruments. Public opinion-based strategies tend to be more competitive. They involve the media, the public, the formulation of conflicts over specific issues in order to have more resources or concession over certain powers. This is a more sulphurous form of competitive action. As for normative differentiation, it belongs to the tradition and possibility of dual federalism. In most cases, in its own right, a federal or subnational government may formulate a cultural policy statement or document that is meant to define culture in a way that is different from how it is defined by other members of a federation. This normative differentiation may be the result of a real heartfelt difference about a government or society's perspective on culture, but it may also be carved out as a political statement—as a way of creating difference in symbols and reiterating different cultural norms and values. In the last chapter, we will further develop how these different instruments and their uses can shape different traditions of intergovernmentalism over cultural affairs.

REFERENCES

Anderson, B. (2006). *Imagined Communities: Reflections on the Origin and Spread of Nationalism.* New York: Verso Books.

Bachmann, R. (2001). Trust, Power and Control in Trans-Organizational Relations. *Organization Studies, 22*(2), 337–365.

Barbalho, A. (2016). O sistema nacional de cultura no governo Dilma: continuidades e avanços. *Revista Lusófona de Estudos Culturais, 2*(2), 188–207.

Baruah, S. (2009). Separatist Militants and Contentious Politics in Assam, India: The Limits of Counterinsurgency. *Asian Survey, 49*(6), 951–974.

Beauregard, D. (2018). *Cultural Policy and Industries of Identity: Québec, Scotland, & Catalonia.* London: Palgrave.

Belfiore, E. (2002). Art as a Means of Alleviating Social Exclusion: Does It Really Work? A Critique of Instrumental Cultural Policies and Social Impact Studies in the UK. *International Journal of Cultural Policy, 8*(1), 91–106.

Belfiore, E. (2006). The Unacknowledged Legacy: Plato, the Republic and Cultural Policy. *International Journal of Cultural Policy, 12*(2), 229–244.

Benz, A. (2007). Inter-Regional Competition in Co-operative Federalism: New Modes of Multi-level Governance in Germany. *Regional and Federal Studies, 17*(4), 421–436.

Bernier, L. (1989). La dynamique institutionnelle des entreprises publiques au Québec de 1960 à aujourd'hui. *Politiques et management public, 7*(1), 95–111.

Bordat, E. M. (2013). Institutionalization and Change in Cultural Policy: CONACULTA and Cultural Policy in Mexico (1988–2006). *International Journal of Cultural Policy, 19*(2), 222–248.

Breton, A. (1987). Towards a Theory of Competitive Federalism. *European Journal of Political Economy, 3*(1–2), 263–329.

Buchanan, J. M. (1995). Federalism as an Ideal Political Order and an Objective for Constitutional Reform. *Publius: The Journal of Federalism, 25*(2), 19–28.

Bulmer, S., & Padgett, S. (2005). Policy Transfer in the European Union: An Institutionalist Perspective. *British Journal of Political Science, 35*(1), 103–126.

Cameron, D., & Simeon, R. (2002). Intergovernmental Relations in Canada: The Emergence of Collaborative Federalism. *Publius: The Journal of Federalism, 32*(2), 49–72. https://doi.org/10.1093/oxfordjournals.pubjof.a004947.

Cardinal, L. (2008). *Le fédéralisme asymétrique et les minorités linguistiques nationales.* Sudbury, ON: Prise de parole.

Chua, W. F., & Poullaos, C. (1993). Rethinking the Profession-State Dynamic: The Case of the Victorian Charter Attempt, 1885–1906. *Accounting, Organizations and Society, 18*(7–8), 691–728.

Commission fédérale d'experts pour l'étude de questions concernant la politique culturelle Suisse. (1975). *Éléments pour une politique culturelle en Suisse.* Bern.

Conforti, J. A. (2001). *Imagining New England: Explorations of Regional Identity from the Pilgrims to the Mid-Twentieth Century.* Chapel Hill, NC: University of North Carolina Press.

Constantelos, J. (2010). Playing the Field: Federalism and the Politics of Venue Shopping in the United States and Canada. *Publius: The Journal of Federalism, 40*(3), 460–483. https://doi.org/10.1093/publius/pjq010.

Csehi, R. (2017). Horizontal Coordination in Federal Political Systems: Non-Centralization in the European Union and Canada Compared. *Journal of European Public Policy, 24*(4), 562–579.

DiMaggio, P. J., & Powell, W. W. (Eds.). (1991). *The New Institutionalism in Organizational Analysis.* Chicago, IL: University of Chicago Press.

Durnova, A., & Zittoun, P. (2013). Les approches discursives des politiques publiques. *Revue française de science politique, 63*(3), 569–577.

Durrer, V., & Miles, S. (2009). New Perspectives on the Role of Cultural Intermediaries in Social Inclusion in the UK. *Consumption, Markets and Culture, 12*(3), 225–241.

Ely, G. S., & Barr, A. (2011). *Where the West Begins: Debating Texas Identity.* Lubbock, TX: Texas Tech University Press.

Erk, J. (2004). Austria: A Federation Without Federalism. *Publius: The Journal of Federalism, 34*(1), 1–20.

Erk, J. (2007). *Explaining Federalism: State, Society and Congruence in Austria, Belgium, Canada, Germany and Switzerland.* London: Routledge.

Fabbrini, S. (2017). Intergovernmentalism in the European Union: A Comparative Federalism Perspective. *Journal of European Public Policy, 24*(4), 580–597.

Faure, A. (1995). *La construction du sens dans les politiques publiques: débats autour de la notion de référentiel.* Paris: Editions L'Harmattan.

Fenna, A. (2012a). Federalism and Intergovernmental Coordination. In B. G. Peters & J. Pierre (Eds.), *The SAGE Handbook of Public Administration* (pp. 750–763). London, UK: Sage.

Fenna, A. (2012b). Centralising Dynamics in Australian Federalism. *Australian Journal of Politics & History, 58*(4), 580–590.

118 J. PAQUETTE

Ford, G. (2007). Constructing a Regional Identity: The Christian Social Union and Bavaria's Common Heritage, 1949–1962. *Contemporary European History, 16*(3), 277–297.

Gardiner-Garden, J. (2009). Commonwealth Arts Policy and Administration. Australian Parliament, Social Policy Section. Retrieved online from the Australian Parliament's website https://www.aph.gov.au/About_Parliament/Parliamentary_Departments/Parliamentary_Library/pubs/BN/0809/ArtsPolicy#_ftnref2.

Gervasoni, C. (2010). A Rentier Theory of Subnational Regimes: Fiscal Federalism, Democracy, and Authoritarianism in the Argentine Provinces. *World Politics, 62*(2), 302–340.

Gibson, C., & Klocker, N. (2005). The 'Cultural Turn' In Australian Regional Economic Development Discourse: Neoliberalising Creativity? *Geographical Research, 43*(1), 93–102.

Gooderham, P. N., Nordhaug, O., & Ringdal, K. (1999). Institutional and Rational Determinants of Organizational Practices: Human Resource Management in European Firms. *Administrative Science Quarterly, 44*(3), 507–531.

Gray, C. (2004). Joining-Up or Tagging on? The Arts, Cultural Planning and the View From Below. *Public Policy and Administration, 19*(2), 38–49.

Gray, C. (2010). Analysing Cultural Policy: Incorrigibly Plural or Ontologically Incompatible? *International Journal of Cultural Policy, 16*(2), 215–230.

Gray, C., & Wingfield, M. (2011). Are Governmental Culture Departments Important? An Empirical Investigation. *International Journal of Cultural Policy, 17*(5), 590–604.

Gupta, P. P., Dirsmith, M. W., & Fogarty, T. J. (1994). Coordination and Control in a Government Agency: Contingency and Institutional Theory Perspectives on GAO Audits. *Administrative Science Quarterly, 39*(2), 264–284.

Hassenteufel, P., & Surel, Y. (2000). Des politiques publiques comme les autres? *Politique européenne, 1*, 8–24.

Hepburn, E. (2008). The Neglected Nation: the CSU and the Territorial Cleavage in Bavarian Party Politics. *German Politics, 17*(2), 184–202.

Hollander, R., & Patapan, H. (2007). Pragmatic Federalism: Australian Federalism from Hawke to Howard. *Australian Journal of Public Administration, 66*(3), 280–297.

Howlett, M., & Ramesh, M. (1993). Patterns of Policy Instrument Choice: Policy Styles, Policy Learning and the Privatization Experience. *Review of Policy Research, 12*(1–2), 3–24.

Huddy, L. (2001). From Social to Political Identity: A Critical Examination of Social Identity Theory. *Political Psychology, 22*(1), 127–156.

Immergut, E. M. (1998). The Theoretical Core of the New Institutionalism. *Politics & Society, 26*(1), 5–34

India Library Association. (1987). Constitution. Retrieved online from the India Library Association website https://www.ilaindia.net/pdf/ilaconstitution.pdf.

Jobert, B. (2004). Une approche dialectique des politiques publiques. *Pôle sud, 2,* 43–54.

Karmis, D., & MacLure, J. (2001). Two Escape Routes from the Paradigm of Monistic Authenticity: Post-Imperialist and Federal Perspectives on Plural and Complex Identities. *Ethnic and Racial Studies, 24*(3), 361–385. https://doi.org/10.1080/713766448.

Karmis, D., & Norman, W. (2005). *Theories of Federalism: A Reader.* London: Palgrave.

Karper, J. H., & Boyd, W. L. (1988). Interest Groups and the Changing Environment of State Educational Policymaking: Developments in Pennsylvania. *Educational Administration Quarterly, 24*(1), 21–54. https://doi.org/10.1177/0013161x88024001004.

Kennedy, J. F. (1963, October 26). Remarks at Ameherst College. Washington, DC: National Endowment for the Arts. Retrieved online from the National Endowment for the Arts' website https://www.arts.gov/about/kennedy-transcript.

Kincaid, J. (1990). From Cooperative to Coercive Federalism. *The Annals of the American Academy of Political and Social Science, 509*(1), 139–152.

Kincaid, J. (1996). *From Dual to Coercive Federalism in American Intergovernmental Relations.* Washington, DC: Georgetown University Press.

Kingdon, J. W. (1984). *Agendas, Alternatives, and Public Policies.* Boston: Little, Brown.

Kyne, S., & Morton, J. (2017). Meeting of Cultural Ministers—The Statistical Advisory Group and the Statistical Working Group—A History. Australian Government.

Lascoumes, P., & Le Galès, P. (2018). *Sociologie de l'action publique.* Paris: Armand Colin.

Laurence, G. (1982). Le début des affaires publiques à la télévision québécoise 1952–1957. *Revue d'histoire de l'Amérique française, 36*(2), 213–239.

Lawton, R. W., & Burns, B. (1996). Models of Cooperative Federalism for Telecommunications. *Albany Law Journal, 71*(6), 72–92.

Lens, V. (2001). The Supreme Court, Federalism, and Social Policy: The New Judicial Activism. *Social Service Review, 75*(2), 318–336.

Lewin, L. S., & Derzon, R. A. (1982). Health Professions Education: State Responsibilities Under the New Federalism. *Health Affairs, 1*(2), 69–85.

Liesbet, H., & Gary, M. (2003). Unraveling the Central State, But How? Types of Multi-Level Governance. *American Political Science Review, 97*(2), 233–243.

Lowies, J. G., & Schrobiltgen, M. H. (2016). L'accord de coopération culturelle entre la Communauté française et la Communauté flamande. *Courrier hebdomadaire du CRISP, 8,* 5–60.

Lownpes, V. (1996). Varieties of New Institutionalism: A Critical Appraisal. *Public Administration, 74*(2), 181–197.

Majone, G. (1992). Regulatory Federalism in the European Community. *Environment and Planning C: Government and Policy, 10*(3), 299–316.

Malaysia, National Department for Culture and Arts. (2018). National Culture Policy. Retrieved online from the National Department for Culture and Arts' website http://www.jkkn.gov.my/en/national-culture-policy.

Mandal, S. K. (2008). The National Culture Policy and Contestation Over Malaysian Identity. In J. Nelson, J. Meerman, & A. R. H. Embong, *Globalization and National Autonomy: The Experience of Malaysia* (pp. 273–297). Singapore: Institute of Southeast Asian Studies.

McKenna, R. (1987). Preemption Reversed: The Supreme Court's Decision in Louisiana Public Service Commission v. FCC. *Administrative Law Review, 39*(1), 43–59.

Migué, J. L. (1997). Public Choice in a Federal System. *Public Choice, 90*(1–4), 235–254.

Miller, T., & Yúdice, G. (2002). *Cultural policy.* Thousand Oaks, CA: Sage.

Monod, D. (2000). Internationalism, Regionalism, and National Culture: Music Control in Bavaria, 1945–1948. *Central European History, 33*(3), 339–368.

Mulcahy, K. V. (2002). The State Arts Agency: An Overview of Cultural Federalism in the United States. *The Journal of Arts Management, Law, and Society, 32*(1), 67–80.

Muller, P. (2000). L'analyse cognitive des politiques publiques: vers une sociologie politique de l'action publique. *Revue française de science politique, 50*(2): 189–207.

Museum and Galleries Australia. (2013). Constitution and Rules. Retrieved online from Museum and Galleries Australia's website https://www.museumsaustralia.org.au/national-council.

National Endowment for the Arts. (2012). How the United States Funds the Arts, NEA, Washington, DC. Retrieved online from the NEA's website https://www.arts.gov/sites/default/files/how-the-us-funds-the-arts.pdf.

Newman, A., & McLean, F. (2004). Presumption, Policy and Practice: The Use of Museums and Galleries as Agents of Social Inclusion in Great Britain. *International Journal of Cultural Policy, 10*(2), 167–181.

Nielsen, G. (1995). L'impasse Canada-Québec et le sort de Radio-Canada: l'autonomie culturelle ou la mort! *Cahiers de recherche sociologique, 25,* 181–212.

Oakley, K. (2006). Include Us Out: Economic Development and Social Policy in the Creative Industries. *Cultural Trends, 15*(4), 255–273.

Oates, W. E. (2005). Toward a Second-Generation Theory of Fiscal Federalism. *International Tax and Public Finance, 12*(4), 349–373.

Ostrom, V., & Ostrom, E. (1971). Public Choice: A Different Approach to the Study of Public Administration. *Public Administration Review, 31*(2), 203–216.

Palier, B., & Surel, Y. (2005). Les «trois I» et l'analyse de l'État en action. *Revue française de science politique, 55*(1), 7–32.

Paquette, J., & Redaelli, E. (2015). *Arts Management and Cultural Policy Research.* London: Palgrave.

Pleshette, E. R. (1998). The National Endowment for the Arts: Crisis or Commitment in America's Art Engagement? *LBJ Journal of Public Affairs, 10,* 11–21.

Prince, M. J. (2006). 'A Cancer Control Strategy and Deliberative Federalism: Modernizing health Care and Democratizing Intergovernmental Relations. *Canadian Public Administration, 49*(4), 468–485. https://doi.org/10.1111/j.1754-7121.2006.tb01994.

Puetter, U. (2012). Europe's Deliberative Intergovernmentalism: The Role of the Council and European Council in EU economic governance. *Journal of European Public Policy, 19*(2), 161–178.

Radaelli, C. M. (2000). Policy Transfer in the European Union: Institutional Isomorphism as a Source of Legitimacy. *Governance, 13*(1), 25–43.

Rector, C. (2009). *Federations. The Political Dynamics of Cooperation.* Ithaca, NY: Cornell University Press.

Riverstone-Newell, L. (2012). Bottom-Up Activism: A Local Political Strategy for Higher Policy Change. *Publius: The Journal of Federalism, 42*(3), 401–421.

Rose-Ackerman, S. (1981). Does Federalism Matter? Political Choice in a Federal Republic. *Journal of Political Economy, 89*(1), 152–165.

Rosenstein, C. (2018). *Understanding Cultural Policy.* London: Routledge.

Royal Commission on the Development in the Arts, Letters and Science. (1951). *Report.* Ottawa: Parliament of Canada.

Ryden, K. C. (1999). Writing the Midwest: History, Literature, and Regional Identity. *Geographical Review, 89*(4), 511–532.

Sabatier, P. A., Schlager, E., Charron, D., & Muller, P. (2000). Les approches cognitives des politiques publiques: Perspectives américaines. *Revue française de science politique, 50*(2), 209–234.

Searing, D. D. (1991). Roles, Rules, and Rationality in the New Institutionalism. *American Political Science Review, 85*(4), 1239–1260.

Selznick, P. (1996). Institutionalism "Old" and "New". *Administrative Science Quarterly, 41*(2), 270–277.

Simmons, J. M. (2017). Canadian Multilateral Intergovernmental Institutions and the Limits of Institutional Innovation. *Regional & Federal Studies, 27*(5), 573–596.

Simon, B., Kulla, C., & Zobel, M. (1995). On Being More than Just a Part of the Whole: Regional Identity and Social Distinctiveness. *European Journal of Social Psychology, 25*(3), 325–340.

Smullen, A. (2014). Conceptualising Australia's Tradition of Pragmatic Federalism. *Australian Journal of Political Science, 49*(4), 677–693.

Solberg, R. S., & Lindquist, S. A. (2006). Activism, Ideology, and Federalism: Judicial Behavior in Constitutional Challenges Before the Rehnquist Court, 1986–2000. *Journal of Empirical Legal Studies, 3*(2), 237–261.

Strom, E. (2003). Cultural Policy as Development Policy: Evidence from the United States. *International Journal of Cultural Policy, 9*(3), 247–263.

Théret, B. (2006). Politiques sociales et fédéralisme politique. Des relations d'interdépendance qui peuvent être positives ou négatives selon le type de fédéralisme. *Lien social et politiques, 56,* 41–56.

Tullock, G. (1969). Federalism: Problems of Scale. *Public Choice, 6*(1), 19–29.

Weingast, B. R. (2009). Second Generation Fiscal Federalism: The Implications of Fiscal Incentives. *Journal of Urban Economics, 65*(3), 279–293.

Weinstock, D. (2004). Towards a Normative Theory of Federalism. *Peace Research Abstracts, 41*(5), 75–84.

Wimmer, M. (1992). *Description and Analysis of Austrian Cultural Policy.* Report Presented at the Council of Europe, Austrian Centre for Cultural Documentation, Research and Mediation.

CHAPTER 4

Cultural Policies, Federations, and Cities

Federations constitute a distinctive pattern of political institutions. In this book, we have insisted on how constitutional acts represent an important element of the political life of federations as they, more or less, divide powers and shape the cultural institutions and realities of cultural policy. Federations also represent a number of challenges when it comes to formulating and implementing cultural policy. Some of these challenges are rooted in structural matters, while others are defined by divergences in cultural aspirations between members of a federation. In this chapter, one more characteristic is added to the distinctive nature of federations: its relationship to land. Federations rely on a distinctive form of territorial imagination. In their political and social imaginaries, federations tend to conceive of land as something that is both divided and reunited—a land that needs all of its components to be complete. In some federations, historical tensions and secessionist movements stimulate how this imaginary works—creating anxieties of secession and fears of territorial loss.

In this chapter, two important elements of federations' specific relationship to their territory are discussed. The first element relates to the question of the national capital—a territory deeply enmeshed in the politics and symbolism of federations. In a rather controversial statement, a famous American political scientist suggested that "[t]rue federal systems do not have capitals; they have seats of governments. 'Capital' implies a place at the top of a governmental pyramid, whereas

© The Author(s) 2019
J. Paquette, *Cultural Policy and Federalism,*
New Directions in Cultural Policy Research,
https://doi.org/10.1007/978-3-030-12680-3_4

123

"seat" appropriately suggests a place of assembly" (Elazar 1987: 75). According to Elazar, Bern was a good example of a subdued city that was not considered a capital, so too was Washington DC, since it has only been in recent years that it has been referred to as the capital of the USA. Whatever Elazar believes, federal capitals benefit from a different treatment than other territories; they have different or preferential forms of planning and urban policies supported by the federal government. In most cases, the constitution has created provisions making the capital city (and its region) a distinct type of subnational government that rests on the dynamics of political, cultural, and regional compromises. Canberra, Brasilia, Ottawa, Washington DC, Kuala Lumpur/Putrajaya, and Bruxelles-Capitale are all good examples of capitals that embody the issue(s) arising from establishing a particular city as the centre of power. Where should the capital be? On what basis should it be a capital? In the first section, the intent is not to provide a systematic history of the political debates surrounding national capitals in federations, but, rather, to focus on the implication of such decisions on cultural policy.

The second element of federations' relationship to their territory has to do with local cultural policy or, more specifically, with federal/local relations. Local cultural policy can be significantly modulated by the institutional and political dimensions of federalism. Municipal governments in federal contexts operate in conjunction with multiple (and higher) levels of government; this multilevel form of governance considerably affects the nature, policy instruments, and capabilities of local governments in the cultural sector. In the vast majority of countries, cities are created by subnational governments through their own legislatures. As such, cultural policy—as an unrestricted area of public intervention— can lead to a greater participation of both levels of government. While municipalities can access two different governmental funders for major cultural infrastructure projects—state and federal governments—they are also prone to the political contests and challenges of either government. In this chapter, discussion will focus on the strengths and weaknesses of this specific situation and show cities and municipal governments navigate the political meanderings of federalism.

4.1   Capital Cities and Cultural Policy

As it was romantically expressed by Elazar (1987: 75), the fact that capital cities imply a certain superiority, the fact that they convey power, makes their selections something prone to political debates and challenges. In a very decentralized view of federalism, the capital of the federation should be the "siege" of power, retaining no glorified or specific status; its purpose is to reunite the legislative, executive, and judicial powers of the federated entities. In practice, capital cities may be deceptively subdued and may even lack character at times. However, capital cities do not lack political and cultural symbolism. When discussing capitals, it is common to distinguish between two types of capital: historical and engineered. Historical capitals are the "natural" centres of power; they tend to be the spaces where politics, commerce, and administration have typically converged. Paris, Rome, Beijing, and London, only to name a few, are certainly the best examples of historical capitals. Engineered capitals, by contrast, are cities that were developed strictly to assume a political function. While engineered capitals can be found outside of federations, the vast majority of these capitals are found in federations. Only a few cases of engineered capitals exist—historically—in unitary States: Belize City and Manila are notable exceptions. But, in most cases, engineered capital cities that still functions in their status as capitals are found in federations: Washington DC, Ottawa, Canberra, Brasilia, New Delhi, and Abuja in Nigeria. Likewise, the new administrative capital of Malaysia, Putrajaya, is also a very recent creation.

These examples all support the fact that federalism raises special considerations when it comes to locate a political centre. Beyond this exceptional situation, federalism may also challenge, in different ways, how we think about capital cities. How do these capitals fit in the big scheme of capitals? This intuition leads to the belief that there may be something distinctive about federal capital cities, which may be furthered when defining capitals and fitting them in models.

According to Hall (2006), there are seven types of capital cities. There are multi-functional capitals, where power, administration, and commerce are concentrated (e.g., Paris, London, Madrid, and Moscow). There are global capitals, cities like London or Tokyo, that are hubs for global commerce and political relations; their reach is beyond that of their single regions. Some cities are "former capitals": cities like Philadelphia (in the USA) and Kingston (in Canada) have played a role as national capital, but the siege of the capital changed over time. The same thing goes for Rio de Janeiro or St-Petersburg in Russia. Other capital cities are super capitals because, while they may not be a national capital in their country, they are the central node for a number of activities, most notably linked to international organizations (e.g., Strasbourg, Geneva, and New York) (pp. 8–9). Building on Hall's capital typology,

126   J. PAQUETTE

we are left with two types of capitals and both apply to federations. First, there are political capitals. These cities, according to Hall, "lack other properties of capitals" and are primarily political in their purpose. Many of the examples that are given by Hall are engineered federal capitals: Ottawa, Canberra, and Washington DC. Second, Hall talks about "provincial capitals" or subnational capitals, which are described as a distinctive reality of federations. It is true that subnational capitals can also be important centres of power and, ultimately, important cultural centres. Therefore, to build on Hall, capital cities in federations tend to retain distinctive characteristics. In particular, in federations, the centre of power is not unique; it is distributed to subnational territories.

Furthermore, when looking more closely at federal capitals, not only do they bring different considerations to the discussion, but there seem to be a great diversity between them. Looking at how capital cities are organized and function, there seems to be multiple answers to the question of capital cities in federations. Building on Van Wynsberghe's work (2014), we can say that there are three types of "national" capitals in federations. This typology derives from one's attention to the place of the capital's territory in the configurations of a federation; it also implies different ideas about the governance of public affairs. These dimensions and types are illustrated more saliently in Table 4.1. The first type implies that a capital city can administratively be defined as the national capital,

Table 4.1 National capitals

Capital	Governance structure	Accession to status
Berlin	City-State	Historical capital
		Reunification 1991
Bern	City	Historical capital
Brasilia	Federal district	Engineered capital
Brussels	City-State	Historical capital
Buenos Aires	Federal district	Historical capital
Canberra	Federal district	Engineered capital
Kuala Lumpur/	Federal districts	Historical capital (KL)
Putrajaya		Engineered administrative capital (Putrajaya)
Mexico City	Federal district	Historical capital
New Delhi	Federal district	Engineered capital
Ottawa	City	Engineered capital
Vienna	City-State	Historical capital
Washington DC	Federal district	Engineered capital

while being territorially in the confines of a subnational entity. Ottawa, the capital city of Canada, is a good example. Ottawa is subject to the municipal administrative dispositions of the province of Ontario; the city has a special status and access to special resources, but it is administratively a city in a subnational territory. The federal public services of Canada are primarily located in Ottawa and the neighbouring city of Gatineau in Québec. While these two cities benefit from a special treatment by the federal government, both are regulated by their provincial governments' policies and standards. The city of Berne, in Switzerland, is another case in point. Berne is the political capital of Switzerland, but it is also the capital of the canton of Berne. Berne does not retain any distinctive political characteristics that would situate it institutionally or provide it with a distinct status apart from the rest of the cities of the country.

The second model is the federal district. In this model, capital cities are situated in a territory that has a special status and a relative degree of freedom. Federal districts are not subnational entities in a country; they do not have equal weight. As reminded by Van Wynsberghe, Washington DC, in 1790, was not only the first federal capital, but the first federal district (p. 324). While the presidency and the Congress have a right to intervene in local affairs in Washington DC, and while that right has theoretically remained in place, since 1973, the city and its municipal council have gained significant power and autonomy in the district. In the same category are Canberra, New Delhi, Kuala Lumpur, Brasilia, Mexico, and Buenos Aires. The City of Mexico is a federal district that has evolved over time as an entity with forms and powers that are technically those of subnational entities. However, from a constitutional basis, it is not considered and cannot be a subnational entity; as such, it remains, de facto, a federal district. Finally, the third model for capital cities in Van Wynsberghe's typology is that of "city States". This model differs from the federal district because it refers to capital cities and subnational entities. Vienna and Brussels fall in this category, as does Berlin since the reunification of its subnational entities.

These different structural and institutional conditions have a considerable impact on local governments' capacities to develop and support their cultural sectors. These structures may also imply different forms of intergovernmental relations. In city-States, municipal and state affairs are merged and may also impose their weight on federal politics, while in capital cities with no specific status, the capital may have to develop its

128   J. PAQUETTE

cultural affairs through a series of complex links between federal, subnational, and local governments. As for districts, the question remains, how much cultural autonomy and power is there in districts? These institutional arrangements, that are typical of federal capitals, should not let us lose sight of the fact that federations also imply subnational capitals, which may cooperate or define themselves as cultural "rivals" and compete over cultural affairs or over one important area of the cultural industries that they claim as part of their distinctive local identity.

4.1.1   Capitals and Cultural Institutions

When looking at federal capitals, the distinction between historical and engineered capitals typically has an important significance on the number and prestige of cultural institutions in place. Historical capitals have been natural sieges of power, but they have also been environments where commerce and culture converge. Cities like Vienna or Brussels have a long cultural history that is reflected in the quality of their artistic institution and echoed in the number and significance of their heritage sites. By contrast, engineered cities and, in particular, recently constructed cities constitute a cultural challenge. In some areas, cultural institutions needed to be built rapidly to serve a growing population, as well as the cultural symbolic of a nation's capital.

The construction of a cultural life is crucial in engineered cities. The construction of a cultural life in Washington DC since 1790 may have evolved organically over the centuries and through the development of national cultural institutions around the Congress and through the development of museums based on collections donated by wealthy patrons of culture. However, capitals cities—like Ottawa and Canberra of Brasilia—that did not possess the bulk of public cultural institutions that a city usually possessed (museums, libraries, archives, opera houses, theatre, etc.) by the mid-1800s represented a monumental challenge for their States. In Brasilia, the construction of a new modern capital in the hinterland of Brazil in the mid-twentieth century offers a rather atypical political trajectory.

The histories of Ottawa and Canberra—as engineered capitals—share many commonalities. Both cities attest to the challenges of creating cultural institutions and a cultural life in a national capital. Québec City, Montréal, and Kingston have all been capitals at some point in Canada's colonial history. As reminded by Gordon (1998), the small lumber city of Ottawa was chosen as the capital of United Canada in 1857 by Queen Victoria after much discussion and much hesitation over the most suitable place to establish such an important political centre (p. 150). Ottawa was, then, not only primarily a lumber-focused city; it had a small population of barely 10,000 people. Situated in the province of Ontario, adjacent to Québec, Ottawa remained the capital of the new confederation in 1867. From a cultural perspective, Ottawa was far from an environment where arts and heritage could thrive. Many politicians thought that Ottawa only needed to have a better-built environment and that planning was the solution. Proposals in the early 1910s were made by the federal government for a massive assistance plan that would "beautify the city" (Gordon 1998). While others preferred to address life quality through the arts and heritage, among the many proponents of this alternative were two governors of Canada, the Earl of Dufferin (1872–1878) and the Marquess of Lorne (1878–1883) did a lot for the development of cultural life in Canada and in Ottawa, in particular.

Leaving the issue of urban planning aside, the development of heritage institutions was a tool to create a cultural life in the new capital. The intention, right from the beginning, was to create cultural institutions of a national status. Despite being close to and in between Toronto and Montréal, Ottawa was a rather isolated city in the late 1800s. These institutions need to be developed in a context where a rich cultural life already existed—in cities like Montréal, Toronto, and Québec. Many politicians and intellectuals who imagined life in the capital city thought that cultural heritage, natural history, and art objects needed to migrate to the political centre. For instance, Pierre-Joseph-Olivier Chauveau, an intellectual and the first prime minister of the province of Québec after the new Constitutional Act of 1867, envisioned the place of museums in the new capital thusly:

> One must hope that the collections and historical statues may someday become the core elements of a future great art gallery with paintings and sculptures, a real national museum. The capital of the Confederation ought to offer these powerful attractions to foreigners who might come visit their beautiful public buildings. The public servants of the federal government are a group of learned individuals and friends of Sciences, [...]. (Chauveau 1876: 341–342)[1]

[1] Authors supplied translation from the French original.

130   J. PAQUETTE

There is a natural association between political capitals and culture; it is almost an expectation. Museums and art galleries are, in most cases, important symbols of political power; as such, it seems that there is a natural sympathy for the combination of museums and politics in capital cities. With all of this being said, the development of new institution in federations can often come with a political price: they are open to political contentions.

One of the first ideas for achieving this vision of a city of culture is to create a museum in the capital. The first step to achieving this museum is through the evaluation of the federal government's museological collections. The small collection of geological specimens assembled by the Geological Survey of Canada and constituted as a "museum" in 1842 by Logan in Montréal was seen as an ideal starting point. This solution was, of course, a controversial one. According to a member of the Senate, the Honourable Mr. Ryan, the removal of the collection from Montréal needed to be rejected since: "The service has been conducted in Montréal with great care, and had been most beneficial to the public" (Senate of the Dominion 1877: 153). Additionally, the senator opposing the bill pointed out many other issues with developing a capital museum, such as the important costs of moving these collections, the integrity of the collections and care to achieve this, the doubts about any appropriate building in the capital to welcome these specimens in, and the much smaller population who would directly enjoy the benefits of this relocation. This position was favourable to retaining the collection in Montréal, in the province of Québec.

In favour of a greater cultural life in the capital city, Senator Haviland's intervention was to be determinant for the future of museums in the federation: "If it belonged to the Dominion Government, he was in favor of it being removed to the Capital, where representatives from all parts of the Dominion could take advantage of it. If it was Dominion property, it should be removed to Ottawa" (p. 154). The faith of the collection, and of the Canadian museum sector, was sealed with this intervention. The collections were removed from Montréal and sent to Ottawa in 1880 to become the basis of a series of museums that eventually emerged as the National Museum in 1927. This vision of an artful capital was pursued by the Marquis of Lorne, Governor General of Canada, who saw in enhancing the cultural life of the capital, a vital element of his work during his mandate. Through his effort in creating the Canadian Academy of Arts in Ottawa in 1880, the Marquis of Lorne made a seminal contribution to the foundation of the National Gallery. Until the late 1990s, Canada's national museums were developed as part of the National Capital projects; they were part of the social and political imagination of the capital. Eventually, in the 2000s, this concentration of heritage in the federal capital was targeted as a potential problem. A movement, favourable to a decentralization—or de-concentration—of national heritage institutions from Ottawa to other places, such as Winnipeg or Halifax, emerged. In sum, in engineered capitals, the development of a cultural life relies heavily on the construction of new—national—institutions. These are important tools for constructing a cultural life, but they also are important markers of cultural status.

Similar logics were at play in Australia. The selection of Canberra as the capital of the federation and its development as a federal territory/district (the Australian Capital Territory) in 1911 constitutes a rich moment for bringing museum-making processes to the federal level of Australia. In federal parliament, one of the first recorded mentions of a federal museum appears in a 1905 Hansard, when parliamentarians discussed the importance of the archaeological discoveries in New Guinea and the necessity of putting them in a trust—perhaps in a State museum—pending future development in the national capital to centralize the collections (Australia, House of representatives 1905). Already, in the early days of the Australian federation, politicians had in mind the production of a cultural life in a new capital city. The logic followed that where there is a capital city, there should be a museum. This is, it would seem, a very general expectation for a siege of power. Additionally, the idea that museums and galleries should be part of the design of the capital was also conveyed in the work of Walter Burley Griffin—an architect and urban planner—whose vision of the capital won over the government at the time (Brockwell and Chippindale 2005; McShane 1998). Following Griffin's vision, Canberra would have an Archaeology museum and a National Gallery. In this case, cultural development went hand-in-hand with urban planning.

The first national museum of the Commonwealth of Australia was the Institute of Zoology. This institution was built from a donation by a scientist from Melbourne, Colin Mackenzie, in the 1920s. In the minds of government officials, this collection would be "the nucleus of a larger collection to be housed in the future at Canberra" (Parliament of Australia 1924). This museum became the National Museum of Australian Zoology—later reorganized as the Australian Institute of

Anatomy in 1931—and would remain in operation until 1985. The National Museum of Australian Zoology was followed—and perhaps surpassed in public interest—by the idea of a War Museum—an idea that took an important place in parliamentary debates at the time—which eventually evolved into a War Memorial project that materialized and opened to the public in 1941. When it comes to envisioning a national museum for Australia, there is no better synthesis of the cultural aspirations and political challenges that creating a new museum in a federation can represent than what is conveyed in a speech given by Arthur T. Woodward, art director of the Bendigo School of Mines, in 1902:

> Sooner or later a National Museum will be founded, and it must be clear to any thinking person that no good can come of having a multiplicity of collections, and no central one. It must not be supposed for one moment that the existing State museums will be stripped of their treasures to such a degree as shall make visible the hand of an invisible desolator, and strike with dismay those who have nobly contributed to and upheld them in the past. Neither would the foundation of such a museum relieve them of the necessity of making future efforts in the many directions in which they are so fully, and we may hope, enthusiastically, occupied. Unless the spirit of magnanimity and patriotism dominates the people of Australia, and those who represent them on the management of such institutions, and those who are in possession of rare and choice specimens, I fail to see how it can ever be possible for a National Museum of Australia to become possessed of a great number of articles, particularly of articles that have an Australian historic interest. The natural home for the latter, now that we are one nation with one destiny, surely would seem to be a National Museum of Australia. (Woodward 1902, cited in Parliament of Australia 2000)

Woodward's plea conveys elements of the social philosophy and political reality and aspirations of federalism; it is not simplistically a nationalist plea. Not only does Woodward discuss the importance of a museum for the nation, but his speech alludes to some sacrifices from the state members, while at the same time recognizing their own pursuits as legitimate. This discourse is quite evocative of the social expectations and political conditions under which cultural ideas evolve in some federations. This speech is important in Australia's cultural policy history as it expresses an important element of the federalist sentiments towards art and the overall importance of cultural institutions in the national capital. As we know today, the development of brand new national museums and art galleries in the capital only materialized almost 80 years after Woodward's speech. The War Memorial, in a sense, represents a turning point for—or the real beginning of—federal heritage projects in the capital.

In a similar vein, the construction of Brasilia as the new capital of Brazil is another ambitious social and political project that aimed to foster the cultural unification of Brazil in its capital—in its geography—by representing a point of junction between a European population, established in coastal cities, and the rest of the population of the country (Stierli 2013: 8). Carrying this vision forward, President Kubitschek was able to secure the legal provisions and constitutional amendments needed to transfer the capital from Rio de Janeiro to a new site, Brasilia, first inaugurated in 1960. The development of this capital was through an intensive planning process that included special attention to architectural elements. The famous architect, Oscar Niemayer, in assistance to the Companhia Urbanizadora da Nova Capital—a federal development society—implemented this vision of a new capital (Cappello 2010). Because of its architectural audacity, now, fifty years later, Brasilia has become a site of significant architectural heritage. In this sense, the vision for culture in the capital was successfully embodied in its bold architectural stance.

In all of these cases, the capital city raises the issue of the geography of cultural institutions; it raises the question of the property of the cultural collections and their accessibility. More importantly, these capital cities raise the question of the existence (or lack thereof) of national cultural institutions. In the cases of Ottawa and Canberra, there was a desire for a national museum predicated on a widely shared idea among politicians and intellectuals that capital cities are relevant to culture: they should embody a country's culture through monuments, art, and heritage institution(s). The desire for a national museum in the capital city was almost rooted in a stereotype of capital cities, based on general ideas of what one might find in these cities. In the case of Brasilia, the removal of the capital city from Rio de Janeiro in the late 1950s was an important political statement against a certain vision of the country—and, similarly, against a certain vision of culture and society. Most of Brazil's national institutions were concentrated in Rio de Janeiro, and most remain concentrated there and on the coast. Heritage institutions were not delocalized; Rio de Janeiro embodied (and continues to embody) cultural policy as a radical statement of culture through arts, architecture, and design. The selection of New Delhi as the capital in India represented similar challenges. Many institutions had flourished in Calcutta for decades; however, when the capital was displaced, it was resolved that national cultural institutions and their collections would remain in the city. This is why the National Library of India is not in the capital, but still in Calcutta.

In federations, the concentration and de-concentration of cultural heritage is a political problem. Concentration of cultural institutions in the capital is based on the legitimacy of this space as a common ground for the federation. On the other hand, the concentration of heritage is seen as a problem for accessibility. Citizens must travel to their national institutions and in countries like the USA, Canada, India, Argentina, Brazil, and Australia, travelling from one end of the country to the other may imply complicated and costly travel arrangements. De-concentration of heritage seems a viable political solution to the question of accessibility, among others. Travelling exhibits, troupes, or programmes may be an interesting alternative, but the development of new institutions—as a strategy of de-concentration of national cultural institutions—causes some serious political problems. The cities designated as the recipients of these new cultural centres—whether they are museums, libraries, or performing arts centres—may seem to be favoured over others. While this problem is not simply one that concerns federations, in this context, it may provide ammunition to fuel old diatribes between federal and sub-national governments.

So far, we have discussed how engineered capitals in federations constitute a unique cultural problem. Through the discussion of a number of cases, we have established that the development of cultural institutions—in capital cities—is seen as an essential element by politicians and civil society at large. Another key element that should be discussed with regard to cultural institutions in federations is their geography. This question brings the place of the capital city into perspective. Are cultural institutions concentrated in the capital city? Or are they de-concentrated, spread across a number of other cities in the federation? In federations, this question is of the highest importance.

Looking at key national institutions in a number of federations (see Table 4.2), a picture of the political geography of heritage institutions can be established. Of course, this picture may not entirely capture every technical and historical process at play in the development of each cultural institution; nevertheless, this picture provides a certain understanding of the cultural sector and of the place and part played by capital cities

Table 4.2 Concentration of cultural institutions in the capital

Capital	Level of concentration
Berlin	De-concentrated
Bern	De-concentrated
Brasilia	De-concentrated
Brussels	Concentrated
Buenos Aires	Concentrated
Canberra	Concentrated
Kuala Lumpur	Concentrated
Mexico City	Concentrated
New Delhi	De-concentrated
Ottawa	Concentrated
Vienna	Concentrated
Washington DC	Concentrated

when it comes to heritage institutions. The observation, here, is based on the national institutions associated with a public service organization. This can be a public sector society, public enterprise, or an organization directly associated with the ministry or department of culture. Table 4.2 is based on organizations that are built on a national mandate. This excludes, of course, subnational public organizations, municipal organizations, and prestigious and prominent private or not-for-profit organizations. Under consideration are the following institutions: national museums, libraries, archives and related collection-based institutions, national theatres, performing art centres, and opera houses.

The first category involves capital cities with low levels of national cultural institutions. In Germany, national cultural institutions tend to be de-concentrated. Many important institutions have been developed outside the capital city. Berlin has the federal *Deutsches Historisches Museum*, but many other federally supported institutions can be found in the former federal capital, Bonn, and in other grand centres, like Munich. The German National Library that was in Berlin is now (since 2010) in Leipzig, with a technical section in Frankfort. As for the German federal archives, they are distributed across the territory, though the main antenna is in Coblenz. Similarly, in Switzerland, the national cultural institutions are not concentrated in Bern. The only national cultural institution in Bern is the National Library. While this cultural institution is perhaps the most important of the Swiss Confederation, there are other collections and museums spread across the territory. These are more modest collections, most of which are housed in heritage sites

136   J. PAQUETTE

(e.g., Oskar Reinhart collection, *Musée des automates à musique*, Museo Vela, and Museum of St-Georges' cloistre). The limited number of national cultural institutions in Switzerland also reflects the traditional reserved attitude of the federal level in cultural affairs.

Other cities also fit into this category. Brasilia has a limited number of national cultural institutions. When the capital was moved from Rio de Janeiro to Brasilia, the collections remained in the former capital. In this case, it can be said that Brasilia is the political capital, while Rio de Janeiro remained the cultural capital thanks to its high concentration of cultural institutions. Similarly, India has an important network of national cultural institutions. The idea to create culture in the capital gained traction rapidly after India's independence. In the process, New Delhi, as the capital city of India, gained a national gallery and national museum. However, most of India's cultural institutions are distributed over the territory. For instance, there are national museums in Mumbai, Bengaluru, and Allahabad. Likewise, the national library and a national museum are still in Calcutta. Additionally, the federal government of India has made an important effort to develop regional centres for performing arts that cover, more or less, the entire territory. Because of India's commitment to intangible heritage, a complex network of regional cultural services provides programming of a national level throughout India.

In a different group are the cities where the national institutions are highly concentrated. Brussels is a good example. Most of Belgium's federal cultural equipment (museums, libraries, archives, institutes) are assembled under the folio of the minister of science policy since cultural affairs belong to subnational entities. There are an important number of federal institutions with a national mandate in Belgium, most of which can be found in Brussels—with the notable exception of the *Musée royal d'Afrique centrale*, which is not technically in Brussels, but in an adjacent city, Tervuren. However, in a general sense, it can be said that every Belgian federal institution is in the federal capital. Buenos Aires in Argentina also has a very high concentration of national cultural institutions. The Museum of National History, the National Museum of Fine Arts, the National Museum of Decorative Arts, and many other collections and heritage sites are located in the Argentinian federal capital. The National Theater—or Teatro Cervantes—is also in Buenos Aires, as is the National Library, which has been housed there since 1992. While it is not uncommon to see attempts at regionalizing the reach of important institutions in some countries, this has not been the case in Argentina. In Australia, every national institution is in Canberra, with the exception of the Australian National Maritime Museum. Mexico City, Kuala Lumpur, and Washington DC all have a high concentration of national cultural institutions. Wien, likewise, is home to an important number of national theaters, performing arts centres, and museums that are all under federal mandate. Federal cultural institutions in Austria are primarily in the federal capital.

Of course, this does not include the heritage site components, because these are often associated with the preservation of a monument, built heritage, or a commemorative park whose cultural values are in situ and part of a nation's collective memory. National battlefields or grave memorials, for instance, are organized as parks which may or may not be in capital cities. These sites cannot be relocated as the event or part of national heritage they commemorate is often dependent on a single site of memory. Therefore, in this section, focus was placed on the idea of cultural institutions are or can be developed independent of any specific site. By looking at collection-based cultural institution, a number of observations can be made. First, collections are rarely moved when a capital city changes. When the capital moved from Calcutta to New Delhi in India in 1912, when the capital moved from Rio de Janeiro to Brasilia in 1960, or when the capital "moved" from Bonn in a reunited Germany in 1991, the collections and national museums and libraries remained in place. There is a political price that could probably not be afforded if such a change were to have occurred.

Second, when new capitals emerge—when they are engineered—there is a tendency to see the political function merging with cultural aspirations. As has been seen in this chapter, this is the case in Ottawa, Canberra, and New Delhi. The case of Brasilia is slightly different as the administration of the most important cultural institutions of the capital has been associated with the federal district's administration. In other words, the federal government gave the capacity and mandate to the special administration of the capital to oversee the country's national institutions. As such, Brasilia, more or less, embodies a national mission in its local administration. Over time, what was implicitly seen as logical may prove to be problematic in the long run. That being said, most new capitals are seen as needing to be part of a cultural project. There are very few cases of collection relocation—though the evolution of the national museum system in Ottawa—as a form of administrative centralization

138   J. PAQUETTE

and geographic concentration of a collection in the capital—is a notable exception.

Third, the de-concentration of national institutions away from the capital results from public service considerations, but also from political ones. Germany, Switzerland, and India have a de-concentrated system of cultural institutions; their national institutions are spread across the territory. In Germany, reunification and regionalism are also part of this political equation, as are linguistic and cultural representations in the location of collections in Switzerland. In the Helvetic Confederation, the small number of federal collections is also associated with heritage sites and points of access that are representative of the countries' cultural diversity. In India, regional and cultural considerations have also shaped the cultural geography of national institutions. In Canada, national cultural institutions have been highly politicized. In the 1980s and more recently (circa 2010), there has been a considerable push to develop national cultural institutions outside the federal capital (Bourgault 2002). Major projects such as the Pier 21 museum in Halifax or the Canadian Museum of Human Rights in Winnipeg are good examples of cultural development driven by the politics of de-concentration. While most major cultural institutions are concentrated in the Ottawa–Gatineau region, the debate about this concentration of institution remains salient.

4.1.2   Governing Culture and Cultural Policy in Federal Capitals

Local and regional cultural policy in national capital districts is bound by ethical requirements whereby it should be representative of regional diversity. Cultural policies are often made with a special care and attention to the national status of the city. If anything, there is a distinct symbolism to cultural policy in federal capitals. Federal capitals not only embody the spirit of the whole nation, they also embody the idea of being the political centre reuniting different regions and subnational entities. Flags, coat of arms, floral emblems, and many other symbols are a common part of the cultural rituals of national capital in federations. From a philosophical perspective, these policies are caught in the politics of recognition: every form of diversity should be recognized symmetrically in cultural events and in urban and regional symbols. In tourism policy, even, there is an implicit acknowledgement that tourists can come from virtually any area of the world, but citizens who travel

4 CULTURAL POLICIES, FEDERATIONS, AND CITIES **139**

to the capital are not simply spending some time—a weekend—they are connecting with what unites a country. In countries like Canada, the USA, and Australia, school visits to the federal capital are part of the civic education of citizens; they are a form of cultural and political ritual. Cultural activities and programming are often constructed as a mirror of the nation's diversity; tourists who come for a pilgrimage to the capital city can find something that is both familiar and different. As a result, the politicized nature of cultural activities, the presence of national institutions, and their style of cultural programming, along with the cultural offerings available to the public can also have an influence on artists, often overshadowing the "local" scene. According to Caroline Agnew, in capital cities "there has traditionally been a high degree of top-down planning in cultural events, some of which is detrimental to the local scene" (Agnew 2016: 204). For Agnew, there is, in capital cities, a "missing middle". Based on her research on the City of Ottawa, Agnew comes to the conclusion that capital cities can overshadow a regional or local art scene. There is a vibrant art scene in national institutions, on the one hand, and an art scene that is primarily associated with amateur art, children's art education, or, simply, leisurely pursuits in the arts with no specific professional ambition. According to Agnew, the money for the arts is absorbed by the national institutions and local educational activities (p. 205).

The context of what Agnew is referring to—the missing middle—cannot really be understood outside the logic of federalism. What Agnew tried to convey is, in fact, the complexity of the distribution of financial and cultural resources in federal systems. A city like Ottawa, for instance, has a cluster of important national institution; as such, the provincial government and local government have tended to reorient their (cultural) funding for other purposes or, in the case of the provincial government, to other cities. Some federal capitals may create a sort of ambivalent situation for local artists and the public. Programming may be done according to the idea of regional, linguistic, or other forms of diversity that characterize a nation. There may be cases where the local population may, at times, feel alienated by cultural choices that tend to be focused on a diversity of normativity that evades them. Similarly, local arts professionals have to navigate the meanders of federal cultural institutions—institutions which may or may not provide them with opportunities for professional development. This is to say that federal capitals are spaces where culture cannot escape politics or, more specifically,

140   J. PAQUETTE

the politics of recognition. On the other hand, it is important to recognize that federal capitals may also present themselves as a different institutional reality for artists, whose perception of the arts scene may be traversed by the perceptions and realities of federal politics at the local level.

Considering all that has been said above, it can be argued that capital cities in federations imply something different when it comes to local cultural policy. These local cultural policies are at the confluence of local and national themes that inform or shape their fabric. More importantly, perhaps, the institutional conditions in which these cities evolve also shape a different reality where the governance of cultural policy may need to involve different layers of government and a variety of stakeholders that can include local, subnational, and federal governments. We will discuss these issues using our typology of reference on the structure of federal capitals: city-States, federal districts, and regular cities.

In city-States, the boundaries between the local and subnational levels of administration are thin. When it comes to cultural affairs, the subnational level of government is technically in a strong situation to impose itself as the dominant actor in cultural governance. Berlin, Vienna, and Brussels are three city-States. In Germany, the move to a new post-reunification capital in Berlin was followed by an important series of measures by the federal government to support culture in the city. The *Hauptstadtkulturvertrag* (Capital Cultural Pact) is one of the federal government's policy instruments aimed at supporting both reunification and the development of cultural infrastructures in the capital. The federal government is also present in local cultural affairs through the *Hauptstadtkulturfonds* (Capital Cultural Funds), established in 1999, which provides direct support for the arts community in a similar manner to that of an arts council. The German federal government also massively invested and participated in a number of projects, in recent years, which involved regional and urban planning. The Museum Island is one of the important projects where the federal government provided supports through subnational transfers to the land-government of Berlin. The Berlin-Bonn act of 1994 that accompanied the transfer of the capital to Berlin is also a federal policy instrument that has impacted on the cultural sector. This act was meant to protect the interests of Bonn and to compensate for some of the costs (financial and otherwise) associated with the transition, but it also included a federal strategy to intervene in local planning through a federal planning office

(*Bundesamt für Bauwesen und Raumordnung*)—which was instrumental in providing funds and expertise to major local cultural projects. As reminded by Anheier and Isar, in Berlin, the city-state government, the subnational level—otherwise known here as the senate—is the most important actor in local cultural policy (2008: 164). The senate also asserts that it is the leading authority in cultural policymaking and—following the German Constitution—cultural decision-making, doing so in a collaborative manner with the advice and participation of the twelve boroughs of Berlin (Berlin, Senate Department for Culture and Europe 2018). Since 2004, the senate has oriented its local cultural policy around the logic of *Kulturwirtschaftsinitiative* (cultural and creative economies).

Berlin is a case where the subnational government assumes cultural leadership in the local cultural governance system. Nonetheless, the governance of local cultural affairs is carried through by federal/subnational agreements that are periodically renegotiated and supported by a federal funding agency and planning office. In the case of Vienna, there is a complex fusion and division of powers between the provincial and municipal governments. This division is theoretical and legal and ensures a provincial status is afforded to Vienna as a member of the federation. The city Senate in Vienna is the place where the provincial legislature meets. In other words, on some affairs, the members act in their capacities as members of the provincial legislatures, while they assume municipal capacities. Similarly, as in the case of Berlin, the boundaries between local and subnational are thin. In the case of Vienna, it seems that the structure of cultural governance, the cultural mandates, and the style of organization has retained all the elements of a municipal style of administration. The cultural mandate is focused on local affairs and on the administration of a number of municipal-level cultural organizations.

Brussels, on the other hand, is a very complex case. Not only is Brussels technically a city-State in Van Wynsberghe's typology of federal capitals (2014), it is also a super capital. Brussels is the capital of the Flemish region, the capital of Belgium, and the siege of most of the European Union's institutions. On social and cultural levels, Brussels' territory is also subject to community governments and legislations. On the territorial side, the Bruxelles-capitale is a regional government, alongside Wallonia and Flanders. Therefore, Brussels is a city-State because it is also a regular subnational component of Belgium. In Belgium, culture is typically a community-level power, more than a

142 J. PAQUETTE

regional-level power. Nonetheless, there are, in the Bruxelles-capitale region, a number of competences—mostly associated with planning and urban landscaping—that fall directly in the purview of the regional government. Culture is, thus, attached to the regional level via issues of urban landscape, built heritage, and monuments. The city government of Brussels—at the communal level—is responsible for arts and cultural development through its "[c]ulture, youth, leisure and sports" folio. To summarize, the situation of cultural governance in Brussels is a rather complex issue. All of the cultural equipment of the federal government is established and concentrated in Brussels. Culture is a community matter by constitution, and Brussels is the home of both Flemish and French populations. Cultural affairs, in Brussels, are governed by some agencies that coordinate cultural action on the territory. For French affairs, the Fédération Wallonie-Bruxelles is the French-community ministry that coordinates a number of community-based public services and cultural policy development for the French-speaking citizens of Wallonia and Brussels. A similar organization and configuration are reflected for the Flemish-speaking population. Now, in Brussels, culture is not only a community affair, it is also, through planning, a regional power (built heritage), though the city—or communal administration—can also intervene in issue of leisure, sports, tourism, and event management. The governance of cultural policy in Brussels is polycentric. This institutional reality has been described as one of the most challenging by some Belgian researchers (Corijn et al. 2009). This is especially the case when actors actively try to promote culture at an international level. It can also be challenging when some actors try to promote cultural policy as a tool for the cultural integration of migrants, since cultural affairs are predominantly defined through the bicultural or bilinguistic divide of Belgium (Comhaire 2012).

In federal districts, local administration of capital cities resides, more generally, in the hands of the federal district administration. These districts differ from city-States, because they are directly subjected to federal powers. In some cases, the federal district is a structural power that can make executive decisions or overturn decisions made by locally elected bodies. This is the case in New Delhi, and it would be the case, theoretically, in Washington DC. In other federal districts, like the Australian Capital Territory, the land is seen as a federal dependency, and the capital city is part of federal land simply to avoid contentions between subnational members and to assure a direct sense of territoriality for the federal government. In federal districts, federal administrations tend to retain a number of powers and a level of discretion over urban planning in the capital region. Issues of architecture, urban bylaws (heights of building, places, etc.), and monuments are areas where the federal administration is most likely to exert its discretionary power. Cultural events and cultural programmes that cater to the local population are less prone to be subjected to any intervention by the federal administration. In fact, the configuration of powers in federal districts has tended to evolve over the last few decades. In acknowledgement of the importance of the quality of life in communities and in recognition of some distinctive regional elements that some capital cities may want to retain or promote, many federal administrations have changed their approach and have tried to create more powers or provide more room for autonomy in local affairs. In this category, many federal capitals have been encouraged by their federal governments to develop their own cultural governance services. In New Delhi, since 1999, the government of the National Capital Territory has developed a cultural service to promote a cultural life that reflects the aspiration of the local population. Since its beginnings, the department has grown institutionally, with cultural targets being part of the strategic plans of the federal district. In Washington DC, since the introduction of the Home Rule in 1973, there have been strong efforts to create and sustain a local cultural life in the federal district. To this end, the District of Columbia Commission on Arts and Humanities was created in 1975. Local heritage functions are assumed by the District of Columbia's Department of Parks and Recreation. In Brasilia, the nature of the territory has made it so that there is an actual municipal tier of government within the federal district. Leadership for local cultural policy is ensured by the *Secretaria de Estado de Cultura do Distrito Federal,* a secretariat that has all the functions of a comprehensive ministry of culture and includes the management of exhibit spaces, a public radio, and many sectorial cultural policies catering to some area of the cultural industries—from publishing to the visual arts. The style of governance and the orientation of this federal district target the creation of a cultural life that is distinctively regional.

In federations, there are only two capital cities that have been established as regular cities—thus creating a clear division between federal, subnational, and local governments. Both Bern and Ottawa, who fall in this category, have a cultural service in their local administration that is commonly attached to leisure and, sometimes, tourism agendas.

In the case of Ottawa, the participation of the provincial government is cultural affairs is rather limited, but the presence of the federal government has always been important in this domain. Cultural policies are developed at the local level, with local stakeholders; however, communication with the federal government is established through different channels. In particular, the federal government has always imagined a capital city in the manner of the District of Columbia, but did not have the power to accomplish this vision. As a result, as early as 1899, the federal government developed a coordination agency—the National Capital Commission—that worked with the municipal and provincial governments to provide the federal government with a voice in matters of urban planning and built heritage in Ottawa. Part of the federal government's strategy was to simply buy land in the region and maintain direct control over it. The federal government developed this strategy in Ottawa and the adjacent territories in the province of Québec (Aylmer, Hull, and Gatineau City). According to Gordon (2006), the approach of the National Capital Commission has changed over time. In the period immediately following World War II, the agency funnelled direct transfers to the local level to facilitate some of the federal government's ambitions: it injected money for "slum clearances", to develop public services suitable for the relocation of some of its departments in the suburbs and to support initiatives that would increase mobility between both Ottawa and Gatineau. In the 1960s and 1970s, the National Capital Commission developed into a body to integrate multiple stakeholders in finding common solutions for and began paying—as in its beginnings— more attention to cultural affairs. In this respect, the commission tries to navigate the complex governance issues related to these multiple layers of government; it also attempts to create common cultural grounds for the local population living in both provinces within the National Capital Region. The cultural rationality of the National Capital Commission has evolved from a concentration on planning and built heritage to issues of leisure and local cultural practices.

The institutional reality of federalism creates a different context for the local governance of cultural affairs in capital cities. As we have seen in this section, the institutional configuration of the capital city—city-State, federal district, or regular city—can have an impact on the style of cultural governance. From all of these examples, a number of principles about the governance of local cultural policies in federal capital cities can be distilled. First, federal governments are interested in local cultural matters. Regardless of the institutional configuration of the capital city, there is a channel on which federal governments can act. The federal government can use incentives (transfers), retain power to overrule local decisions, or (try to) create an instrument to actively pursue its interests. Second, the local reality—the local fabric and tastes—seems to be a problematic issue in federal capitals. Cities can have a rich cultural life of their own (Vienna, Brussels, Buenos Aires, etc.), but the contribution of municipal governments in most cities is often limited by the division of powers and the institutional realities of federalism.

4.2   Federalism and Local Cultural Policy

Cities are an essential component of a citizen's life, and many of the most important public services used on a daily basis—most public utilities needed for a decent lifestyle—are provided by local administrations, city governments, or cooperative associations between cities. According to Gibbins, cities occupy an important role in public service delivery and their contribution is vital; however, historically, their place in federations has been minimal. Very few constitutions define the powers of cities; in most cases, they are seen as being under the purview of subnational administrations. As such, to put it in Gibbins words, "local governments [have] left scarcely any imprint on the constitutional or institutional structures of federal systems" (2001: 163). It is true that, in most federations, cities are created by an act that emanates from subnational legislature. Cities can be created, dissolved, or amalgamated by an act of the subnational legislature (Schuster 2002). This is true of most federations, with the exception of federations in Latin America where federal/municipal relationships tend to be more formalized and institutionalized in constitutional affairs. In Mexico, for instance, the federal constitution has set the number and characteristics of local governments in each subnational entity.

These institutional realities are extremely important for cultural policy research. In recent years, cities have been seen as an increasingly important centre for cultural policy development. Funding strategies of cities have important consequences for art scenes and institutions (Breux and Colin 2007; Paquette 2008; Henningsen et al. 2017). New trends in local cultural policy may also exert an ideological impact, helping to change the normativity and orientation of other levels of cultural policy (Gilmore 2004). Local cultural policy may also help validate and popularize the importance of new values in cultural policy development, as well as help spread them institutionally (Griffiths et al. 2003; Mommaas 2004; Redaelli 2013). Many of the ideas conveyed in local cultural policy also circulate widely at a global level, influencing other cities and national governments (Sassen 2010; Paquette 2015). All of these recent trends tend to support the fact that cities are extremely important for cultural policy development; they are important sites for policy formulation and often serve as important social and intellectual laboratory for culture. Therefore, the question raised is: What is the place of cities in federations, and, in particular, what is the place of culture in the city/federal relationship? How are these articulated?

This question brings us back, once more, to issues of intergovernmentalism. The best possible answer to this complex question requires a consideration of intergovernmental instruments. How and by which means is this intergovernmental relationship made possible?

The first instrument of cultural relations between federal governments and cities is (financial) transfers—which may include targeted investments for cultural facilities (Leighninger 1996). Major cultural projects may require investments from every level of government. In Canada, the patterns of funding for major cultural infrastructure have evolved in the last few decades to rely on investments from all levels of government as equal partners (Champagne 2013). Cultural investments are funded by the federal, provincial, and municipal governments who typically agree to invest as equal partners in the project (Duxbury 2008). The only problem with this model of cultural funding for cities is that if they are pushing for a project—if they are the leader of a cultural infrastructure project—they will need to convince the federal and subnational levels of government of the suitability of their initiative. As such, cities may be caught in a complex politics where they have to ensure that the other levels of government agree on the specificities of a project, as funding from one level of government may be conditional on the participation of the other level. Cultural infrastructures may, therefore, be caught up in the politics of public finances, as well as in politics in the plain and most simple of senses.

In a different vein, the German reunification was an important opportunity for the development of federal/local relationships. As part of the reunification strategy, the federal government has made available some funding for cultural infrastructures as well as for other kinds of cultural projects (Zimmer and Toepler 1996; Burns and Van der Will 2003; Friedrichs and Dangshats 1993).

The second instrument of intergovernmental relations may be found in expertise and direct collaborations between federal administrations and city governments. Federal municipal relationships may, in this sense, take the form of a collaboration to develop the capacity to formulate policy. In other words, these relationships suggest the transmission of cultural policy practices as expertise diffused from the federal to the local level of government. These strategies may take on a number of different forms. In the USA, the National Endowment for the Arts has been a catalyst for cultural ideas. According to Michael Rushton, "[t]he NEA's 'Our Town' grant programs reward communities that invest in the arts as part of 'creative placemaking' [strategies]" (2015: 26). As such, the NEA is contributing to the dissemination of new ideas on local cultural policy development. In Canada, building on the model of the European capitals of culture, the federal government has, since 2002, invested in the municipalities through its own Canadian Cultural Capitals programme. This programme symbolically recognizes the importance of different cities' cultural landscapes across the country. The selection of grant recipients is based on merit, but also on a certain idea of geographical representation of the different parts of the country enmeshed in the selection process. Additionally, this programme was not strictly targeted at major metropolises, but included mid-size cities and small towns. The programme required that cities develop their own cultural policy. As such, the programme offered seed funding for developing capacities and expertise at the local level. These are good examples of a top-down relationship geared towards the development of local (cultural policy) skills and knowledge. However, this relationship may be understood in different terms. Sometimes, the quest for expertise and policy solutions may come from the city, itself. For instance, the work of Redaelli and Haines (2014) shows to what degree cities look to federal and subnational governments to establish their own (cultural) structures. The structuration of municipal services in cultural affairs, whether it is in terms of arts or heritage, is commonly inspired by strategies and solutions borrowed from the higher levels of government. The work of Redaelli and Haines shows how this inspiration can have institutional consequences, influencing how cultural services are structured in cities.

Third, cities may be participant in federal politics. In this sense, they may try to develop direct access to federal governments. It is not uncommon for major cities to establish strong relationships with the federal government. Major cities in this sense, metropolises, tend to have direct access to federal institutions and politicians. Other cities may try to advocate their agendas through associations designed to represent municipal interests. The National League of Cities and the National Association for Towns and Townships in the USA, the *Deutscher Städtetag* in Germany, or the Federation of Canadian Municipalities in Canada are all good examples of associations where the interests of municipal governments are discussed. In these associations, advocacy with the federal government is always a crucial element of the collective actions developed by these organizations. Culture is one of the many themes discussed in these associations' meetings. Another alternative for the participation of cities in cultural affairs—through intergovernmental relations—can occur through federal/subnational forums. In Australia, the meetings of cultural ministers—which reunite the federal and state ministers of arts and culture—have typically invited a representative of the municipal sector to join in the discussions. Agents from the municipal level not only take these opportunities to convey their own demands, they use them to provide higher levels of government with useful information about the realities of cities that may evade federal and subnational politicians. Moreover, these opportunities allow municipalities to provide strategic information when it comes to the viability of a policy alternative and the potential challenges associated with its implementation at the local level.

Cities are not immune to politics and their cultural exchanges with federal governments. In Argentina, urban-led regeneration projects are caught in the middle of federal, subnational, and local politics. According to Dinardi, some projects, like that of the development of a cultural centre in a former post office, serve as good examples of the political landscape in which local cultural policy evolves in Argentina. The post office project, in particular, was seen as representing the values of federalism; it was seen as a tool for bringing forward "a long-cherished dream" or bringing all of the country and its diverse cultures together in a national cultural project (Dinardi 2015: 14). While this may, of course, appear benign at first sight, in the political context of Argentina this also implied an important positioning. Local cultural policy needs to navigate through what Dinardi calls binomial thinking—it needs to navigate and avoid pitfalls and divisive subjects structured along dichotomic political thinking. Similarly, in Canada, as is the case with many other forms of local policy, municipal cultural policy is a tool for increasing the visibility and participation of the federal government in citizens' lives. Local cultural policies provide an additional and

4 CULTURAL POLICIES, FEDERATIONS, AND CITIES   149

unrestricted field of social intervention for federal governments, helping them circumvent certain constitutional limitations—notably in health or education. Politically, direct transfers to cities from the federal government can also be seen as a test of strength or a way of challenging subnational (provincial) authorities (Paquette 2008; McCaughey et al. 2014) since some of these cultural pursuits converge with political debates about Canadian identity.

References

Agnew, C. (2016). Being Part of the 'Supercreative Core': Arts, Artists and the Experience of Local Policy in the Creative City Era. In J. Paquette (Ed.), *Cultural Policy, Work and Identity: The Creation, Renewal and Negotiation of Professional Subjectivities* (pp. 197–213). London: Routledge.

Anheier, H. K., & Isar, Y. R. (Eds.). (2008). *Cultures and Globalization: The Cultural Economy.* Thousand Oaks, CA: Sage.

Australia, House of Representatives. (1905). *Question—Thursday 27th July 1905.* Canberra: Parliament of Australia.

Australia, Parliament of Australia. (1924). *Zoological Museum Agreement Bill— Second Reading.* Canberra.

Berlin, Senate Department for Culture and Europe. (2018). *Actors.* Retrieved online from Berlin Senate's website https://www.berlin.de/sen/kultur/en/cultural-policy/actors/.

Bourgault, J. (2002). *Horizontalité et gestion publique.* Québec: Presses Université Laval.

Breux, S., & Collin, J. (2007). La politique culturelle des villes québécoises face à la récente réforme municipale. *Cahiers de géographie du Québec, 51*(142), 9–27. https://doi.org/10.7202/015894ar.

Brockwell, S., & Chippindale, C. (2005). Walter Burley Griffin and a Museum of Archeology at the Heart of Australia's Capital. *Australian Archaelogy, 60*(1), 52–54.

Burns, R., & Van der Will, W. (2003). German Cultural Policy: An Overview. *International Journal of Cultural Policy, 9*(2), 133–152.

Cappello, M. B. C. (2010). A revista brasília na construção da Nova Capital: Brasília (1957–1962). *Risco: Revista de Pesquisa em Arquitetura e Urbanismo,* (11), 43–57.

Champagne, E. (2013). Les programmes d'infrastructures municipales du gouvernement fédéral: une analyse de la gouvernance multiniveau au Canada. *Télescope: Revue d'analyse comparée en administration publique, 19*(1), 43–61.

Chauveau, P.-J.-O. (1876). *L'instruction publique au Canada. Précis historique et statistique.* Québec: Imprimerie Augustin Côté et cie.

150   J. PAQUETTE

Comhaire, G. (2012). Activisme urbain et politiques architecturales à Bruxelles: le tournant générationnel. *L'Information géographique, 76*(3), 9–23.

Corijn, E., Vandermotten, C., Decroly, J. M., & Swyngedouw, E. (2009). Bruxelles, ville internationale. *Brussels Studies, 13*, 1–10.

Dinardi, C. (2015). Unsettling the Role of Culture as Panacea: The Politics of Culture-Led Urban Regeneration in Buenos Aires. *City, Culture and Society, 6*(2), 9–18. https://doi.org/10.1016/j.ccs.2015.03.003.

Duxbury, N. (2008). *Under Construction: The State of Cultural Infrastructure in Canada*. Vancouver: Centre of Expertise on Culture and Communities.

Elazar, D. J. (1987). *Exploring Federalism*. Tuscaloosa: University of Alabama Press.

Friedrichs, J., & Dangshats, J. (1993). *Hamburg: Culture and Urban Competition*. Manchester: Manchester University Press.

Gibbins, R. (2001). Local Governance and Federal Political Systems. *International Social Science Journal, 53*(167), 163–170.

Gilmore, A. (2004). Local Cultural Strategies: A Strategic Review. *Cultural Trends, 13*(3), 3–32. https://doi.org/10.1080/0954896042000260924.

Gordon, D. L. (1998). A City Beautiful Plan for Canada's Capital: Edward Bennett and the 1915 Plan for Ottawa and Hull. *Planning Perspectives, 13*(3), 275–300.

Gordon, D. L. (2006). *Planning Twentieth Century Capitals*. London: Routledge.

Griffiths, R., Bassett, K., & Smith, I. (2003). Capitalising on Culture: Cities and the Changing Landscape of Cultural Policy. *Policy & Politics, 31*(2), 153–169.

Hall, P. (2006). Seven Types of Capital City. In D. Gordon (Ed.), *Planning Twentieth Century Capital Cities* (pp. 24–30). London: Routledge.

Henningsen, E., Håkonsen, L., & Løyland, K. (2017). From Institutions to Events—Structural Change in Norwegian Local Cultural Policy. *International Journal of Cultural Policy, 23*(3), 352–371. https://doi.org/10.1080/10286 632.2015.1056174.

Leighninger, R. D., Jr. (1996). Cultural Infrastructure: The Legacy of New Deal Public Space. *Journal of Architectural Education, 49*(4), 226–236.

McCaughey, C., Duxbury, N., & Meisner, A. (2014). Measuring Cultural Value in Canada: From National Commissions to a Culture Satellite Account. *Cultural Trends, 23*(2), 109–119. https://doi.org/10.1080/09548963.2014.8974.

McShane, I. (1998). Building a National Museum of Australia: A History. *Public History Review, 7*(1), 75–88.

Mommaas, H. (2004). Cultural Clusters and the Post-industrial City: Towards the Remapping of Urban Cultural Policy. *Urban Studies, 41*(3), 507–532.

Parliament of Australia. (2000). *National Museum of Australia Amendment Bill 2000—Bill digest no. 85 2000-01*. Canberra.

Paquette, J. (2008). Engineering the Northern Bohemian: Local Cultural Policies and Governance in the Creative City Era. *Space and Polity, 12*(3), 297–310. https://doi.org/10.1080/13562570802515184.

Paquette, J. (2015). Recomposition de l'action culturelle locale. Production et circulation des logiques d'action publique culturelle au Royaume-Uni et dans l'espace anglo-saxon. In M. Roy-Valex & G. Bellavance. *Arts et territoires à l'ère du développement durable*. Québec: Presses de l'Université Laval.

Redaelli, E. (2013). Assessing a Place in Cultural Planning: A Framework for American Local Government. *Cultural Trends, 22*(1), 30–44.

Redaelli, E., & Haines, A. (2014). Framing Cultural Resource Policies in Comprehensive Plans: A Neo-institutional Analysis. *Journal of Planning Education and Research, 34*(4), 409–419. https://doi.org/10.1177/07394 56X14546167.

Rushton, M. (2015). Cultural Districts and Economic Development in American Cities. *Poetics, 49*(Complete), 20–29. https://doi.org/10.1016/j.poetic.2015.02.003.

Sassen, S. (2010). The City: Its Return as a Lens for Social Theory, *City, Culture and Society, 1*(1), 3–11. https://doi.org/10.1016/j.ccs.2010.04.003.

Schuster, J. M. (2002). Sub-National Cultural Policy—Where the Action Is: Mapping State Cultural Policy in the United States. *International Journal of Cultural Policy, 8*(2), 181–196.

Senate of the Dominion of Canada. (1877). *Fourth Session—Third Parliament*. Ottawa: Citizen Printing and Publishing.

Stierli, M. (2013). Building No Place: Oscar Niemeyer and the Utopias of Brasília. *Journal of Architectural Education, 67*(1), 8–16.

Van Wynsberghe, C. (2014). Brussels, DC: le rêve américain? *Outre-Terre, 40*(3), 321–332.

Zimmer, A., & Toepler, S. (1996). Cultural Policies and the Welfare State: The Cases of Sweden, Germany, and the United States. *The Journal of Arts Management, Law, and Society, 26*(3), 167–193.

CHAPTER 5

Federations and Subnational International Cultural Relations

In this chapter, we engage with subnational cultural relations. As we shall immediately see, this idea may be theoretically challenging in some disciplines—like Political Science, International Affairs, and other related fields. External affairs and international relations are often assumed to be the resort and responsibility of countries—that is to say, the specific domain of nation states. The international relations literature has typically focused on the study of State-to-State relationships defined as relationships between at least two sovereign states. Every constitution recognizes the importance of foreign affairs, and federal constitutions generally recognize that this is a federal jurisdiction. The capacity to develop relationships with other States, the capacity to establish formal diplomatic relationship with them, and the capacity to sign treaties and participate in international political institutions (United Nations, Unesco, European Union) are all powers reserved to States; constitutions do not typically allow for subnational partners to engage formally in foreign affairs. The body of literature from international relations has, thus, typically developed on the study of State-to-State relationship defined as relationships constructed between two or multiple sovereign states.

That being said, inspired by different views of international relations, there has been a growing body of literature that invites a redefinition of international relations in a way that is less focused on the States and national administrations, in particular. In recent years, this body of work on transnationalism has invited an acknowledgement of the number of

© The Author(s) 2019
J. Paquette, *Cultural Policy and Federalism,*
New Directions in Cultural Policy Research,
https://doi.org/10.1007/978-3-030-12680-3_5

153

ties and relationships between populations and actors of the civil society across State boundaries. International relations ought not to be simply seen as relations between States, they should involve a diversity of agents. This line of research suggests that the conventional definition of international relations (provided above) as a State-to-State relationship is something that needs to be debated—and has, in fact, been debated in the field for a good number of decades (Blanc et al. 1995; Kingsbury 1998; Waldinger and Fitzgerald 2004; Westwood and Phizacklea 2013).

Where do subnational governments or states fit into this conversation? International relations are now either seen, in the most orthodox sense, as the relations between two or more States or as any relations between actors at the international level. Subnational governments remain difficult to situate in contrast to these two polar opposite views of foreign relations. On the one hand, subnational governments are governments; they are state apparatuses. And while the interregional and international relations of subnational governments speak to the growing number of exchanges and networks that develop beyond what is classically understood as international relations, their activities remain no less governmental and state-related. On the other hand, as much as their external relations may not be carried out with the same level of authority or sovereignty as that of a country, it remains that subnational governments can engage with other governments in areas that are constitutionally defined as their shared or specific area of power and legislation. In federal contexts, in particular, subnational governments may benefit from exclusive powers over a certain areas of activities such as education, health, or environment, among many others, which brings to salience the potential necessity of conducting their own foreign and interregional affairs. In Germany, as we have seen, the rigorous understanding of the dual federalism has made it necessary to create a platform of exchanges between the federal government and the *Länders* on cultural matters. European integration, and the signature of international treaties, may well have important cultural implications for the *Länders* in Germany, and this is why this dialogue is important in this case.

To account for the distinctive situation in which subnational governments conduct foreign affair activities, and to better categorize it in relation to other foreign affairs activities, the notion of paradiplomacy was developed by political scientists and public affairs scholars. Paradiplomacy is defined by Lecours (2002: 92) as the "third world" or world politics as it goes beyond the two main conceptions of international politics described above (in reference to James Rosenau views of world politics as being defined and structured by States and non-State actors).

As a notion, paradiplomacy was developed in the 1980s (Aguirre 1999: 186). Paradiplomacy conveys the basic idea that regions and subnational governments engage in international relations and, sometimes, in "formal diplomatic" relationships. From the literature, we can distinguish two common yet complementary understandings of paradiplomacy (Duchacek 1984). The first view of paradiplomacy insists on region-to-region cooperation and discussions in transborder contexts; it insists on interregional relations (Aguirre 1999: 187). In recent years, it is this perspective on paradiplomacy that has attracted the most interest among scholar. Interregional cooperation and cross-border agreements have been studied in context of environment (Chaloux and Paquin 2013; Johns and Thorn 2015), economic integrations, and commercial relations (Sideri 1997; Dąbrowski 2013), and even in peace-building research (Klatt and Wassenberg 2017). Much of this literature has now been meshed and is increasingly re-problematized under the governance and multilevel governance literature (Mingus 2006; Dickson 2014).

The second understanding of paradiplomacy is rooted in the political dynamics of federalism and supposes a tension between the central State's diplomacy and one or many of the federated states' international or interregional interests (Michelmann and Soldatos 1990). Regional or subnational diplomacy is characterized by the changing dynamics of competition and cooperation commonly observed in federal contexts. This literature has typically emphasized the conflictual nature of subnational diplomacy vis-à-vis the central State's distinct economic and political interests (Mitchell 1995; Tatham 2013; Royles 2017). Conversely, some literature also documents how sub-states have used paradiplomacy in their quest for national recognition. This has been documented in the cases of Flanders (Paquin 2003), Québec (McHugh 2015), Scotland (Rioux Ouimet 2015), Catalonia (Paquin 2002), and the Basque Country (Totoricagüena 2005). By insisting on identity politics, some of these researches may, in fact, be underscoring a variety of social expectations with regard to subnational states' role, as well as a variety of enduring economic and cultural aspirations that may play well beyond the confines of identity politics.

This chapter aims to explore the issue of subnational cultural relations, an area of activity otherwise known as cultural diplomacy. As an area of foreign relationships, cultural diplomacy is often described, more broadly, as "public diplomacy" and associated with branding and the promotion of brand, image, and identity (Gilboa 2008; Zamorano and Rodríguez Morató 2015). While culture and cultural relations may seem like more peripheral activities in comparison with economic affairs or defence, they are far from trivial. For instance, the literature on subnational paradiplomacy tends to see in cultural affairs a special means for promoting some nationalistic agendas (in Québec, Flanders, Catalonia, etc.). But to ascribe cultural diplomacy to the confines of nationalism is a rather limiting view. Cultural diplomacy, it is argued, serves a more important function than simply promoting nationalist agendas; it can also support economic and social objectives. If anything, cultural relationships are a means of maintaining diplomatic relationships; they are also a mean to sustain continuity in subnational diplomacy.

Subnational international relations typically follow four patterns. First, some subnational governments establish direct relationships with countries. These subnational governments may engage directly with foreign governments, but they may also try to engage with another country's civil society. Second, subnational governments may establish relations with other subnational governments. These relations are commonly for trade purposes, but can also be for cultural reasons. The cultural dimension, as we know, is an important tool in developing business relations. Third, a number of subnational states may reunite to engage with and establish communications over a number of important policy issues. Fourth, in some cases, subnational governments may, with federal governments, participate in international relations. In this fourth scenario, subnational and federal governments act collaboratively in foreign affairs.

To achieve their international goals, subnational governments may sometimes rely on a series of different instruments. The most common instrument is participation in official visits, through which subnational governments will engage directly with other government. For example, in recent years, some Swiss cantons have increased their international presence. This is the case of the canton of Basel. In terms of its attempts to conduct its cultural diplomacy, the canton—famous for its annual Art Basel art fair—signed an agreement in 2011 with the municipal government of Miami to establish a cultural collaboration around the event. Basel has also established direct diplomatic links with Shanghai through which they have actively pursued a programme of cultural diplomacy that supports student exchanges, professional performing art companies, and visual arts events. Basel also borders France and Germany and has developed direct economic and cultural links with their regional governments. This is all, now, centrally coordinated by the canton's external relations office. Other Swiss cantons, like Zurich, for example, have an external relations office and conduct their relations through this department.

Often, members of subnational government will liaise with other governments on important matters, including cultural ones, with official visits serving as part of the repertoire of diplomatic actions used to this end. In the same category, the government of Baden-Württemberg has developed formal relations with the Canadian provincial government of Ontario, signing a memorandum of cooperation on scientific and cultural affairs. The government of Baden-Württemberg has also developed long-standing relationships with the regions of Liaoning and Jiangsu in China. In terms of subnational/national cultural cooperation, the government of Saarland in Germany has established a formal relationship with France and has a cultural development strategy that aims at developing cultural exchanges and French language capacity in the region as a potential tool for economic development.

Another frequent form of subnational international relations now takes form in trades missions. Trade missions are international visits where politicians and a number of important commercial—and sometimes cultural—stakeholders travel to develop relationships with prospective foreign partners. Subnational governments may decide to organize their own trade missions, but they may also join a trade mission organized by their federal government. In recent years, the educational sector has given a lot of traction to subnational diplomacy as States compete in attracting more foreign students to their countries and educational systems. In India, subnational governments have been particularly active at this level (Sridharan 2003).

Finally, a less frequent, but important tool used by subnational governments for establishing formal relationships is the establishment of an office abroad. Subnational governments have developed many trade or tourism offices in different cities around the world. For example, in recent years, the State of California has opened its own China Trade Office in Shanghai to promote commercial exchanges between China and California. In the context of European integration, the province of Salzburg in Austria was the first to establish subnational relations in Austria with the European Union in 1992 and the first to establish a delegation in 1996. Austria is not alone; the German lands, like Baden-Württemberg, also have their own delegations in the European Union.

These are only a few examples of the instruments and strategies used by subnational government to develop their foreign affairs and pursue their own interests. In this chapter, we will discuss in further details three approaches to subnational cultural diplomacy. The first approach has to do with a tradition dating back to the British Empire: the agent-generals in Canada and Australia. Agent-generals have existed in virtually every part of the British Empire, but in Canada and Australia, this function was the seed for a different kind of international relationship. The second approach has to do with cultural diplomatic activities related to identity affirmation. There are many subnational states that have strong claims to cultural distinction, and these claims are not simply part of how they engage with their federal administration or other partners of the federation; they are also a tool for international relations. Finally, the third approach relates to situations in which subnational entities participate in international forums and international organizations. In this case, we wish to illustrate how subnational states not only engage in bilateral relations, but make use of existing organizations to conduct their own subnational paradiplomacy.

5.1   The Agent-General Tradition in Australia and Canada

In Australia and Canada, most subnational governments have established official delegations in London. These delegations are contact points between British authorities and the subnational governments and legislatures. These delegations cannot engage in consular activities; they simply do not have these powers. Nonetheless, these delegations do provide a range of services: information about higher education, trade advice, organizing a subnational visits, and organizing cultural activities. While London is an important centre, these delegations have evolved and many subnational governments have established their quarters in other countries over time. Cultural activities that offer a distinctive view of the state or province are among the most important tasks of agent-generals; it is a tool that assists states in their work at the international level. In this section, we will present the reasons behind the development and persistence of this unusual institution that is linked to the British imperial history, as well as to the development of Australian and Canadian federalisms.

Examining the State-formation processes of Canada and Australia is important in understanding why the function of the agent-general was first developed. A first and fundamental element that led to the creation of the agent-general function was the colonial status of Canada and Australia— both of which were part of the British Empire. Despite the existence of local colonial governments, affairs conducted in London remained crucial to the administration of Canada and Australia up until the introduction of the Statute of Westminster in 1931, which granted both countries autonomy from the acts promulgated in the British parliament.

For a long period of time, the foreign affairs of Britain's colonies were strictly conducted by the British government; for the better benefits of its Empire, British colonies were forbidden from establishing their own representation abroad. However, colonies were allowed to establish offices in and send representatives to London as it was not considered foreign territory (Hilliker 1990: 5). To administer and coordinate colonial affairs with London, colonies—from the Americas and the West Indies, in particular—relied on envoys established in London to act as liaison officers. The origins of the term "agent-general" are difficult to trace. However, as was reported in a correspondence from a former agent-general, annexed to the Hansard of parliamentary debates of New Zealand in 1879, at the occasion of a new nomination for an agent-general: "The designation is, I believe, from that which was formerly borne by the representatives of the New England States before the declaration of American independence" (New Zealand, Parliament 1879: D3-2). Before American Independence, the colony of Nova Scotia (Canada)—a territory adjacent to New England—also had a presence in London through an agent-general, dating back to 1762 (Elliott 1988). Similarly, it is in 1787 that New South Wales (Australia) established its first agent-general office in London (New South Wales 2017). In sum, the function of agent-general takes its roots in the complexity of colonial governments of the eighteenth century; agents-general was acting as liaison officers, centralizing information and coordinating decision-making for the colonies from their London offices. In many cases, the existence of an agent-general was also seen as a status symbol for the colony in question—a position that inferred a measure of influence and clout in the metropolis.

The persistence, not to say survival, of the agent-general function following the development of both the Canadian and Australian federations remains puzzling. In Canada, the British North America Act of 1867 federated the Provinces of Canada (Ontario and Québec), New Brunswick, and Nova Scotia. The federation grew with the addition of new colonies and territories, a process that was still active well into the twentieth century—most notably with the introduction of Newfoundland and Labrador in 1949. Provinces that had representation in London kept it active, and, in some cases, new delegations were established for provinces where representation was inexistent. The provinces of Ontario and Québec developed their representations in London after the confederation, despite the creation of a High-Commission of Canada in London that would have otherwise served as representation for Canada as a whole.

The persistence and institutionalization of the agent-general function in the governments and public services of Canadian provinces and Australian states is the result of four converging forces. The first force was driven by transformations affecting Britain and the organization of its public administration. Published in 1854, the Northcote-Trevelyan Report raises concerns about patronage and the efficiency of the public sector. While this report may be somewhat mythicized in the grand narratives of modern State development, it does point to the fact that the organization and efficiency of the civil service were being debated at the time, with some stakeholders calling for greater professionalism and expertise in the conduct of public duties. The same year, the (re)creation of a mechanism and institutional entity to manage colonial affairs—the Colonial Office—marked a new era in the colonial/metropolis relationship, wherein colonial matters were expected to be handled with greater efficiency (Newbury 2014). Before this period, agents-general primarily handled commercial duties, such as securing payments for colonial enterprises or handling trade-related matters with shipping companies, for instance. Some agents-general would also, on occasion, act as "emigration agents" on behalf of their colonial patrons as a means of promoting the circulation of labour from the metropolis to the colonies.

The organization and development of the Colonial Office contributed to the institutionalization of the "representational" and political duties of agents-general. On the one hand, the broad areas of policy covered by the Colonial Office required that agents-general become more fluently versed in political affairs. On the other hand, the Colonial Office contributed to formalizing the channels of communications and lines of command between London and its colonies. Published in 1890, this excerpt from a paper published by a well-known British politician who had travelled the colonial sphere—Stanley Leighton—is revealing of the agents-general's place in the colonial administration:

> The States which enjoy responsible government possess a highly-trained staff of public men equal to our own. The Colonial Ministries are represented in London by Agents-General, and are in constant communication with them. The Agents-General are, in fact, the Ambassadors of the Colonies to England and the Governors are the Ambassadors of England to the Colonies. The influence of the latter is on the wane, of the former is on the increase. [...]. (Leighton 1890:147)

However, beyond the basic architecture of colonial administration and the place of agents-general therein, the firsthand observations of Leighton (1890) also convey a growing perception that the Colonial Office might not have been the most appropriate and efficient place to liaise about colonial affairs and raise the following questions:

> Should a Colony provide itself with some authoritative channel of communication with Parliament independent of the Colonial Office? Is it expedient to attach to the office of the Agents-General some representatives in Parliament authorized to express without intermediary the Agent-General's opinion when the interests of a Colony are at stake? (p. 158)

To these questions, Leighton's answers were highly in favour of a greater and more direct role for the agent-general in matters of colonial governance. Despite this response, the Colonial Office did contribute to the institutionalization of the agent-general function; it helped define its function in greater political terms, as a representative of colonial self-government interests.

The second defining force that shaped the nature of agents-general is related to the development of the Canadian and Australian federations. Agents-general had assumed an important role in the negotiations that led to the development of the Canadian federation in 1867 and the Australian federation in 1901. For instance, the Colonial Office's records speak to the technical importance and political influence of agents-general in the processes that led to the formation of the Commonwealth of Australia (Great-Britain, Parliament 1900). Agents-general had also been performing some commercial duties on behalf of the colonies: they would assume payments or sign receipts for transactions conducted with the self-governing colonies.

162   J. PAQUETTE

A third force that shaped the function of agents-general was a distinctively cultural one and can be found in the Colonial Exhibitions of the late 1800s and early 1900s. From the Great Exhibition of London in 1851, to the Intercolonial exhibitions in Australia (between 1866 and 1876), all the way to the series of Colonial Exhibitions that occurred in London and throughout the world beginning in the 1880s up to the start of World War II (Hoffenberg 2001), these exhibitions all contributed to a demand for cultural and administrative representatives by "natives" who knew the colonies and had their interests at heart. These exhibits contributed to the need for cultural representatives, thus shaping an important element of the agent-general function. The participation of agents-general in the colonial exhibits significantly contributed to defining the symbolic aspect of the function.

Finally, the fourth force that contributed to the institutionalization of the function of agents-general from the Australian states and Canadian provinces has to do with the fact that these were extremely useful agents in providing information for prospective migrants. In both federations, there was a competition to attract European migrants to help expand their respective labour forces, and agent-generals were strategic in this competition between subnational governments. Migration from the British Isles and Ireland, in particular, was seen as desirable by Canadian and Australian subnational governments. The desire to increase migration from the British Isles and Ireland was particularly well-conveyed by a public allocution delivered by W. C. Noxon, who occupied the function of agent-general for Ontario in the 1920s. According to Noxon, the focus on attracting people from the British Isles was a question of character—the "quality of the people" of the British Isles—that made them highly desirable (Noxon 1924: 138). As a result of these efforts to actively attract migrants, in 1913 alone, more than 190,800 individuals of Irish or British descent had elected British North America (Canada or Newfoundland) as their new homes, while a total of 56,800 chose Australia (p. 140).

In the 1920s, the province of Ontario offered better support to prospective migrants and guaranteed "employment at good wages on arrival," with employment offers that exceeded those of "rival" provinces (Noxon 1924: 143). This competition—and the pressures placed on agents-general to sufficiently recruit migrants—is saliently highlighted in an article published in a 1912 issue of the Sherbrooke Daily Record—a newspaper published in the province of Québec. Notably, this article includes an interview with a Québec migration officer working with the agent-general who reportedly had to compete with representatives of other provinces. In this respect, public relations were a key element of the work undertaken by agents-general:

> England and Scotland are flooded with Dominion literature pertaining largely to the West. There is also, an abundance of literature on Ontario and the Maritime provinces, [...] I booked two families for points in Stanstead county [Quebec]. Before sailing other agents switched them off and sent them to Winnipeg [Manitoba], [...] We must advertise. Big results cannot be accomplished without it. [...] The need of the hour is advertising matter. (Sherbrooke Daily Record, April 3, 1912: 1)

Over the years, the need for attracting more migrants necessitated that governments expand the scope of their recruitment beyond the British Isles and Ireland, into other Northern European countries. London offices acted as a pivotal coordination point for agents-general to organize and plan the passages of new populations of (im)migrants. Beyond London, the province of Québec, notably, sent an agent-general to Paris to establish diplomatic relations and support any potential immigration to the province.

The bureaucratization of colonial administration, the political value of the role, the cultural function it could assume in the British Empire, and the strategic place it occupied all contributed to keeping the function of the agent-general active—and, even, to popularizing it. Why would subnational governments keep their delegation? In Australia, after federation, governments maintained their delegations. In Canada, some provinces kept their agents-general after the 1876 confederation, while others who did not have representation decided to create one. Why is that? Answers to these questions can be found in the dynamic and politics of State-formation and federalism.

In April 1903, the agent-general function was greatly discussed during the Commonwealth Conference between Australia's state premiers. The question of agents-general was widely discussed. While it was argued—mainly by the Tasmanian representative to the conference—that the establishment of a High-Commission[1] [an embassy] should suffice

---

[1] High-Commission is the term used for a diplomatic office between members of the Commonwealth. It is a symbolic term, but it refers today to an embassy, to a diplomatic representation.

164 J. PAQUETTE

and the agent-general function should be abolished, the other state representatives were not of the same opinion. According to Sir John See, then-Premier of New South Wales:

> In regard to the Agent-General, I have given this matter a good deal of thought, and cannot see my way clear to delegate to a High Commissioner, when he is appointed, the business arrangements of this State, because they are considerable, [...] As far as I am concerned, I will be very sorry to see, and certainly would not consent to hand over, the great commercial affairs or our State to a High Commissioner, who would not be in touch with us at all, and could not very well serve six masters, [...] we most emphatically prefer to have our own Agent-General. (Australia, Legislative Assembly of NSW 1903: 53)

This excerpt from the meeting of Australian state premiers suggests that the agents-general were maintained and redefined by the dynamics and politics of cooperation and competition that characterizes federations. Given the constitutional structure and history of colonial relationships following federation, it is significant that agents-general remained in office and was not supplanted by the development of High-Commissions. Similarly, in Canada, it was the idea of increasing the subnational presence in London—not removing it—that became widely discussed. As suggested by this excerpt from an article written by a London correspondent of *The Globe*—a Canadian newspaper—the contribution of agents-general in other jurisdictions was an item of political discussion and debate in Canada:

> That Canada should be represented in the English labour market makes no doubt. Each of the principal Australian colonies now has its Agent-General in this country, and when necessary, these gentlemen act in consort for the great benefit of the communities they represent. [...] Various theories have been broached from time to time, as to the representation of the colonies in the Imperial Government, but apparently insuperable difficulties stand in the way of such arrangement. (The Globe 1869: 2)

Columnists in the Canadian province of Ontario, in particular, were eager for greater representation in London as a mean of better accessing both the British and world markets. This also conveys the social and political dynamics of a federal society, where representation and presence of subnational partners on the international scene—then, mostly,

London—was of an important value. In some federations, there are implicit ideas or suspicions that some members' interests will be better represented than others. As such, having representation is of the utmost important in terms of ensuring member states are not completely ignored or forgotten.

To summarize, the agent-general function is rooted in the development of the British Empire. Agents-general were agents of coordination between London and the colonies, with the function eventually developing into a semi-diplomatic role. Two important elements must be kept in mind when considering the role of the agent-general. First, the agent-general's function and relationship with London should have, technically, disappeared with the Canadian and Australian federations being put in place. However, what happened is opposite: subnational governments that did not have similar functions decided to create their own agent-general positions after they joined the federation. Second, as Australia and Canada gained autonomy between 1907 and 1939, they normalized their relations with London in diplomatic terms. Therefore, subnational governments were entering into a "grey zone" when it came to their capacity to conduct foreign affairs on a bilateral level because foreign affairs are federal powers. As a result, cultural affairs were an important and non-threatening way for subnational governments to maintain an international relationship in London.

Over time, on the seeds of this former colonial institution of the agent-general, a series of subnational offices were developed across the globe. After World War II, Australian and Canadian subnational governments developed representations that were no longer centred exclusively in London. Over the span of three decades beginning in the 1960s, subnational governments in Canada and Australia began to engage with governments in Europe and the USA. For example, New South Wales opened an office in New York in 1958 and another in Los Angeles in 1978. Similarly, the Government of Victoria used its London office as a hub to further its relations with continental Europe and, eventually, opened an office in Frankfurt in 1982. In Canada, the Government of Ontario opened offices in Chicago (1953), New York (1956), and Los Angeles (1967), as well as in Milan (1963), Stockholm (1968), and Brussels (1969), among a host of others. The Government of Québec opened general delegations in New York (1940), Paris (1961), Munich (1971), Brussels (1972), and Mexico City (1980), and a series of more modest offices (delegations) in Rome (1965), Los Angeles (1970), and

166   J. PAQUETTE

Boston (1970) among others. Ontario, Alberta, and Québec also opened offices in Japan as early as 1969, 1970, and 1973, respectively. Japan was also a focus of attention for Australian subnational governments who established offices in Tokyo throughout the 1960s, 1970s, and 1980s (e.g. Western Australia and New South Wales in 1968, Victoria 1978, and Queensland 1980) (Rix 1999: 90).

During this period, the function of agent-general was not only characterized by a new focus on activities that extended beyond London to other areas of the globe, it was also characterized by a progressive redefinition of the function's role that included not only trade, but tourism and cultural activities. The following excerpt from a speech delivered at the Empire Club in Toronto in 1974, by Ward Cornell, then-Ontario agent-general in London, presents an interesting self-reflection and presentation of the duties of an agent-general during this era:

> Last year, 1973, the present Minister of Industry and Tourism, the Hon. Claude Bennett, re-defined in the Legislature the role of the Agent General in this modern era to reflect, more accurately, the responsibilities assumed. The Agent General has dual responsibilities–operational and representational. [...] Operational responsibilities refer to the programmes and. activities of the Ministry of Industry and Tourism. [...] In the area of business development, which is the trade and industry side of our operation, Ontario House entertains about thirteen missions per year, a little bit better than one per month. [...] Tourism is another important part of our United Kingdom operation. Our thrust over the past two years has been to focus our attention and energy on what we call the travel trade. [...] If a management consultant doing a job description analysis were to ask me how my time was spent (they always ask that question, don't they?) I would say 50/50 between operations and representation. [...] Representation involves supporting visiting Ontario cultural groups ranging from the Toronto Symphony and the Mime Theatre to an under-fourteen boys' all-star soccer team from Kitchener. It involves making contact with both the elected British Government representatives and the British civil servants. (Cornell 1974)

This excerpt conveys the main duties for which an agent-general was responsible, which can broadly be divided into operational and representational activities. On the one hand, operational activities included day-to-day operations related to the office and its attachment to a ministry. This operational dimension also involved the organization of visits (missions): economic missions from small businesses; exhibition missions where select businesses were invited to present their products; and "product prospecting missions and business opportunities missions". On the other hand, the representational activities were, arguably, primarily related to cultural events. Despite the great variety of activities described in the excerpt above—from highbrow cultural events to minor sporting events—these activities conveyed that cultural relations were an important element of an agent-general's representational work. In the absence of real diplomatic mandates, agents-general specialized in social and cultural events as a way of engaging in political activity. Sustaining fairs, cultural events, and film festivals were important facets of the work carried out by the agents-general in their delegations abroad.

The 1960s, 1970s, and, to some extent, the 1980s were the most prolific decades for state and provincial government paradiplomatic activities (in terms of the number of agent-general offices established and resources made available to them). During this era, agent-general offices and activities had an official—not to say very "diplomatic"—flare to them. In the 1970s, some offices—like the New South Wales office in London—exceeded fifty staff members. During the 1980s and entering into the 1990s, Canadian provinces and Australian states began to dramatically review their presences abroad. Ontario, for instance, closed all its agent-general missions—including its missions in London—in 1993; Tasmania did the same in 1992. Many Canadian provinces and Australian states opted for more modest operations and kept their agent-general delegations to a minimum, preferring, instead to join operations with their federal governments.

Towards the end of the 1990s—after a decade of detraction and disinterest where global representation was concerned—Canadian provinces and Australian states began, anew, to entertain the idea of establishing their presences abroad. Since the late 1990s, the "agent-general" term has been increasingly reserved for provincial/state representatives located in London offices. In recent years, a new terminology has emerged to describe the agent-general function in other jurisdictions: (trade and investment) commissioner or delegate. With this new nomenclature, there has also been a new wave of activities characterized by a new geographic focus on China, Southeast Asia, and India. For instance, Alberta, Western Australia, Québec, and Queensland have all significantly expanded their paradiplomatic activities in Asia since the late 1990s. The nature of an agent's (or commissioner) work has remained largely associated with providing expertise to, and establishing contacts for, businesses, as well as facilitating the international visits of business and trade partners. Since the late 1990s, the representational activities of agents have had less to do with events and formal cultural diplomacy, and more to do with branding and providing opportunities to market a regional identity. Assisting university tours and attracting foreign students have also become important parts of an agent's yearly activities.

The most striking and important changes that came during this latter period have had to do with the scale and focus of the agent-general's (or commissioner's) work: Canadian and Australian delegations have placed less emphasis on being satellites that connect with a country's national government, and more emphasis on developing regional relationships and collaboration. First, delegations follow a new geography and operate on a regional scale. State and provincial governments establish offices to connect with regions (e.g. Guangdong, Tamil Nadu, Shandong, etc.). This logic is also perceptible in the offices Canadian provinces and Australian states have established throughout Europe and North America, where a focus on regions has become more salient. Second, the formalization of relationships with other governments also comes from a statement of mutual collaboration—a twinning agreement—that officialises interregional relations. These twinning agreements rely primarily on cultural material. Culture acts as a tool to create the symbolism of political relationships. Collaborations are defined as being based on exchanges in performing arts; they may also take form in the development of a festival or a series of cultural events celebrating the relationship between regional governments. The new regional scale of subnational relations has also been used to further business relations with fewer possibilities for entering into politically hostile relationships with federal governments. Additionally, this emphasis on collaboration also speaks to the capacity of states and provinces to engage with regions and other subnational governments to further their governance capacity in a variety of policy areas—from trade, to environment, to energy issues. Cultural relationships are a key component in the articulation of these paradiplomatic exchanges. Agents-general—or, now, trade officers—will sponsor "South-Australian Arts Week" or the venue of an exhibit for a British Columbian artist in London to support their presence and visibility, and create a more or less neutral platform to initiate discussion on commercial or political affairs.

5.2 Affirming Identity and Cultural Aspirations

As reminded by Chad Rector (2009), most federations proceed by federating members who may have similar institutional weight—from a constitutional perspective; however, some members may, in fact, have more or less powers at the economic level than others. Other federations are uneven because some of their members aspire to different social objectives than the majority of the members of a federation. In other circumstances, these differences can be fuelled by a difference in language or culture that is spoken in some parts of a country and that differs from the majority culture or language. In some federations, national minorities (Beauregard 2018) are in majority in a subnational state, and this contributes to the cooperative and competitive dynamics of federalism. Foreign affairs have to do with commercial interests; they have to do with prestige and political recognition. For some subnational states, while these are important elements, the pursuit of foreign affairs is done, also, to affirm their identity or, at the very least, to affirm a form of difference. Implicitly, the federal government is seen as unable to fully represent the subnational states at the international level. This is, at least, the claim. Therefore, establishing direct bilateral or multilateral relations is seen as politically important by these states.

Whether it is for a cultural, linguistic, or regionalist affirmation, occupying the international scene is important for subnational states. In this section, we will talk about the cases of Flanders, Québec, and Bavaria. As much as these cases are about the expression of something different about their national or regional identities, their actions in the international sphere should not be seen as divorced from economic and other political interests. In fact, issues of culture and economy are often mutually reinforced (Beauregard 2018); they often act in unison. Therefore, as much as identity is a thrust, this should be nuanced and contrasted with other rationalities for acting on the international scene.

In Flanders, the international relations are carried out by the regional Department of Foreign Affairs. Following the constitutional reforms of 1993 in Belgium, the country's regions were allowed to carry out their own diplomatic activities and international relations (Criekemans 2010). What this constitutional reform recognized was the capacity for the regions to represent themselves on matters that are constitutionally defined as regional competences—which includes cultural affairs. Since this confirmation of regional powers in international relations, the region of Flanders has expended its presence all throughout the globe. Particularly, Flanders operates in five key areas of international affairs: European Union-related diplomacy, sustainable development, trade and infrastructures, peace and security, and culture and science.

In Flanders, cultural diplomacy is conducted as an interdepartmental affair and is, therefore, shared between the Department of Culture and the Department of Foreign Affairs. The cultural diplomacy of the Flemish state is described according to this mandate and these objectives:

> The cultural dimension in its international relations is of great importance to Flanders. The Flemish cultural diplomacy:
>
> - supports the cultural sector and creative industries in their international ambitions and networking where useful, always aiming at promoting cooperation and exchange,
> - enhances the international visibility and reputation of Flanders through the arts and heritage sector,
> - considers culture as a bearer of values and believes in the international relations of Flanders and the European Union,
> - fosters mutual understanding and trust in the relations with foreign countries.
> - The Department of Foreign Affairs acts as bridge between the broad cultural field and the diplomatic network of the Government of Flanders. It supports specific projects or initiatives abroad either representing the shared interests of the cultural sector and the government, or by means of exchange of ideas, values or traditions, fostering relations with other countries. For each of these cases the department consults with other entities such as the Department of Culture, Youth and Media, Tourism Flanders and Flanders Investment & Trade. (Flanders, Department of Foreign Affairs 2018a)

Since the early 1990s, Flanders has developed a series of official diplomatic representations across the globe. It has permanent missions in Berlin, Paris, New York, Vienna, Madrid, Pretoria, London, The Hague, and Warsaw. Flanders has also established trade offices in other countries. Flanders' diplomacy operates on three levels: bilateral (direct relations with countries), multilateral (participating in international organizations), and bi-regional (or bilateral) relations between regions. In recognition of its specific aspirations and its status in the Belgian federation, Flanders has assumed a certain leadership in developing bilateral relations with regional or subnational governments. It has relationships with Catalonia, the Basque Country, Bavaria, Wales, Northern Ireland, Scotland, and Québec. In fact, the development of international relations at the regional or subnational level was one of the first steps taken by Flanders in the development of its international affairs. In fact, one of the first formal international relations established by Flanders was with Québec in the early 1980s through scientific cooperation. The Flemish Department of Foreign Affairs describes the nature of its relationship with Québec as follows:

> Quebec is one of the ten provinces of the Federal State of Canada. The official language is French. Quebec was one of the first partners with whom Flanders established bilateral relations. The cooperation between both regions originates in the parallels between the status of Quebec within Canada, and that of Flanders in Belgium. From the outset, language and culture assumed an important role within relations. (Flanders, Department of Foreign Affairs 2018b)

Alienation from Belgian politics has been a sentiment shared by many Flemish citizens, some of whom aspire to create their own country. There has been, in Flanders, a general sympathy for the case of Québec in Canada. There is certainly, in this sense, a form of solidarity between the two subnational states.

Flanders is also active in cultural cooperation, having established cultural cooperatives with Bavaria and Australia—the latter of which revolves around the heritage of the two World Wars. Cultural affairs are important for Flanders as they help sustain the visibility of the state and its culture—which has been an important challenge for many subnational communities who aspire to be recognized globally. Culture is, in this sense, a powerful instrument.

As much as we have established that some of the international affairs activities undertaken by Flanders have been done in relation to a quest to affirm their identity, these activities are also heavily driven by commercial and altruistic political interests—such as the quest for world peace. Additionally, these powers have been made and became recognized by the Belgian Constitution. However, these powers are also found in the French-speaking part of Belgium. Wallonie-Bruxelles International is the international Department of Foreign Affairs for French-speaking Belgians. Like Flanders, Wallonia is active in the cultural sector, through support for activities, events, and international programmes in architecture, dance, visual arts, fashion, publishing, literature, and music. Similarly, Wallonia has delegations in Alger, Berlin, Bucharest, Paris, Dakar, Hanoi, Beijing, Québec City, Tunis, and Warsaw, among many more. The approach differs from that of Flanders, but Wallonia also has its own international interests and conducts its cultural diplomacy around the world.

In Canada, Québec is the province with, perhaps, the most different social and political aspirations vis-à-vis the nation and other provinces. It should be noted that Québec is not the only place in Canada where there is a French-speaking population; there are important populations of francophones in Ontario (Franco-Ontarians) and New Brunswick (Acadians), as well as a number of French-speaking (minority) communities scattered across the different Canadian provinces. The case of Québec is different, however, since the province is comprised of a majority of French-speakers. Additionally, in the late 1960s and early 1970s, a movement in favour of secession took place, with some of these energies having been channelled into political parties. The Parti Québécois, a social-democrat and secessionist party, came to power and variously governed the province of Québec throughout the 1980s, 1990s and early 2000s. In 1980 and 1995, the Parti Québécois organized referendums on Québec's sovereignty, though it was unsuccessful in achieving its objective of a majority mandate to secede in both cases. Nevertheless, this strong will to express Québécois identity could not be more strongly expressed than through the idea of creating a country of its own.

Interestingly, Québec has established its foreign affairs along the lines of the agent-general system—a system that is deeply rooted in the British Empire. In other words, the institution used by Québec to conduct its foreign affairs is, in fact, a very common catalyst for subnational relations in Canada. Of course, by comparison, Québec is certainly one of the most active provinces on the international scene, and it is certainly one of the better equipped in terms of having permanent offices abroad. Another important nuance that should be specified is that Québec had established diplomatic relations years before secessionist parties existed. In this sense, diplomatic relations are not a creation to be understood strictly along the lines of a secessionist agenda. Additionally, the idea of affirming a distinctive identity in Québec should not necessarily or automatically be understood as a will to create a country. There is, in the political tradition of Canada and Québec, a political sentiment that Québec is different—a sentiment shared by some federalist politicians and members of the civil society. In fact, a certain version of "nationalism" has been intellectually and politically held by the Liberal Party of Québec, the main—if not only—federalist political party in the province. The Liberal Party of Québec and the Parti Québécois have contributed to both the development of Québec's foreign affairs and the establishment of cultural diplomatic relations with a number of States.

Notably, Québec has had an agent-general in London for a long time, which facilitated its reconnection with France on diplomatic terms when Britain and France were in good standing. In fact, the collaboration between Britain and France around the War in Crimea, in 1854, can be seen as a turning point for the colony (Chartier 1996: 54). In 1882, Canada established diplomatic representation in Paris; Hector Fabre was nominated as both ambassador for Canada and agent-general for Québec. During Fabre's mandate, Québec's delegation in Paris was a vitrine for French–Canadian artists. Diplomatic relations between Québec and France were organized around educational and cultural missions. Since then, the Délégation Générale du Québec à Paris was established in 1961, which recognizes and grants Québec with diplomatic immunity and other diplomatic privileges.

While Paris has been a focal point for cultural diplomacy for Québec, over the years the province has developed representation around the world. In the 1940s, Québec opened delegations in the USA; and in the 1970s, it established delegations in Brussels, Tokyo and Munich. In total, Québec has eight general delegations focused on bilateral relations; five delegations focused on economic affairs; twelve regular offices in Europe and Asia; four antennas where it currently develops relationships with regional partners in emerging technologies; and two multilateral delegations.

International cultural affairs are governed by Québec's Ministry of Culture, established in 1961, in collaboration with its Ministry of Foreign Affairs, established in 1967. In conducting its international cultural affairs, Québec acts on principles that are similar to those recognized in Flanders insofar as the province operates and collaborates internationally in fields that fall within its jurisdiction according to the constitution. Education and culture are powers that can be claimed by the provincial legislature. Since 1965, the Government of Québec has established a principle known as the Doctrine Gérin-Lajoie—named after a cabinet minister who established that Québec was constitutionally capable and had the political interest to conduct its own foreign affairs in the jurisdictions over which it is sovereign (Paquin 2014).

174   J. PAQUETTE

Culture is a central element of Québec's subnational diplomacy. Québec subnational diplomacy includes a focus on economic and global development, the promotion of the French language around the world, and cultural affairs. In 2017, the federalist government of the Parti Libéral du Québec defined the three main priorities of is foreign policy as follow: "(1) Build a more prosperous Québec; (2) Contribute to a more secure, sustainable and equitable world; (3) Promote Québec creativity, culture, knowledge and specificity" (Québec, Relations internationales et francophonie 2017). Additionally, Québec's cultural industries are an important part of its foreign activities. As suggested by the ministry: "Europe is Québec's largest cultural market for Québec creators and, like us, is concerned with preserving cultural diversity" (Québec, Relations internationales et francophonie 2017).

Bavaria is another case where customs, traditions, and religion, not to mention sentiments towards the federation, all play in favour of affirming its own sense of identity abroad. Bavaria has its own extensive network of international delegations and is active at the international level. The Free State of Bavaria also has its own constitution that affirms its distinction and commitment to preserving and promoting its distinctive social and cultural differences. Bavaria's international activities are carried out by the Ministry of Economic Affairs, Energy and Technology. Since the 1990s, Bavaria has established delegations around the world. Bavaria now has almost thirty foreign delegations—including delegations in Argentina, Canada, the USA, Chile, Asia, China, Hungary, and many other places around the world. Bavaria's foreign relations and delegations tend to be driven by economic missions and orientations, though they can also entail collaborations with the Ministry of Arts and Culture as a means of structuring its mandates in cultural diplomacy. According to the Ministry of Arts and Culture:

> Since the fall of the Berlin Wall and the Iron Curtain, the Free State of Bavaria has concentrated its efforts most particularly on encouraging intercultural activities with the Central, South Eastern and Eastern European States. Thanks to numerous bilateral and multilateral projects and the exchange of experts, it has been possible to discover common ground in a variety of ways, and to provide fresh stimuli. [...]
>
> Cultural exchange must not be allowed to stop at Europe's borders. Historical connections and political considerations have led to institutionalised partnerships with South Africa (the Provinces of the West Cape and Gauteng), Brazil (Sao Paulo), China (Shandong Province) the USA

(California) and Canada (Québec). The most recent partnership has been established with Karnataka in India. (Bavaria, Ministry of Arts and Culture 2018)

According to Criekemans (2010), these are similar instruments, but they also share noticeable differences. In the case of Bavaria, trade plays an essential role, but the foreign delegations are used as points of entry to achieving other purposes, including cultural diplomacy (p. 40). In the case of Flanders, the region's initial foreign activities focused on cultural and bilateral subnational relations; however, since the 2000s, Flanders' foreign activities have evolved in ways that better mesh with other important agendas of economic and technological importance (p. 39). As for Québec, and Wallonia for that matter, Criekemans notes that "both international cultural policy and initiatives in the area of educational cooperation remain very much central in the paradiplomatic activities of these regions" (p. 41).

5.3   International Organizations and the European Union

So far, this chapter has insisted on bilateral relations—on the development of subnational international relations—by focusing on diplomatic relations and cultural cooperation between States and subnational governments (Flanders and France, Germany and Poland), or between two subnational governments (Québec and Flanders, Bavaria, Wallonia). There are, however, important multilateral forms of cooperation in cultural affairs. Some institutions, like UNESCO or the Francophonie, are important international organs that govern cultural affairs at a multilateral level. Similarly, issues of European integration also concern matters that are important to cultural affairs—whether it is labour laws and living conditions of artists, the promotion of a European citizenship through the arts, or matters of education or heritage preservation—and the integration may have important impacts for subnational governments.

For federations like Germany and Austria, the European integration represents a number of important and interesting institutional challenges. According to Sassatelli, "European cultural policy, which was conceived, even more self-consciously than at other levels, as an instrument to build a cultural identity for the Europe of the European Union" (2002: 436). And there is, according to Sassatelli, a federalist sentiment for unity and identity that is at play in European integration and, more specifically, in the European Union's approach to cultural identity (p. 438). The European Union's cultural policy instruments include a number of measures and programmes. In its main areas of artistic intervention, the European Union funds educational projects; provides grants for artists; administers the famous programme, European Capital of Culture; and has established a "Creative Europe" policy with a budget of close to €1.5 million (European Union 2018). Because culture is a subnational matter in Germany and Austria, the participation of subnational governments in cultural matters is required; it is a key component of their institutional reality. In both cases, inter-ministerial conferences can help to inform the federal government in which direction to go; in practice, however, the presence of subnational delegations as part of European Union activities is crucial for cultural affairs. In Austria, the province of Vorarlberg has been a very active participant in multilateral activities; it has been actively represented and working at the European level with its own subnational delegation, but has also been participating in a variety of instances—such as the committee for the regions—made to give voice to regions (Vorarlberg 2018). The European Union's regional policy also has important elements that can affect regions in a country. The capacity to access European Union information and debate it is crucial, which makes the organization of an office in Brussels a strategic point of entry for acquiring the necessary information for domestic policymaking.

Other multilateral institutions—like UNESCO—are important for the future of culture and cultural policy. In Canada, the federal government agreed in 2006 to include a representative of the Government of Québec as part of its permanent UNESCO delegation. While this may have practical implications, it also has a symbolic nature and is an important instrument in working towards a cooperative federalism in cultural affairs. Similarly, on some occasions, the Québec government was used strategically in the negotiations by the federal government. The negotiation around the Convention on the Protection and Promotion of the Diversity of Cultural Expressions is a good example. The Government of Québec was determined to make sure that cultural protection also meant that governments around the world could keep subsidizing and protecting their cultural sectors against pushes for liberalizations. The Québec government was, then, in a better position to establish relations with partners on cultural affairs in Europe, using a strategy that did not compromise Canada's competing agendas on commerce and free trade.

The *Organisation internationale de la francophonie* is another good example of multilateral organizations where cultural affair is widely discussed. The organization is the result of a long history of multilateral collaborations on education and culture between ministers of French-speaking countries. In the 1960s, the organization was first embodied through a higher education cooperation that, in the 1970s, became the *Agence de cooperation culturelle et technique*—which represented a more formalized cooperation between members, and gave the impetus to create the ensemble of programmes and platforms that the organization has become known for today. The idea behind the organization was to reunite the political elite of French-speaking countries to carve out strategies to protect and promote the French language. Many innovations developed from this multilateral cooperation—including the funding of TV5, a French international channel that airs programmes and news from public broadcasters of France, Belgium, Switzerland, Luxemburg, and Canada, as well programmes of its own aimed at providing a better representation of the interests of the global south. The francophonie is also widely used by subnational governments in the promotion of their cultural interests. Switzerland has a national delegation, as does Belgium (since the 1970s) and its subnation, the Fédération Bruxelles-Wallonie (since 1980). Canada has a total of four delegations: Canada (since 1970), Québec (since 1971), New Brunswick (since 1977), and Ontario (since 2016)—though the latter's delegation holds only an observer status and, thus, cannot vote on any francophonie motions. Similarly, Louisiana was recognized as an observer in 2018.

References

Aguirre, I. (1999). Making Sense of Paradiplomacy? An Intertextual Enquiry About a Concept in Search of a Definition. *Regional & Federal Studies, 9*(1), 185–209. https://doi.org/10.1080/13597569908421078.

Australia, Legislative Assembly of NSW. (1903). *Report of the Proceedings of the Conference Between the Premiers of the States of the Commonwealth of Australia*. Sydney: W. A. Gulick, Government Printer.

Bavaria, Ministry of Arts and Culture. (2018). *International Cultural Affairs*. Retrieved from the Ministry of Arts and Culture's website https://www.km.bayern.de/art-and-culture/international.html

Beauregard, D. (2018). *Cultural Policy and Industries of Identity: Québec, Scotland, & Catalonia*. London: Palgrave.

Blanc, C. S., Basch, L., & Schiller, N. G. (1995). Transnationalism, Nation-states, and Culture. *Current Anthropology, 36*(4), 683–686.

Chaloux, A., & Paquin, S. (2013). Green Paradiplomacy and Water Resource Management in North America: The Case of the Great Lakes-St. Lawrence River Basin. *Canadian Foreign Policy Journal, 19*(3), 308–322. https://doi.org/10.1080/11926422.2013.845582.

Chartier, D. (1996). Hector Fabre et le Paris-Canada au coeur de la rencontre culturelle France-Québec de la fin du XIX e siècle. *Études françaises, 32*(3), 51–60.

Cornell, W. (1974, October 24). *The Empire Club of Canada Addresses* (pp. 58–70). Toronto, ON, Canada: The Empire Club. Retrieved online from the Empire Club's website http://speeches.empireclub.org/60461/data

Criekemans, D. (2010). Regional Sub-State Diplomacy from a Comparative Perspective: Quebec, Scotland, Bavaria, Catalonia, Wallonia and Flanders. *The Hague Journal of Diplomacy, 5*(1–2), 37–64.

Dąbrowski, M. (2013). Europeanizing Sub-national Governance: Partnership in the Implementation of European Union Structural Funds in Poland. *Regional Studies, 47*(8), 1363–1374. https://doi.org/10.1080/00343404.2011.628931.

Dickson, F. (2014). The Internationalisation of Regions: Paradiplomacy or Multi-level Governance?, *Geography Compass, 8*(10), 689–700. https://doi.org/10.1111/gec3.12152.

Duchacek, I. D. (1984). The International Dimension of Subnational Self-Government. *Publius, 14*(4), 5–31.

Elliott, S. (1988). *Nova Scotia in London: A History of Its Agents Generals, 1762–1988.* London: Office of the Agent General of Nova Scotia.

European Union. (2018). Culture in Cities and Regions. Policy document. Retrieved online from the European Union's website https://www.ec.europa.eu/culture/policy/culture-policies/cities-regions_en.

Flanders, Department of Foreign Affairs. (2018a). *Culture.* Retrieved from the Department of Foreign Affairs' website https://www.fdfa.be/en/culture-science/culture.

Flanders, Department of Foreign Affairs. (2018b). *Quebec.* Retrieved from the Department of Foreign Affairs' website https://www.fdfa.be/en/quebec.

Gilboa, E. (2008). Searching for a Theory of Public Diplomacy. *The Annals of the American Academy of Political and Social Science, 616*(1), 55–77. https://doi.org/10.1177/0002716207312142.

Great-Britain, Parliament. (1900). *Australia. Further Papers Relating to the Federation of the Australian Colonies.* Presented to Both Houses of Parliament by Command of her Majesty. London: Her Majesty's Stationery Office.

Hilliker, J. (1990). *Canada's Department of External Affairs* (Vol. I). Kingston: McGill-Queen's University Press.

Hoffenberg, P. H. (2001). *An Empire on Display: English, Indian and Australian Exhibitions from the Crystal Palace to the Great War.* Berkeley: University of California Press.

Johns, C. M., & Thorn, A. (2015). Subnational Diplomacy in the Great Lakes Region: Toward Explaining Variation Between Water Quality and Quantity Regimes. *Canadian Foreign Policy Journal, 21*(3), 195–211. https://doi.org/10.1080/11926422.2015.1035296.

Kingsbury, B. (1998). Sovereignty and Inequality. *European Journal of International Law, 9*(4), 599–625.

Klatt, M., & Wassenberg, B. (2017). Secondary Foreign Policy: Can Local and Regional Cross-Border Cooperation Function as a Tool for Peace-Building and Reconciliation? *Regional & Federal Studies, 27*(3), 205–218. https://doi.org/10.1080/13597566.2017.1350652

Lecours, A. (2002). Paradiplomacy: Reflections on the Foreign Policy and International Relations of Regions. *International Negotiation, 7*(1), 91–114. https://doi.org/10.1163/157180602401262456.

Leighton, S. (1890, October). The Colonial Office and the Colonies. *The National Review,* (92), 45–160. Document from the Foreign and Commonwealth Office Collection from John Rylands University Library, University of Manchester.

McHugh, J. T. (2015). Paradiplomacy, Protodiplomacy and the Foreign Policy Aspirations of Quebec and other Canadian Provinces. *Canadian Foreign Policy Journal, 21*(3), 238–256. https://doi.org/10.1080/11926422.2015.1031261.

Michelmann, H. J., & Soldatos, P. (1990). *Federalism and International Relations. The Role of Subnational Units.* Oxford: Oxford University Press.

Mingus, M. S. (2006). Transnationalism and Subnational Paradiplomacy: Are Governance Networks Perforating Sovereignty? *International Journal of Public Administration, 29*(8), 577–594. https://doi.org/10.1080/01900690500455305.

Mitchell, J. (1995). Lobbying 'Brussels'. *European Urban and Regional Studies, 2*(4), 287–298. https://doi.org/10.1177/096977649500200401.

Newbury, C. (2014). Patronage and Professionalism: Manning a Transitional Empire, 1760–1870. *The Journal of Imperial and Commonwealth History, 42*(2), 193–214. https://doi.org/10.1080/03086534.2013.851872.

New South Wales, State Archives and Records. (2017). The New South Wales Office, Sydney, Australia. Retrieved online from the New South Wales State's Archive's website. https://www.records.nsw.gov.au/agency/5133

New Zealand, Parliament. (1879). *Journals of the House of Representatives. Appendix. 7th Parliament, First Session, Vol. II. Wellington, New Zealand.* Retrieved online from the New Zealand's Parliament's website https://paperspast.natlib.govt.nz/parliamentary/AJHR1879-II.2.1.5.4?query=agent-general

Noxon, W. C. (1924). Empire Settlement. *Proceedings of the Royal Society of Arts, 72*(3713), 138–151.

Paquin, S. (2002). Paradiplomatie identitaire en catalogne et les relations Barcelone-Madrid. *Études Internationales, 33*(1), 57–90. https://doi.org/10.7202/704382ar.

Paquin, S. (2003). Paradiplomatie identitaire et diplomatie en Belgique fédérale: Le cas de la Flandre. *Canadian Journal of Political Science/ Revue Canadienne De Science Politique, 36*(3), 621–642. https://doi.org/10.1017/S0008423903778792.

Paquin, S. (2014). Le fédéralisme d'ouverture et la place du Québec (et des autres provinces) dans les négociations internationales: rupture dans la continuité? *Canadian Foreign Policy Journal, 20*(1), 29–38.

Québec, Relations internationales et francophonie. (2017). Europe. Retrieved online from the Ministère des relations internationales et de la francophonie website http://www.mrif.gouv.qc.ca/fr/relations-du-quebec/europe

Rector, C. (2009). *Federations: The Political Dynamics of Cooperation.* Ithaca, NY: Cornell University Press.

Rioux Ouimet, H. (2015). From Sub-State Nationalism to Subnational Competition States: The Development and Institutionalization of Commercial Paradiplomacy in Scotland and Quebec. *Regional & Federal Studies, 25*(2), 109–128. https://doi.org/10.1080/13597566.2014.992886.

Rix, A. (1999). *The Australia-Japan Political Alignment: 1952 to Present.* London: Routledge.

Royles, E. (2017). Sub-State Diplomacy: Understanding the International Opportunity Structures. *Regional & Federal Studies, 27*(4), 393–416. https://doi.org/10.1080/13597566.2017.1324851.

Sassatelli, M. (2002). Imagined Europe: The Shaping of a European Cultural Identity Through EU Cultural Policy. *European Journal of Social Theory, 5*(4), 435–451.

Sherbrooke Daily Record, Anonymous. (1912, April 3). Eastern Townships Requires Advertisement, E. T. Immigration's Experience.

Sideri, S. (1997). Globalisation and Regional Integration. *The European Journal of Development Research, 9*(1), 38–82. https://doi.org/10.1080/09578819708426677.

Sridharan, K. (2003). Federalism and Foreign Relations: The Nascent Role of the Indian States. *Asian Studies Review, 27*(4), 463–489. https://doi.org/10.1080/10357820308713389.

Tatham, M. (2013). Paradiplomats Against the State: Explaining Conflict in State and Substate Interest Representation in Brussels. *Comparative Political Studies, 46*(1), 63–94. https://doi.org/10.1177/0010414012453031.

The Globe, Anonymous. (1869, January 19). Our London Correspondence, p. 2.

Totoricagüena, G. (2005). Diasporas as Non-Central Government Actors in Foreign Policy: The Trajectory of Basque Paradiplomacy. *Nationalism and Ethnic Politics, 11*(2), 265–287. https://doi.org/10.1080/13537110591005757.

Vorarlberg. (2018). Options for the States to Contribute Towards the Formulations of Objectives in the EU. Retrieved online from the Land of Vorarlberg's website http://www.vorarlberg.gv.at/english/vorarlberg-english/regions_europe/europe/vorarlbergandeurope/optionsforthestatestocont.htm.

Waldinger, R., & Fitzgerald, D. (2004). Transnationalism in Question. *American Journal of Sociology, 109*(5), 1177–1195.

Westwood, S., & Phizacklea, A. (2013). *Trans-nationalism and the Politics of Belonging*. London: Routledge.

Zamorano, M. M., & Rodríguez Morató, A. (2015). The Cultural Paradiplomacy of Barcelona Since the 1980s: Understanding Transformations in Local Cultural Paradiplomacy. *International Journal of Cultural Policy, 21*(5), 554–576. https://doi.org/10.1080/10286632.2014.943752.

CHAPTER 6

Conclusion:
Governing Culture in Federations

In the literature on federalism, the notion of cultural federalism has most commonly been used in reference to federations constructed on cultural diversity (Hueglin and Fenna 2015). Cultural federalism, in this sense, refers to a federation that has been designed in a way to associate a diversity of cultures—mostly nationally recognized cultures, living together in the geographic region constituted as a country. This meaning of cultural federalism could probably be used to describe Belgian, Swiss, Canadian, Russian, Indian, Malaysian, Iraqi, and Nepalese federalisms. Therefore, what this definition of cultural federalism conveys is the idea of a federation that assembles—that federates—different nations. This definition is most certainly the one that political scientist would retain when referring to cultural federalism.

That being said, cultural policy researchers have increasingly used the notion of cultural federalism to talk about intergovernmental relations and the structural forms of cooperation or competition of cultural policy. In Kevin Mulcahy's work (2002), cultural federalism constitutes a field of forces—a power structure—between federal and subnational players. For Rosenstein, cultural federalism refers to the idea of "responsive, collaborative intergovernmental relations" (Rosenstein 2018: 100). In Rosenstein's work, the idea of cultural federalism implies collaboration, while in the work of Noonan on the American system, cultural federalism supposes a more reserved place of federal powers and more room for the states. In other words, cultural federalism is made possible by a less predominant

© The Author(s) 2019

J. Paquette, *Cultural Policy and Federalism*,
New Directions in Cultural Policy Research,
https://doi.org/10.1007/978-3-030-12680-3_6

183

place for the federal level and a more democratic place for states (Noonan 2015: 41). In Erk's work on media policy in Germany (2003), cultural federalism is a form of cooperation—one which requires collaboration and may be seen as an oppressive configuration of power by either federal or subnational governments. Cultural federalism may also mean a division of cultural powers (Saint-Pierre and Audet 2011; Gattinger and Saint-Pierre 2008). Looking back at these different definitions, we can come to two conclusions. First, cultural policy researchers have claimed the concept of cultural federalism and made it their own. As a result, since cultural federalism has a meaning of its own, and since it conveys meaning to a research community, it is perfectly legitimate to use this expression even if it may—at times—create confusion vis-à-vis its use in fields like political science, for instance. Second, researchers in cultural policy seem to use cultural federalism to refer simultaneously to a number of different—albeit complementary—ideas. Cultural federalism is a structure of cooperation; it is also implicitly, in some cases, a normative position—a "good" thing. In other cases, cultural federalism means that there is a systemic division of power. All of these definitions are perfectly defendable. In this book, and in this chapter in particular, we use cultural federalism not as a specific kind of intergovernmentalism that implies cooperation, but as something that refers to different types of intergovernmental arrangements in federations. Therefore, cultural federalism, here, can be defined as the cooperative or competitive form of intergovernmental relations developed to govern cultural affairs in a federation. By this, we mean that there are different types of cultural federalism.

The main objective of this book has been to offer a view of the basic principles and dynamics at play in federalism—to offer a map of the institutional patterns that can influence and shape cultural policymaking and implementation in federations. To provide this map of institutional patterns, we relied on four parameters—the first two of which are the most important. First, we discussed the importance of the constitutional division of cultural powers. In this perspective, we looked at formal power, delved into constitutional documents, and tried to understand how the structure of cultural powers was shaped. We emphasized the legislative capacities of governments over cultural policy. The second parameter is that of intergovernmentalism. Of course, we argue that intergovernmentalism implies strategies of cooperation, but it also implies strategies of competition. At this level, we focused on executive capacities, looking at capacity to negotiate, make decisions, and implement policies. We also approached, in this sense, the administrative arrangements over cultural policies in federations. These are the two most important parameters in defining federalism for cultural policy. In addition to these two parameters, we tried to understand other areas that are fundamental to cultural policy. We discussed the place of cities in federations. We know, now, that in most cases, cities are closely tied to subnational governments. Therefore, we raised two main issues: What is the nature of intergovernmental relations between cities and federal governments, and what is the place of culture in capital cities? How are they governed? Finally, we also added another element that is important to address when talking about cultural policy: the place of cultural diplomacy and international cultural relations. The unique history of some federations and the unique cultural diversity of others offer interesting approaches to cultural policy that all speak to the influence of federalism in cultural affairs—even at the international level.

In this chapter, we want to talk about cultural federalism as encompassing different approaches to cultural governance. We have seen, throughout this book, a vast number of commonalities in principle, but also a vast amount of diversity between the cases we have discussed. Therefore, building on observations made in previous chapters, this chapter will discuss patterns that emerge and that can help us distinguish between different types of cultural federalism. Looking at their distinctive approaches to the four parameters discussed throughout this book, we can identify four types of cultural federalism. Before going any further, we should recall a number of important principles about typologies. First, typologies are mostly imperfect systems of classification. Typologies are constructed on a number of criteria, characteristics, and parameters to classify ideas, objects, or structures into different categories or types. Second, typologies are useful for examining commonalities and differences; they provide a useful way of organizing social realities. Third, typologies work on basic principles, looking at basic commonalities and basic differences. However, typologies can be very imperfect when it comes to making certain nuances and taking stock of aspects of social reality that are, in fact, much more complex than what is presented in different types. Types are an intellectual reduction; they are imperfect tools for accounting for nuances, but they are intellectually helpful. Types help us to recognize broad, generalizable aspects of the social reality we are studying. The value of types is primarily pedagogical. They are reductions, but they offer a "short-cut" to discuss some important elements of society. Finally, a fourth element that should be kept in mind is the

186   J. PAQUETTE

fragility of types and typologies when it comes to public policy. Systems of public policy evolve over time, and the formulation and implementation of cultural policy in some countries have changed over history. The idea that cultural policies will continue changing and evolving is a perfectly reasonable hypothesis. Types give a certain sense of fixity, while society is perhaps more fluid than it is presented in typologies.

As a result, we wish to offer a typology based on basic principles, knowing that countries may fit more in one category than another, and that some countries may seem like outliers. In other words, these types are not definitive, and each country can present a number of examples or situations where we would be required to revise our judgement, here. The types presented in this chapter are based on the intersection between the division of power and the practices of intergovernmentalism as described in previous chapters. These types are also informed by the nature of the federal/local relationship over cultural affairs and the subnational government's capacities in cultural diplomacy and international cultural relations. It should be noted that these types are created in relation to cultural policy—exclusively—defined by governmental interventions and instruments in the cultural sector. A look over other jurisdictions, or other policy areas, would potentially provide a whole different form of classification and encompass a whole range of different countries, depending on the division of power related to these other policy areas (e.g. energy, education, environment, trade, natural resources, etc.) and the styles of intergovernmental relations at play. This typology is simply reproducing institutional and political patterns with regard to cultural governance in federations.

In the next sections, we will present the four types of cultural federalism that result from a synthesis of these different parameters. The first type we will present is that of federal leadership. The second type we will discuss is that of competitive cultural federalism. The third and fourth types are, respectively, veto point cultural federalism and developmental cultural federalism.

6.1   Type 1—Federal Leadership

This first type of cultural governance is characterized by a strong dominance of the federal government in cultural affairs (see Table 6.1). The cases of Mexico and Argentina (Bordat-Chauvin 2014, 2018) are the ideal types of this kind of cultural federalism. In terms of the formal division

6 CONCLUSION: GOVERNING CULTURE IN FEDERATIONS 187

Table 6.1 Federal leadership type of cultural federalism

Parameters	Characteristics
Division of power	• State-formation: imperial dissolution • Predominantly centralized at the federal level • Diversity is not a counterbalance to federal power
Intergovernmentalism	• Coercive cooperation • Policy transfers • National training programmes, national standards • Courts not used to challenge power • Little horizontal or subnational/subnational relations
Local/Municipal	• Predominance of federal powers
International	• Subnational cultural diplomacy: inexistent or limited

of power, the federal leadership model tends to be structured on a formal definition of power as being the property of the federal government. The constitutions of the States that fall under this type of federalism would typically define cultural policy as a federal power. This is the case in Mexico, Argentina, and Brazil. The tradition of constitutionalism pertaining to strong federal leadership often specifies, to a very important degree, the level and nature of powers attributed to the federal government. Constitutional documents in this form of federalism also tend to be more favourable to federal powers, creating more capacity for the federal government to act in cultural affairs, while also creating obligations for subnational government (ex: Brazil and Mexico). It could be said that this form of cultural governance is characterized by an overly centralized federal government. As for issues of diversity, they can be mentioned and defined in constitutional documents, which may create cultural obligations, but they are not part of the dynamics of the federation at this stage.

The case of the Brazilian Constitution is a good example one that acknowledges cultural diversity, as is the Argentinian Constitution. While both documents express a will to protect and promote cultural diversity, this has not translated into cultural policy instruments at this point. It may be part of a cultural promotion programme, but these constitutions do not open a space for self-governance in cultural affairs, nor do they indicate a dual/multiple system of cultural governance where minority or Indigenous populations could be part of the federal dynamics of cultural policy. While there could be significant changes in the future for some of these countries, at present, the cultural governance of these countries is in the hands of federal powers. In other words, diversity cannot offer any counterbalance to relativize federal authorities in these countries. These federations resulted from a dissolution of imperial power; they were created from different and diverse regionalisms, and even different cultures, but these are not widely acknowledged by their political institutions. These countries do not, in this sense, reflect "federal societies" (Elazar 1987). The social and cultural aspects of federalism are not relayed at the institutional level of these countries.

In terms of intergovernmental relationships, cultural policies in the federal leadership type of cultural federalism are defined as more cooperative. But the form of cooperation implied, here, is generally more coercive than it is a way of achieving the mutual cultural interests of the federation's partners. In fact, mutual interest tends to be defined centrally by the federal government. The input of subnational administrations is, generally, more permissible or perceptible at the implementation level of cultural policy. In other words, cultural policy is nationally defined and regionally implemented. Cultural policy circulates from the federal to the subnational level in the form of policy transfer. Even the forums made for policy formulation are not reflective of the ideal of a regional representation based on subnational membership. The case of the museum policy formulation platform in Brazil is a good example of a context where diversity is imagined from a sectorial perspective (visual arts, performing arts, heritage), but not on a regional level. In other words, in this type, the cultural development processes do not retain characteristics of federative representations—like federal senates, in general, would for political representation. Also, while there are some important exceptions, the civil society of this type of federation may be less prone to reproduce these structures of federalism in their own activities as it may not be a tradition or may not necessarily serve any political purpose to their organizations.

Federal government in the federal leadership type is predominant players, and the circulation of their expertise is important in providing guidance and standards at the local level and creating capacities at the subnational level. Finally, at the intergovernmental level, there are very few subnational/subnational bilateral relations. Cultural initiatives remain dominated by the federal institutions; the federal power is not being challenged by it subnational governments and certainly not being challenged in court.

Looking at federal/municipal relations, these are almost as important as federal/subnational relations in the federal leadership context. In some constitutions, like the Mexican Constitution, subnational powers are limited; federal powers give shape to the subnational/municipal relationship. In other words, the subnational governments and the cities are almost on equal grounds when it comes to transacting with the federal government. Additionally, this type of federalism is also characterized by an inexistent or very scarce level of international cultural diplomacy. While cities can play a role in some areas or in trying to attract international events, there are very limited attempts to do so at the subnational level.

Historically, the case of Austria could also have been categorized in the federal leadership type of federalism for a number of reasons. First, while the Austrian Constitution does not clearly define cultural powers, it is assumed that they fall into the purview of subnational authorities. However, education in Austria is defined as a federal power, and the notion of education conveyed in the constitution could also fall in what we think of, today, as being relevant to cultural policy. The place of culture as a subnational power is relatively debatable. Second, Austria has been traditionally seen as a federation without a federal society (Erk 2004). For this reason, the federal government has been historically present and has served as a leader of cultural policy in the country. The circulation of cultural policy models and ideas in Austria follows a top-down approach, not so much by an expression of authority, but by a certain passivity at the subnational level. Austrian subnational governments do not typically use or invest their cultural powers. That being said, in recent years, and through the European Union, some Austrian regions have started to develop new patterns of actions and are, more or less, experimenting with regional powers in different ways. Some provinces, like Tyrol or Vorarlberg, have helped in transforming the landscape of cultural federalism in Austria by moving it away from a de facto federally dominated scene where cultural aspirations and leadership are concerned. Inter-ministerial conferences are also increasingly, in the European integration process, becoming a significant platform for intergovernmental action at the subnational level.

6.2   Type 2—Competitive Cultural Federalism

Competitive cultural federalism does not mean that there is no cooperation or that there is only conflict. Competitive cultural federalism implies that the governance of cultural affairs is traversed by asymmetries (cultural, linguistic, and regional) and that actors are using institutional

190   J. PAQUETTE

Table 6.2   Competitive cultural federalism

Parameters	Characteristics
Division of power	• Subnational power or shared authority
	• Importance of diversity
Intergovernmentalism	• Transfers
	• Departmental/ministerial conferences as forms of coordination
	• Low bilateral subnational collaborations
	• Public opinion
	• Courts to challenge, respect, or acquire powers
	• Normative differentiation in cultural policy referentials
Local/Municipal	• Cities as part of federal dynamic
International	• Active subnational cultural diplomacy

levers to achieve their own ends (Table 6.2). Federal and subnational agents may agree on policy issues and often collaborate, but a number of their interests may be constitutively different right from the start. Federations often reunite competing cultural interests—this is simply a fact of federalism. The federal government may, at times, have competing interests with subnational members. In other cases, there may even be a competition between subnational members, to gain more resources or more power and autonomy from the federal government. In this category of federalism, the cases of Germany, Canada, and Belgium serve as good examples. To a certain degree, the Australian case can be said to also share many of the characteristics of this model of cultural governance. The Australian case, however, is a bit of an outlier—though, in recent years, there has been an increasing conscience in Australia about inequalities in federal funding. Data on federal and subnational cultural funding in Australia show that some member states receive much more support from the federal government than others (ex: New South Wales), while they also invest less than other members (Australia, Meetings of Cultural Ministers 2017). These revelations information has sparked the outcry of many regional and sectorial arts organizations. Cultural federalism in Australia has evolved through cooperation, but is prone to competitiveness.

Looking at division of power, competitive cultural federalism implies a strong presence of subnational members in cultural affairs. The constitution may define culture as a subnational power (as is the case in Germany and Belgium, for instance). In other cases, the constitution may define culture as belonging to both levels of government and legislatures. In these cases, subnational governments either have vested interests in cultural affairs or they have developed a tradition of governmental interventions in social affairs that has included the arts and heritage (as is the case in Australia and Canada). These cases suppose an important tradition of government participation in social affairs, where the subnational government plays a certain leadership role in the process of developing and implementing cultural policy. This model supposes competition because it implies that either the federal government's ambitions or the subnational governments' cultural aspirations must be negotiated. In this type of federation, the two levels of government are active in cultural affairs which create a field of force that is channelled through federal institutions.

Federal transfers can be an important source of intergovernmental relations and the result of a subnational collective action in competitive cultural federalism. Cultural policy formulation implies a number of other instruments. In cooperative strategies, competitive federalisms have established forums and conferences as a mean of negotiating their interests in the cultural sectors. Departmental and ministerial conferences are an important tool for policy coordination. Collaboration between subnational members remains low except in instances of collective actions to gain more autonomy or resources from the federal government. Public opinion plays a certain role in intergovernmental affairs as culture is generally higher in the political agenda than in other places, and it can be prone to political controversies. In Belgium, Canada, and Australia, for that matter, cultural affairs are now increasingly taking place in the mediatic spheres, where cultural controversies can play a part in the political dynamics of their federations. In other cases, where competition is stronger, courts are used to challenge powers or to acquire new ones. A court judgement may be necessary to have a federal intervention in its area of jurisdiction, while in other cases, a court judgement may be used to have the federal government take a step back and retract its interventions into areas of competency that belong to subnational governments. The logics of cultural policies—their rationales—may differ greatly between subnational members and be very different from the orientations desired by the federal government. In this sense, cultural policies are a space for normative differentiation; they help assert different identities and distinctive values.

In this context, federal/municipal politics possess three characteristics. First, federal/municipal politics can be used by federal governments to achieve their agenda while bypassing negotiations with subnational governments. Transfers to major cities are often a way for federal powers to achieve their cultural policy goals. Second, cities have to negotiate the politics of federalism; they can rely on two levels of government which, at times, may be strategically good. If a party in power is less supportive of culture at one level of government, a city can always try to access and convince the other level, which may be more sympathetic to its cultural aims. In other occasions, this negotiation between multiple levels of government may create more complicated scenarios. Sometimes, where major cultural investments are concerned, there may be an implicit requirement that a city convinces both levels of government to complete cultural funding for a project, which may complicate the municipal strategy if the other levels of governments are not responsive or are hostile towards each other. As such, cities can benefit from or be caught in the crossfires of the politics of federalism. Third, in competitive types of cultural federalism, cities tend to organize themselves collectively to have representation—and a measure of power—in federal/subnational discussions.

Finally, an important characteristic of competitive cultural federalism is that of a strong subnational cultural diplomacy. In the case of Canadian provinces and Australian states, the agent-general model has been an important foundation on which cultural diplomacy developed and evolved in recent years at the subnational level. Flanders, Wallonia, Québec, Bavaria, and many other subnational governments have also had an active and evolving presence (and strategies) at the global level. Subnational cultural relations and cultural diplomacy are a means through which a subnational government can become more visible at the global level. This is an indication of a more competitive view of cultural federalism.

6.3   Type 3—Veto Points Cultural Federalism

The notion of veto points comes from the institutionalist side of the public policy literature. Veto points are junctions in political systems where agreements are necessary for a policy to go forward. According to Ellen Immergut, "[p]olitical decisions require agreement at several points along a chain of decision made in different arenas" (1990: 396). Each opportunity there is for a policy—in our case, cultural policy—to be overturned constitutes a veto point. In the USA—as a result of the division of power stemming from the constitution and the presidential system, where the legislative, executive, and judicial are separated—the veto points are numerous. In cultural policy, the states, and many other administrative units can also be seen as contributing to the multiplication of veto points in the system. The more veto capacity there is, the more actors and institutions can conceivably challenge decision-making in culture. Similar to the USA, Switzerland has a number of institutional veto points where decisions can be overturned along a complex decision-making chain. For instance, in 2018, the youth movement of the Liberal radical party organized a federal referendum on taxation in support of national public broadcasting to ask the Swiss if they wanted this system to stop. The Swiss voted "no" in a majority of approximately 70%, however, should they have voted yes, the result would have been a defunding of the plurilingual national public broadcaster. This was, in part, the objective of this popular initiative. This example serves to show how veto points are not just numerous in the Swiss political system, their capacity to impact decisions can be quite important.

Every political system has veto points; theoretically, we could analyse the veto points in cultural policymaking for every State in the world. Federalism is, by definition, a political structure that offers many veto points to its members. However, we use the notion of "veto points" because it represents, quite saliently, the characteristic of some cultural federalism, like those of the USA and Switzerland. By comparison, in a system where power is less perfectly divided—such as in the parliamentary systems of Australia and Canada—there is a fusion of the executive and legislative branches that create a fundamental difference for cultural policy. In Australia and Canada, it is technically easier to initiate or end a cultural policy at the federal level. By contrast, in the American and Swiss system, the number of veto points makes it difficult to initiate policy development at the federal level.

In veto points cultural federalism, the constitution prevails and reinstates the dualism and division of power between federal and subnational levels of administration and legislature. Veto points are numerous, which can be challenging for cultural policy development. This complex institutional assemblage also creates a different civic culture wherein cultural policy advocacy is informed by institutional divisions and collective actions require strategies that target every actor in the decision-making process. This institutional assemblage may also involve a greater sense of federalism in collective actions and may require the mobilization of partners in

194   J. PAQUETTE

Table 6.3   Veto points cultural federalism

Parameters	Characteristics
Division of power	• Constitution prevails
	• Dualism
	• Multiplication of veto points
Intergovernmentalism	• Transfers
	• Higher bilateral relations at the subnational level
	• Public opinion
	• Courts are used to challenge, respect, or acquire powers
Local/Municipal	• Part of federal politics
International	• Respect of division of powers
	• Relatively active

other parts of the federation. Federal/municipal politics are also deeply enmeshed in this system of institutional collaboration and veto.

In terms of intergovernmental relationships, in veto point cultural federalism, these are typically structured along the lines of a number of instruments that, while respecting the constitution and its division of power, draw on numerous opportunities for cooperation and competition. Courts have been used in the American system to clarify the states' powers in cultural affairs—especially in the radio-broadcasting sector. In Switzerland, reforms to the federal constitution were necessary to establish a federal office of cultural affairs. International cultural relations exist, but they are conducted in a manner that respects the division of power; none of the strategies employed build on the symbolic of autonomy in international relations and cultural affairs (Table 6.3).

6.4   Type 4—Developmental Cultural Federalism

Our final type does no justice, in its label, to the important and ambitious measures put in place by many states, like India, to support a thriving cultural sector through a very comprehensive cultural policy. By developmental cultural federalism, we mean cultural policymaking in developing countries, of course, but, likewise, the expression also alludes to contexts where cultural policy development is extremely asymmetric (Table 6.4). The federal government is disproportionately more active than subnational governments. Although subnational states have the

6 CONCLUSION: GOVERNING CULTURE IN FEDERATIONS   195

Table 6.4 Developmental cultural federalism

Parameters	Characteristics
Division of power	• Mixed cultural powers
	• Subnational governments cannot/do not act on their power
	• Minority rights
Intergovernmentalism	• Transfers
	• Capacity development
	• Standards and norms
	• Professionals
Local/Municipal	• Asymmetric
International	• Organizational level

power to intervene in cultural affairs, they do not because of a lack of resources, expertise, and/or there are other, more pressing priorities. In India and Malaysia, the federal government is disproportionately more active, although some states (ex. Tamil Nadu and Penang) have developed and maintained an important level and tradition of cultural policy-making. In these federations, minority rights can colour or give a certain political texture to cultural policy development, and may alter, in some areas, the capacity of the federal government to act, while also securing some specific powers for some subnational members.

In this context, it is expected that the federal government offers financial support to its subnational governments to fulfil their cultural ambitions, but it can also act in support of cultural development by providing expertise, national standards, and training programmes. While there is an impression of centralization of cultural powers in the developmental cultural federalism type, in reality, it is the structural incapacity or difficulties of many subnational states to occupy their cultural sector that engenders this impression. In the cases of India and Malaysia, developing heritage capacities and cultural tourism are both high in the policy agenda, which shapes different logics and brings in different agents which may have stakes in the economics of cultural tourism.

The experience of cultural policy development in the context of developmental cultural federalism is probably better seen and observed at the professional and organizational levels. These are the actors, arguably, have had the most say in constructing a system of cooperation for cultural affairs. Metropolises have a disproportionately higher capacity to engage with the federal government in developmental cultural

196   J. PAQUETTE

federalism and may, in fact, be better equipped than some subnational states to develop and implement cultural policy. International activities in this form of federalism are non-inexistent at the subnational level and are probably best found in professional and organizational collaborations. With certain fundamental nuances, the case of the current Russian Federation's cultural system would probably fall into this category.

6.5   GENERAL CONCLUSION

For cultural policy research, federalism, for many reasons, is a non-negligible institutional reality. Among the reasons sustaining this importance is the fact that an important number of nations and a fundamental number of populations live in federal systems. Cultural life—from arts education in elementary school, to the annual programme of the national arts centres, to the programming of cultural events at regional museums, to the national cultural policy—is all organizations and moments that are typical of citizens living in a federation and are all shaped by the complex political reality offered by federalism. Federalism informs the fabric of cultural policy, it mirrors the questions of identity and the division of powers in the very manner it approaches each of its statements. Does the policy respect the division of powers? Is it representative? Federations are a complex institutional reality that relies on an implicit system of political symbols to inform how political affairs—including cultural policy—are being discussed. For artists, heritage professionals and, cultural organizations, federalism is a system that may present them with opportunities for cultural funding, but this redistribution of cultural powers may also constitute a constraint and require a more complex manoeuvre when it comes to structuring a collective action. All of these questions are crucial for cultural policy research.

When we approach cultural policies, we are influenced by our preconceptions: we are influenced by the knowledge we have of our own political institutions. This influence is typical to comparative work and has had two consequences for this book. First, it was important to keep in mind that Canadian federalism is not the only type of federalism; many other forms of federalism could have a number of different influences on cultural policy. In other words, extreme caution has been taken not to over-impose Canadian federalism into the reading grid of every federation and cultural federalism that has been discussed in this book. Second, this book is meant as a tool for double mediation between scholars. In this sense, the book was meant as a tool for scholars who are studying cultural policy—comparatively or not—in different parts of the globe; it is meant to help scholars retrieve some basic ideas and elements about the influence of federalism on cultural policy. Similarly, this book can also be seen as a reference tool for those who are in federal systems, but need to relativize their system's functioning when comparing it with other federations.

Cultural policies change over time and so do federations. This book was not meant as a definitive comparative research. Rather, the book's objective was to provide a map—a number of conceptual resources to help understand the relationship between federations and cultural policy. As such, the book has aimed to provide elements that inform about the institutional intricacies that cultural policy actors face in federations.

References

Australia, Meetings of Cultural Ministers. (2017). *Cultural Funding by Government 2015–2016.* Canberra: Australian Bureau of Statistics.

Bordat-Chauvin, É. (2014). De la mobilisation à l'institutionnalisation: une analyse comparative historique des politiques culturelles au Mexique et en Argentine. *Pôle Sud, 2,* 49–64.

Bordat-Chauvin, E. (2018). *Les politiques culturelles en Argentine et au Mexique.* Paris: Editions L'Harmattan.

Elazar, D. J. (1987). *Exploring Federalism.* Tuscaloosa, AL: University of Alabama Press.

Erk, J. (2003). Federalism and Mass Media Policy in Germany. *Regional & Federal Studies, 13*(2), 106–126.

Erk, J. (2004). Austria: A Federation Without Federalism. *Publius: The Journal of Federalism, 34*(1), 1–20.

Gattinger, M., & Saint-Pierre, D. (2008). Can National Cultural Policy Approaches Be Used for Sub-National Comparisons? An Analysis of the Québec and Ontario Experiences in Canada. *International Journal of Cultural Policy, 14*(3), 335–354. https://doi.org/10.1080/10286630802281921.

Hueglin, T. O., & Fenna, A. (2015). *Comparative Federalism: A Systematic Inquiry.* Toronto: University of Toronto Press.

Immergut, E. M. (1990). Institutions, Veto Points, and Policy Results: A Comparative Analysis of Health Care. *Journal of Public Policy, 10*(4), 391–416.

Mulcahy, K. V. (2002). The State Arts Agency: An Overview of Cultural Federalism in the United States. *The Journal of Arts Management, Law, and Society, 32*(1), 67–80.

Noonan, D. S. (2015). Arts of the States in Crisis-Revisiting Determinants of State-Level Appropriations to Arts Agencies. *Poetics, 49,* 30–42.

Rosenstein, C. (2018). *Understanding Cultural Policy.* London: Routledge.

Saint-Pierre, D., & Audet, C. (2011). Les Tendances et les Défis des Politiques Culturelles-Cas Nationaux en Perspective. France-Angleterre-États-Unis-Allemagne-Espagne-Belgique-Suisse-Suède-Pays de Galle et Écosse-Québec-Les Organisations Internationales. Québec: Presses de l'Université Laval.

INDEX

A

Administration
cultural, xiv, 3, 31, 32, 80, 81, 85, 86, 90, 92, 93, 97, 98, 101, 111, 113, 115, 125, 126, 137, 140–143, 145, 147, 158, 163, 188, 193
federal, xiv, 3, 31, 64, 81, 85, 86, 90, 92, 94, 97, 98, 101, 111, 113, 115, 126, 137, 140–143, 145, 147, 158, 188, 193
local and municipal, xiv, 3, 4, 80, 94, 137, 140–143, 145, 147, 159, 187, 190, 194
subnational, xiv, 3, 31, 32, 90, 93, 97, 98, 111, 113, 115, 126, 140–143, 145, 158, 163, 188, 193
Agent-general, 158–168, 172, 173, 192
Althusius, Johannes, 11, 12
Archeology (archeological), 37, 38, 50, 98, 104, 131

Archive, 33, 35, 36, 45, 46, 51, 128, 135, 136
Argentina, 17, 21, 32, 38, 52, 57, 62, 63, 65, 69, 97, 111, 113, 134, 136, 137, 148, 174, 186, 187
Art
advocacy, 111
artists, 99, 108, 109, 139, 140, 173, 175, 176, 196
galleries, 130, 132
performing, 34–36, 134–137, 156, 168, 188
professional, 111, 139
theater, 128
Australia, xi, xiii, 17, 20, 21, 24, 32, 34, 36–38, 48, 65–67, 69, 84, 89, 95, 96, 106, 107, 110, 114, 131, 132, 134, 137, 139, 148, 158, 159, 161–167, 171, 190, 191, 193
Australian Capital Territory, 131, 142
Austria, 17, 20, 21, 32, 40, 46–48, 69, 70, 93, 100, 104, 137, 157, 175, 176, 189

© The Editor(s) (if applicable) and The Author(s), under exclusive license to Springer Nature Switzerland AG 2019
J. Paquette, *Cultural Policy and Federalism*, New Directions in Cultural Policy Research, https://doi.org/10.1007/978-3-030-12680-3

199

200 INDEX

Autonomy, 3, 6, 8, 10, 15, 18, 22, 23, 39, 51, 54, 58, 79, 80, 127, 128, 143, 159, 165, 190, 191, 194

B
Baden-Württemberg, 157
Basel, 156
Bavaria, 21, 103, 106, 169, 171, 174, 175, 192
Belgium, xiii, 17, 21–23, 32, 40, 44, 45, 57, 63, 64, 68, 69, 99–101, 107, 136, 141, 142, 169, 171, 177, 190, 191
Berlin, 126, 127, 135, 140, 141, 170, 172
Berne, 127
Bonn, 135, 137, 140
Brasilia, 124–128, 133, 135–137, 143
Brazil, xi, 17, 21, 32, 38, 52–54, 57, 62, 63, 65, 67, 69, 97, 113, 128, 133, 134, 187, 188
British-Columbia, 104
Broadcasting, x, 16, 35, 37, 115
 laws, 43, 49, 90, 100, 103
 radio and television, 34, 36, 42, 43, 45, 48, 49, 51, 90, 100–103, 115, 194
 standards, 42, 43, 45, 102, 103
Broadcasting corporation
 Australia, 34, 37
 British, 37
 Canadian, 16, 101, 103
 Radio-Québec, 103
 TV Ontario, 103, 115
Brussels (and Bruxelles-Capitale), 64, 107, 124, 126–128, 135, 136, 140–142, 145, 173, 176
Budget, 176. *See also* Funding (funds)
Buenos Aires, 52, 126, 127, 135, 136, 145

C
Calcutta, 134, 136, 137
California, 92, 157
Canada, xi, xiii, 4, 6, 7, 13, 15, 17, 20–24, 32, 34–38, 48, 49, 57–62, 65–69, 86, 87, 89, 95, 96, 98, 101–104, 107, 109, 114, 115, 125, 127–130, 134, 138, 139, 146–148, 158–160, 162–165, 171–174, 176, 177, 190, 191, 193
Canberra, 36, 124–128, 131, 133, 135, 137
Cantons, 9, 20, 43, 64, 70, 86, 97, 106, 157
Capitals
 Cultural Funds, 140
 Cultural Pact, 140
 engineered, 125, 126, 128, 131, 134, 137
 historical, 125, 126, 128
China, xi, 3, 157, 167, 174
Citizenship, 2, 5, 10, 11, 13, 15, 20, 50, 52, 57, 58, 61, 62, 82, 92, 105, 175
City-State, 126, 140–142, 144
Colombia (Gran Colombia), 17, 22
Colonial (colonialism), 20, 37, 38, 60, 128, 159–165
Colonial Office, 160, 161
Commemoration, 53
 anniversary, 94
 Bicentennial, 94
 Centennial, 94
Competition, xii, 17, 25, 78–82, 89, 91, 93, 101, 112–115, 155, 162, 164, 183, 184, 190, 191, 194
Confederation, 12, 13, 18, 19, 34, 35, 39, 70, 86, 94, 100, 129, 135, 138, 160, 163

INDEX 201

Conference
Canadian Intergovernmental
Conference Secretariat, 96
Cultural Ministers Council (CMC),
95
inter-ministerial, 94, 176, 189
Kultusministerkonferenz, 94
Congress, 5, 8, 33, 52, 56, 92, 127,
128
Constitution (constitutional), xi, xiii,
xiv, 4–9, 13, 18, 21–23, 32, 33,
38–70, 78, 84, 86, 88–90, 94, 97,
98, 102, 110, 112, 113, 123, 124,
127, 129, 133, 141, 142, 145,
149, 153, 164, 169, 171, 173,
174, 184, 187–190, 193, 194
Cooperation, xii, 17, 25, 48, 78–82,
89–91, 93–95, 97–101, 112–115,
155, 157, 164, 171, 175, 177,
183, 184, 187–190, 194, 195
Cosmopolitan (cosmopolitanism), 11, 15
Court. *See* Judicial power
Creative industries, 104. *See also*
Cultural industries
Cultural affairs, xi, xiii, xiv, 9, 24,
31–33, 35, 39, 41–43, 45–48, 51,
53, 54, 65–67, 81–83, 85, 86,
88, 89, 91, 92, 94, 96, 97,
100–102, 104, 105, 113, 114,
116, 128, 136, 140–142, 144,
147, 148, 153, 154, 156–158,
165, 169–171, 173–177,
184–187, 189–191, 194–196
Cultural development, x, 20, 33, 35,
40, 41, 59, 61, 85, 92, 114, 115,
128, 129, 131, 134, 138, 140,
142, 147, 148, 157, 186, 188,
194, 195
Cultural diplomacy, xiv, 25, 37, 43,
44, 155, 156, 158, 168, 170,
172–175, 185–187, 189, 190,
192

Cultural industries, 50, 77, 95, 96,
111, 128, 143, 174
Cultural nationalism, 81–87, 89, 113
Cultural policy
development, x, xi, xiv, 1, 31, 56,
57, 63, 77, 142, 145–147, 194,
195
implementation, xiv, 1, 3, 25, 54,
56, 57, 77, 81, 91, 184, 186,
188
instruments, 91, 114, 176, 187
local, xi, 124, 140, 141, 143,
145–148
making, 25, 141, 184, 193–195
research, x, xi, 3, 15, 19, 32, 57,
145, 196
Cultural relations, xiv, 6, 8, 32, 47,
66, 67, 97–99, 115, 124, 146,
153, 155, 156, 167, 173–176,
183–186, 188, 191, 192, 194
Cultural rights, 19, 32, 38, 41, 45, 49,
50, 52, 53, 57–60, 62–65, 68,
69, 102
Czechoslovakia, 1, 8

D
Department
Conaculta, 97
Department of Canadian Heritage,
96
department of culture, 99, 135, 170
Federal Office for Culture, 97
Ministry of Culture, 92, 143

E
Education, 6, 39, 47–49, 61, 63, 69,
70, 92, 94, 99, 100, 103, 104,
139, 149, 154, 157, 158, 173,
175–177, 186, 189, 196
Elazar, D.J., 1, 2, 5, 124, 188

202 INDEX

Empire, 20, 34, 39, 40, 69, 158, 159, 163, 165, 166, 172
European Union, 2, 12, 13, 17–19, 44, 92, 100, 141, 153, 157, 170, 175, 176, 189

F
Federal district, 50, 54, 126, 127, 140, 142–144
Federalism
  cooperative, 79, 81, 90, 91, 99, 101, 169, 176, 184, 188, 191
  counter-power, 13, 16
  dual, 90, 91, 101, 115, 154
  executive, 4, 13, 90, 95, 97, 110, 193
Federalist
  Paper, 13
  politician, 99, 172
  thought, thinker, 11, 13
Federal society, 61, 84, 107, 111, 133, 164, 173, 188, 189
Flanders, 44, 102, 107, 141, 155, 156, 169–173, 175, 192
France, xi, 1, 3, 4, 47, 59, 80, 111, 156, 157, 173, 175, 177
Francophonie, 104, 174, 175, 177
Funding (funds), xiii, 24, 35, 45, 53, 54, 62, 77, 92–94, 99, 104, 113, 139–141, 145–147, 176, 177, 190, 192, 196

G
Germany, xii, xiii, 17, 20, 21, 32, 39, 43–45, 69, 90, 94, 100–102, 106, 115, 135, 137, 138, 140, 148, 154, 156, 157, 175, 176, 184, 190
Gray, Clive, 19, 77, 101, 108

H
Hamilton, Alexander, 11, 13
Heritage, x, 16, 34–36, 41, 43, 45, 49, 52, 56, 61, 65, 66, 77, 82, 84, 88, 92, 94, 97–99, 104, 105, 108, 111, 129, 131, 133, 135, 142–144, 147, 171, 175, 188, 191, 195, 196
  protection, 32, 43, 49, 53, 63, 96
  site, 53, 128, 135–138

I
Identity
  affirmation, 158
  cultural, 37, 52, 88, 175, 176
  politics of, 2, 62, 155
  regional, 4, 102, 106, 107, 168
Ideology, 15, 90
India, xiii, 17, 20, 21, 23, 32, 37, 38, 49, 50, 69, 98, 104, 107, 109, 110, 114, 133, 134, 136–138, 157, 167, 194, 195
Indigenous, 21, 57, 58, 60–63, 65–70, 87, 88, 95, 96, 107, 187
Infrastructure, 37, 39, 113, 124, 140, 146, 170
Institution
  cultural, xi, xiv, 16, 17, 19, 31, 33–38, 40, 43, 45, 49, 51, 57, 65, 80, 93–100, 105, 108, 114, 123, 127–129, 131–139, 141, 143, 145, 147, 175, 176, 184, 186, 188, 189, 191, 193, 196, 197
  federal, 1, 2, 8–17, 20, 22, 24, 33–36, 38, 40, 43, 45, 46, 61, 65, 67, 78–80, 83, 89, 90, 92, 95, 97, 98, 100, 106, 111, 112, 124, 127, 130–132, 135–140, 144, 145, 147, 175,

176, 188, 190, 191, 193, 194, 196

national, x, xii, xiii, 2, 20, 33–35, 37, 38, 40, 41, 43, 45, 80, 86, 92, 93, 97, 99, 100, 102, 104, 108–110, 128, 129, 131–140, 193, 196

Intergovernmental, xii, xiv, 6, 14, 32, 48, 80, 81, 90, 91, 95, 97, 98, 113, 114, 127, 146–148, 183–186, 188, 189, 191, 194

Intergovernmentalism, xiv, 44, 80, 90, 94, 95, 100, 116, 146, 184, 186, 187, 190, 194, 195

Italy, xi, 1, 3, 80, 111

J

Judicial power, 4, 9, 13, 31, 105, 125, 193

   courts, 45, 102, 114, 115, 187, 188, 190, 191, 194

   tribunals, 102

K

Kant, Immanuel, 11, 14, 15

Kuala Lumpur, 50, 124, 126, 127, 135, 137

Kymlicka, Will, 11, 15

L

Länder, 39, 43, 102, 154

Language, 14, 21, 32, 41, 45, 49, 53, 57–61, 63, 64, 69, 87, 88, 107, 157, 174, 177

Leadership, 34, 35, 38, 40, 43, 47, 48, 51, 52, 54–57, 66, 93, 95, 96, 112, 141, 143, 170, 186–189, 191

Library, 33, 36, 38, 109, 110, 134–136

London, 60, 125, 158–160, 162–168, 170, 173

M

Madison, James, 11, 13

Malaysia, xiii, 17, 20, 21, 32, 37, 38, 50, 57, 58, 68, 69, 88, 89, 98, 99, 107, 114, 125, 195

Mexico, xi, 4, 5, 17, 32, 38, 55, 56, 69, 97, 107, 113, 126, 127, 135, 145, 186, 187

Mexico City, 4, 126, 127, 135, 137, 165

Mill, John Stuart, 11, 13, 14, 17, 19

Ministry. *See* Department

Minority, 23, 69, 172

   cultural, 21, 22, 57, 62, 68, 99, 102, 187, 195

   linguistic, 21, 22, 44, 57, 58, 68, 102

Montesquieu, C.L., 12

Montréal, 128–130

Mulcahy, K.V., 32, 92, 93, 183

Multicultural, 21, 49, 58, 61, 107

Multiculturalism, 15, 49, 61, 62, 69

Multilateral, 169, 170, 173, 175–177

Museum (museum policy), x, 33–38, 43, 45, 46, 50, 51, 92, 98, 109, 110, 128–138, 140, 188, 196

N

National Capital Commission, 144

National Endowment for the Arts (NEA), 24, 33, 43, 84, 92–94, 147

Nepal, xiii, 17

New Brunswick, 34, 160

204 INDEX

New Delhi, 38, 125–127, 133, 135–137, 142, 143
Newfoundland, 8, 160, 162
New South Wales, 36, 159, 164–167, 190
New York, 92, 125, 165, 170
Nova Scotia, 34, 160

O

Ontario, 7, 16, 22, 34, 99, 103, 104, 115, 127, 129, 157, 160, 162–167, 172, 177
Organization
cultural, x, xi, 38, 56, 77, 97, 109, 114, 141, 177, 196
inter-departmental, 114
international, 104, 125, 158, 170, 175, 177, 196
not-for-profit, 95, 135
organizational level, 98, 100, 114, 195
public service, 95, 100, 135, 160
Ottawa, 4, 124–131, 133, 135, 137–139, 143, 144

P

Paradiplomacy, 154–156, 158
Paris, 59, 125, 163, 165, 170, 172, 173
Policy
formulation, 81, 97, 146, 186, 188, 191
implementation, xii, 3, 81
instruments, 52, 77, 91, 96, 114, 124, 140, 176, 187
social, xiii, 48, 55, 61, 83, 91
transfer, 98, 100, 113, 114, 187, 188

Power
federal, 5, 6, 10, 42, 47, 48, 50, 52, 66, 67, 90, 101, 102, 115, 142, 165, 183, 184, 187–189, 192
relationship, 9, 33
subnational, xi, 2, 4, 7, 21, 22, 40, 41, 43, 46, 47, 51, 56, 70, 81, 184, 189, 190, 192, 194, 195
Profession, xii, 80, 92, 97, 99, 100, 105, 109–112, 114, 139, 156, 195, 196
professional groups, 81, 108, 111
professionalization, 98
Province, 2, 4, 6–9, 16, 22, 34, 35, 37, 46, 49, 52, 61, 66, 93, 99, 101, 103, 104, 107, 115, 127, 129, 130, 144, 157, 158, 160, 162–164, 167, 168, 172, 173, 176, 189, 192
Public opinion, 114, 115, 190, 191, 194
Puerto Rico, 23, 93
Putrajaya, 124–126

Q

Québec, 15, 109, 155, 156, 165–167, 169, 175–177
province, 7, 16, 22, 34, 35, 61, 99, 103, 104, 107, 115, 127, 129, 130, 144, 160, 162, 163, 171–173, 192
Québec City, 128, 129, 172, 174
Queensland, 36, 106, 166, 167

R

Regionalism, 113, 138, 188
Regulation, 18, 42, 43, 45, 48, 51, 77, 103
regulatory agency, 101, 115

regulatory federalism, 90
Religion, 14, 32, 57–59, 61, 89, 107, 174
Report, 85, 87, 93, 160
   Clottu Commission, 85, 86
   Massey Commission, 35
   Whitlam report, 85
Representation, 16, 67, 97, 99, 106, 109–112, 138, 147, 159, 160, 163–168, 170, 173, 177, 188, 192
Reunification (German), 23, 39, 138, 146
Rhodesia, 1
Riker, W.H., 9
Rio de Janeiro, 125, 133, 136, 137
Russia (Federation of Russia), xiii, 17, 21, 32, 51, 69, 125

S
Saarland, 157
Sabah and Sarawak, 38, 50, 58, 69, 107
Self-governing, 2, 8, 20, 34, 36, 48, 69, 161
Senate, 9, 18, 55, 110, 130, 141, 188
Singapore, 8, 17, 38, 59
South Australia, 36
Spain, 15, 17–19
State-formation, 32, 34, 37–41, 68, 69, 159, 163, 187
Strategy, 91, 104, 105, 108, 111, 112, 114, 115, 134, 140, 144, 146, 157, 176, 192
Subnational
   communities, 45, 105, 171
   government, 2, 4–10, 13, 21–23, 33, 34, 36, 37, 39, 40, 45, 49–52, 54–59, 63, 65–67, 79, 82, 89–91, 93, 94, 97, 98, 101, 104–106, 108, 109, 113,

115, 124, 128, 134, 140, 141, 143, 145–147, 154–158, 162, 165, 166, 168, 171, 175–177, 185–189, 191, 192, 194, 195
   level, 2, 8, 9, 37, 46–49, 55, 56, 63, 67, 89, 93, 94, 97, 98, 100, 108, 113, 114, 140, 141, 146, 154, 171, 188, 189, 192–194, 196
   power, xi, 2–4, 7, 21, 22, 40, 41, 43, 46, 48, 51, 56, 70, 81, 184, 189, 190, 192, 195
   relations states, xiv, 7, 33, 56, 66, 83, 93, 94, 99, 127, 141, 148, 153–157, 165, 168, 169, 171, 172, 175, 187, 189, 192, 195
Switzerland, xiii, 17, 20–22, 32, 57, 63, 64, 68, 70, 83, 85, 86, 89, 96, 106, 127, 135, 138, 177, 193, 194

T
Tamil Nadu, 98, 168, 195
Toronto, 99, 129, 166
Training, 53, 100, 114, 187, 195
Transfers, 91–94, 100, 113, 114, 133, 140, 144–146, 149, 187, 188, 190–192, 194, 195. *See also* Policy

U
UNESCO, 52, 104, 153, 175, 176
United Kingdom (UK), 17–19, 111, 166
United States, xi, xiii, 4, 5, 8, 13, 17, 20–24, 32, 33, 41, 42, 65–68, 70, 83, 84, 89, 92–94, 99, 101, 106, 107, 124, 125, 134, 139, 147, 148, 165, 173, 174, 192, 193

206 INDEX

Urban, 86, 124, 129, 131, 138, 140, 142–144, 148
USSR, 16, 17

V
Values, 19, 47, 78, 80, 84, 88, 90, 91, 96, 116
  normativities, xiv, 145
Veto points, 186, 192–194
Victoria, 36
  Queen Victoria, 129
  State of Victoria, 37
  Victorian government, 37, 165
Vienna, 126–128, 135, 140, 141, 145, 170

Vorarlberg, 104, 176, 189

W
Wallonia, 40, 141, 142, 171, 175, 192
Washington DC, 4, 43, 124–128, 135, 137, 142, 143
Western Australia, 36, 166, 167
West Indies (Federation), 1, 17, 159

Y
Yugoslavia (ex-Yugoslavia), 1, 8, 16, 17